NOMADS AND FARMERS:
A STUDY OF THE YÖRÜK OF SOUTHEASTERN TURKEY

Frontispiece: A Spring Camp

ANTHROPOLOGICAL PAPERS

MUSEUM OF ANTHROPOLOGY, UNIVERSITY OF MICHIGAN
NO. 52

NOMADS AND FARMERS:
A STUDY OF THE YÖRÜK OF SOUTHEASTERN TURKEY

BY
DANIEL G. BATES

ANN ARBOR
THE UNIVERSITY OF MICHIGAN, 1973

© 1973 by the Regents of the University of Michigan
The Museum of Anthropology
All rights reserved

ISBN (print): 978-0-915703-64-7
ISBN (ebook): 978-1-951519-19-3

Browse all of our books at sites.lsa.umich.edu/archaeology-books.

Order our books from the University of Michigan Press at www.press.umich.edu.

For permissions, questions, or manuscript queries, contact Museum publications by email at umma-pubs@umich.edu or visit the Museum website at lsa.umich.edu/ummaa.

PREFACE

THE research on which this study is based was supported by fellowships from the Foreign Area Fellowship Program and from The University of Michigan Project for the Study of Social Networks in the Mediterranean. I wish to express my appreciation to both organizations for their generous support. In preparing for this study and in my training at The University of Michigan I have received assistance from many, both students and faculty, but especially from Professors William D. Schorger, my advisor, John F. Kolars, Eric R. Wolf, and Aram A. Yengoyan. They have provided guidance and encouragement throughout the entire period of my study. I am indebted to John Kolars and Eric Wolf for taking time to visit me in Turkey during the research period. Also, it was the earlier work of John Kolars in Antalya Province which suggested the particular ethnographic focus of this study. Prior to beginning actual field work I was fortunate to be able to meet with two scholars whose own studies in Turkey set standards for accurate and insightful analysis of processes in rural Turkish agricultural and nomadic societies: Professor Wolf-Dieter Hütteroth and Professor Paul Stirling. I am grateful to both for their hospitality and good advice.

During the two years I lived in Turkey I was shown hospitality and assistance by numerous individuals and institutions. It is possible to mention only the most active contributors. I wish to thank the Turkish Government, in particular the Foreign Relations Section of the Ministry of Education, for its understanding support of the study. Professor Nusret Fişek of Hacettepe University kindly arranged for much of my economic and sociometric data to be punched on computer cards. Dr. Fredrick C. Shorter was of immeasurable assistance in the preparation of the systematic economic and demographic survey. While in the field, local officials of many departments and of all ranks were unfailingly courteous and often of much help. The then Museum Director of Maraş, Mr. Gengiz Köseoğlu, offered encouragement in countless ways. Professors Halet Çambel, Erol Tümertekin, Duran Taraklı, and Ahmet Demir were unstinting not only in their professional assistance but also in giving their time and friendship. Most of all I own a strongly felt debt of gratitude to the many Yörük friends who took me into their homes during my long stay with them, and who offered great personal warmth and hospitality. Due to lack of space I can name only my two field assistants from the tribe, Mr. Mustafa Gezgin and Mr. Güzel Ateş. I want to thank Mrs. Shirley Jong, who not only typed the manuscript but met the series of unreasonable demands imposed by my schedule. George Stuber painstakingly prepared the maps, figures and tables, often translating that which in its original form was rather less than comprehensible. Finally, I would like to acknowledge my considerable debt to the associate editor of this series, Barbara Z. Bluestone, who has contributed greatly to the final shape of this report. A grant from the Center for Near Eastern and North African Studies at The University of Michigan has helped to make the publication of this monograph possible.

The patience, assistance, and encouragement of my wife Ülkü have made this study not only possible but also enjoyable.

FOR MY PARENTS

TABLE OF CONTENTS

INTRODUCTION 1

I. PASTURES, MIGRATORY ROUTES, AND THE
SOCIAL LANDSCAPE......................... 5
The Area of Study........................... 5
The Geographic Dimension.................... 7
The Social Landscape 21

II. THE IDEOLOGY OF AGNATIC DESCENT, DESCENT
GROUPS, AND SEGMENTATION 35
Tribe and Lineage Conceptions................ 38

III. YÖRÜK NORMATIVE AND ALTERNATIVE SYSTEMS
OF MARRIAGE.............................. 59
Culturally Stipulated Preferences of Marriage 60
Observed Marriage Frequencies................. 64
Bride Price and Kidnapping 68
The Contexts and Causes of Kidnapping 74
Kidnapping and the Dispersion of Kinship Ties........ 79
Summary and Final Remarks on Marriage 85

IV. RESIDENCE AND THE FORMATION OF NEW
HOUSEHOLDS THROUGH SEPARATION AND
INHERITANCE 87
Rules of Post-Marriage Co-Residence and Stated
    Preferences 88
Extended Patrilocality: Fratrilocality............. 95
Filiolocality 98
Women and Post-Marriage Residence 99
Inheritance and the Formation of New Domestic Units. . . 101
Residence Defined by the Proximity of Tents......... 113
The Problem of Dyadic Kin Ties 114

V. CAMP GROUPS AND THE ACQUISITION OF
   PASTURE RIGHTS..........................121
   The Contractual Nature of Pasture Rights..........125
   Migration................................130
   Leadership, Economic Differentiation, and Pasture
      Acquisition..........................133

VI. DOMESTIC PRODUCTION, CONSUMPTION, AND
   THE DETERMINANTS OF VARIATIONS IN WEALTH..143
   The Herd as the Unit of Production...............143
   Consumption of Market Purchased Commodities......156
   Limited Partnerships........................160
   Distribution of Wealth in Nomadic Society..........161
   The Domestic Mode of Production................168

VII. NOMADIC SETTLEMENT AND CHANGES IN
   SOCIAL LIFE.............................191
   Distribution of Wealth and Settlement.............194
   Group Settlement..........................197
   Social Change After Settlement.................201

VIII. CONCLUSION..............................223

Bibliography.................................227

Plates......................................237

LIST OF TABLES

1. Variations in snowfall during winter quarters......... 12
2. Temperature variations in winter pastures.......... 13
3. Monthly temperature variations in İslahiye.......... 14
4. Rainfall for years recorded in winter pastures....... 15
5. Summary of meteorological data for areas traversed
   by Yörük............................... 16
6. Named descent groups at the Kabile level.......... 40
7. Origin by descent group of presently married women
   as compared with descent group of husband......... 62
8. Bride price and the degree of consanguinal kinship of
   wife to present husband....................... 62
9. Marriage types by degree of kinship of wife to present
   husband................................ 66

10.	Arranged and kidnap marriages by relationship of wife to husband	73
11.	Histogram of bride prices paid for presently married Yörük women over the last 55 years	75
12.	Arranged and kidnap marriages by quartile of bride price	76
13.	Kidnapping and exogamy	80
14.	Distribution of domestic statuses as defined by domicile and relationship to head of household	90
15.	Post-marital residence for presently married nomad males	91
16.	Post-marital residence for presently married nomad females	91
17.	Marriage stability among nomadic Yörük	94
18.	Post-marriage residence of dependent sons by household	96
19.	Relationship of the number of people co-resident in the household and wealth in sheep	97
20.	Household size among sedentary and nomadic Yörük	103
21.	Scatter plot of years separated from natal tent and age of living heads of household	107
22.	Histogram of inheritance of sheep among nomads	109
23.	Percentile ranking of inheritance in sheep among nomads	110
24.	Camping decisions involving close affines among tents of one lineage during one year	119
25.	Distribution of tents according to named yaylas and cost of pasture rental (1969)	128
26.	Summary table of village agricultural cycles for areas traversed by Yörük	132
27.	Annual estimated cash purchases for domestic consumption	158
28.	Distribution of households by quartile of wealth and family type for each descent group	165
29.	Chi square test for association between family type and number of people co-resident in tent	172
30.	Circumstantial variables affecting wealth according to quartile of wealth	173
31.	Percentage of variation in wealth: curvilinear coefficient of determination according to amount of inheritance	173
32.	Percentage of variation in wealth: curvilinear coefficient of determination according to age of head of household	175

33.	Percentage of variation in wealth: curvilinear coefficient of determination according to years separated	175
34.	Circumstantial variables affecting wealth arranged by family type	177
35.	Chi square test for association of wealth and type of family	178
36.	Coefficient of determination of variation in wealth by type of family	178
37.	Composition of households by quartile of wealth in sheep	179
38.	Composition of households by quartile by type of family	180
39.	Chi square test of association of wealth in sheep and number of people in tent	181
40.	Scatter plot of wealth in sheep and number of people in tent	183
41.	Sheep/worker index of productivity vs. consumer/worker index (total group)	185
42.	Sheep/worker index of productivity vs. consumer/worker index (first quartile of wealth in sheep)	185
43.	Sheep/worker index of productivity vs. consumer/worker index (second quartile of wealth in sheep)	186
44.	Sheep/worker index of productivity vs. consumer/worker index (third quartile of wealth in sheep)	186
45.	Sheep/worker index of productivity vs. consumer/worker index (fourth quartile of wealth in sheep	186
46.	Composition of Yörük households in Nogaylar Köyü	206
47.	Joint land use by independent Yörük households in Nogaylar Köyü	208
48.	Nogaylar Yörük households by lineage	214

LIST OF FIGURES

1.	Map of Turkey	facing page 5
2.	Area of research	facing page 7
3.	Sequence of pastoral land use and movements of households	8
4.	Population pyramid: total	29
5.	Population pyramid: nomads	30
6.	Population pyramid: İslahiye	31
7.	Population pyramid: both villages	32

8.	Diagram of Satĭlar descent group	53
9.	Variability in household size among sedentary and nomadic Yörük	104
10.	Changes in mean inheritance of sheep over the past 25 years	111
11.	Age distributions in median sized herd of sheep	148
12.	Herd size, lambing, and mortality	150
13.	Herd size, lambing and mortality	152
14.	Wealth in sheep among nomadic Yörük households	163
15.	Herd size variations among lineages	164
16.	Plot rankings in wealth by percentile for nomad herds	167
17.	Variations in family size and type of family	171
18.	Distribution of population in households in Nogaylar	205
19.	Land use by family in Nogaylar Köyü	212

LIST OF PLATES
(following p. 236)

1. (Frontispiece) A spring camp
2. Girl leading her family's camels
3. First day of spring migration
4. Packing the caldron
5. Hasan Baba, prominent member of the Satĭlar lineage
6. Three brides
7. Bride making bread
8. Woman washing clothes
9. Camp group in migration
10. Cheese makers in the ağa's dairy tent
11. Preparing wool for felt rug
12. Weaving a rug for the tent
13. Admiring neighbor's newly born camel

INTRODUCTION

OBJECTIVES

THIS analysis has two primary objectives. First, although Turkic tribes of Iran are well documented in ethnographic literature, there have been few comparable anthropological studies of Turkish-speaking tribes in Anatolia.[1] The investigation described in the subsequent pages will hopefully fill that lacuna with respect to the Yörük tribes of southeastern Turkey. Here the organizing principles of nomadic and sedentary Yörük society will be treated in detail through an analysis of nomadic pastoral patterns of land use.

The study is set in the Middle Taurus range of southeastern and central Turkey. The populations and communities described represent different adaptations to what is a shared environment. Conversely, the ethnographic heterogeneity and associated patterns of production might be seen as giving rise to populations inhabiting differing socio-economic environments, all within one overarching state political structure, and often making use of the same basic array of resources. However, ethnicity establishes the outer limits of the groups studied.[2] This is true with respect to marriage in particular: but political and economic processes reinforce the lines drawn by ethnic ascription. At the same time, all communities, ethnically defined or not, come under the political jurisdiction of

---

[1] It should be mentioned that there are a number of good geographical and historical studies which deal with Yörük. Reference will be made to these in the text. Johnson provides a good summary bibliography of geographical works on Turkish nomads (1969:177-185) as does Kolars (1963). Also, Dr. Ulla Johansen, Heidelberg University, conducted extensive ethnographic investigations among Yörük tribes in Adana and Maras provinces in the 1950's.

[2] Following Barth (1969:13) the minimal criteria for ethnicity as used here are the characteristics of ascription by others and self-ascription.

the Turkish state, and all are integrated into a supra-regional market economy.

This is mentioned here because there is an understandable, although often unwarranted, tendency to make a dichotomy between tribal and state forms of political organization in which one form is held to preclude the other. In much of the Near East, tribal systems serve an important function in mediating relations between local communities and the government. The tribe, of course, need not be the only such mediating political instrument in a region. While among the Yörük ethnicity and the political concept of tribe are virtually coterminous, this is not always true for the sedentary populations with which they are in contact. For example, Kurdish, Türkmen, and Çerkes communities[3] often deal with the nomadic Yörük via channels external to descent-based political structures. They have elected officials whose authority does not derive in the final analysis from the local community. Thus the Yörük—in terms of involvement in a wider market economy and because of their relations with ethnically different sedentary populations--are similar, despite local peculiarities, to a broad range of nomadic pastoral societies.

[3] Çerkes is the Turkish term for Circassian Sunni Moslem immigrants to Ottoman provinces during the years 1857-1898, with most coming to western Anatolia and to what is today Jordan. Local terms will be employed for ethnic groups mentioned in the text, for example Türkmen in place of Turkoman. The orthography and phonology of Turkish given by G. L. Lewis (1967:1 *et seq.*) is followed:

Form	Value	Form	Value
A a	French *a* in *avoir*	M m	m
B b	b	N n	n
C c	j in jam	O o	French *o* in *note*
Ç ç	ch in church	Ö ö	German ö
D d	d	P p	p
E e	e French *e* in *etre*	R r	r
F f	f	S s	s in sit
G g	g in gate or in angular	Ş ş	sh in shape
Ğ ğ	lengthens preceding vowel	T t	t
H h	h in have	U u	u in put
İ i	French *i* in *si*	Ü ü	German *ü*
I ı	a in serial	V v	v
J j	French j	Y y	y in yet
K k	c in cat or in cure	Z z	z
L l	l in list or in wool		

INTRODUCTION 3

Rather than give equal weight to all of the variables which affect continued inter-specialization exchange, the following analysis will treat in depth those variables concerned with the processes of pasture acquisition and utilization by the pastoral nomads. This restriction is useful not only for clarity of presentation, but also because gaining access to a primary resource such as land is fundamental to the maintenance of the nomadic pastoral adaptation. The way in which this is achieved is crucial to an understanding of Yörük internal organization. The political economy of the nomadic population represents an adjustment to the need for negotiated rights to pasture owned by non-Yörük populations. The process of acquiring access to land, together with the nature of animal husbandry in a market economy, generates many of the organizational features of contemporary Yörük society, and largely establishes the range of options available to the herd owners.

The individual families, apart from choosing from a number of alternative strategies as they deploy their capital in sheep and labor, have also to contend with the decision of whether or not to settle. Although current economic pressures in southeastern Turkey favor increasingly rapid rates of settlement, nomadic pastoralism for many is a highly profitable economic activity. For others it is the only alternative to becoming part of the growing rural proletariat, the fate of the landless. Because of this, settlement will be discussed here as an integral aspect of nomadic pastoral adaptations in the region, and not as a special case encountered under unusual circumstances. Furthermore, a discussion of sedentarization will help elucidate changes which have occurred within Yörük society as responses to a shift in the mode of production when land was given to them, and when a highly flexible residence pattern was abandoned for village life.

OUTLINE

The analytic chapters are distributed through three broadly sketched sections. The first is concerned with identifying the topics and specifying the variables treated, the theoretic basis for the analysis and describing the geographical and social landscapes.

Chapters in the second section describe the nomadic pastoral population, in particular, the structure and organization of the domestic mode of production with reference to the prerequisites of animal husbandry, the social parameters of production, and the supra-domestic political structure. Relations with sedentary communities are relevant here. Statistical data are analyzed to establish household and herd variability. Also this analysis will be the base line for a general discussion of alternative economic strategies for households. Differing patterns of residence, migration, sedentarization, and market involvement become intelligible when viewed this way.

The third and final portion of the study will describe the settlement of formerly pastoral nomadic families of Yörük in the area of winter pastures. It will discuss some of the factors which select families out of the pastoral nomadic society and lead them to settle. The joint settlement of related families will be distinguished from the isolated settling of individual households acting alone. It will be shown why some are successful in the new economy and why others are not, and what changes have arisen in social life as adjustment to changes in production.

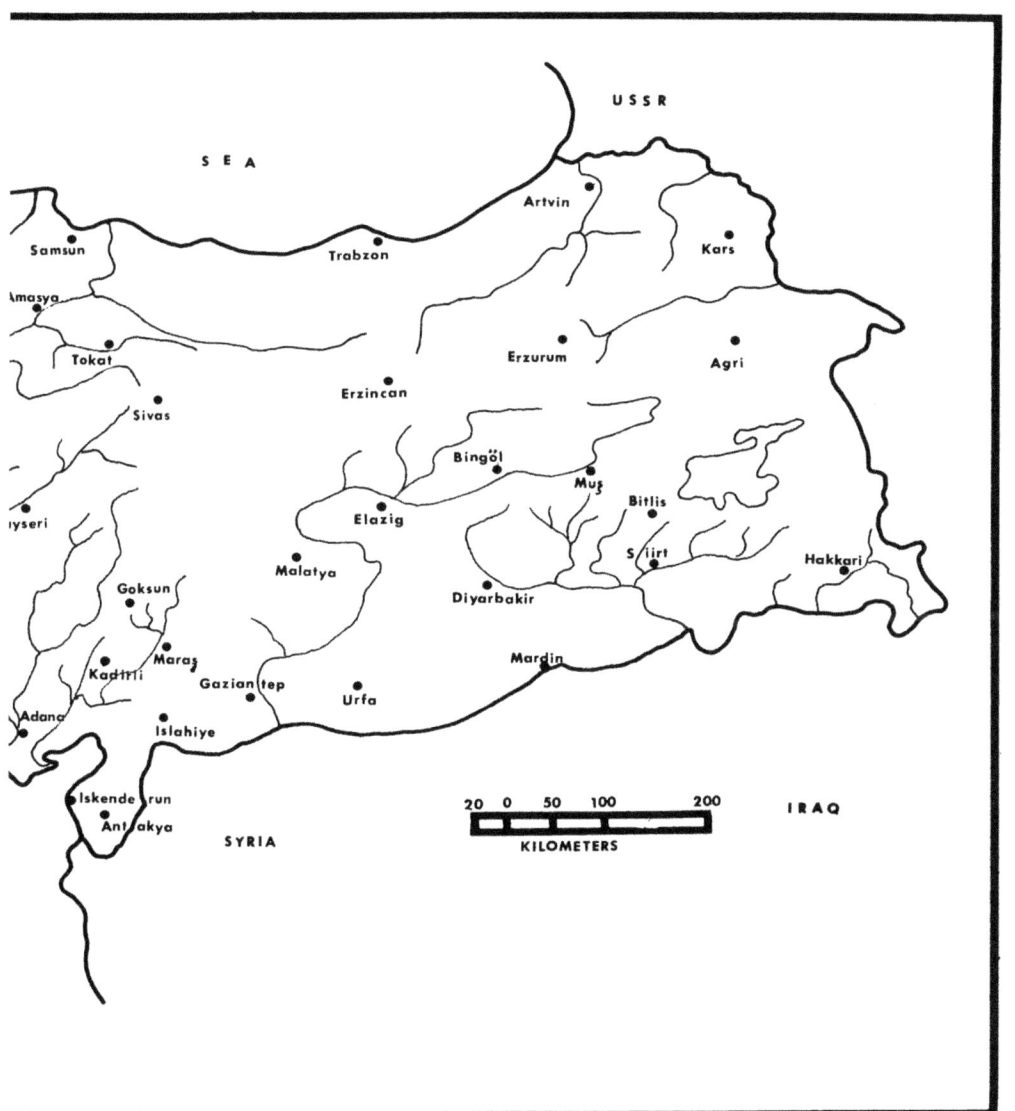

Fig. 1. Map of Turkey.

I
PASTURES, MIGRATORY ROUTES, AND THE SOCIAL LANDSCAPE

THE Yörük tribes whose movements define the area of research migrate semi-annually between two relatively fixed points. Members of the tribes move with their flocks and tents from the lowland plains of Maraş, Gaziantep, and Hatay provinces in the southeast of Turkey, passing over the Anti-Taurus Mountains, to arrive at summer pastures in the Middle Taurus range of central Anatolia, Kayseri Province. The migratory pattern is that common in most mountainous regions of the Near East. Domestic animals, here sheep and to a lesser extent goats, are supported in numbers beyond the year-round carrying capacity of any given pasture by the successive exploitation of climatically different altitudinal zones. The nomadic population which manages and subsists on these herds passes twice yearly through plains and mountain villages along the 200 kilometer trek leading from the Kırıkhan (elevation, 300 meters) and İslahiye (500 meters) districts in the south to points where, following mountain trails, camp groups leave the road to attain the windy, cold summer pastures of the Binboğa (peak, 2,830 meters), Tahtalı (2,850 meters), and Dumanlı (2,875 meters) mountains of the Taurus range along the edge of the central Anatolian plateau.

THE AREA OF STUDY

Like migratory water fowl in other climes, the movement of these peoples in search of grasslands marks the seasonal progression of winter to spring and summer to fall for the sedentary communities along their routes.[1] For the purposes of the following

[1] Sedentary communities in the summer pastures refer to the increasingly crisp cool weather at the end of summer as Yörük weather: *Yörük havası*, or *Yörüğ'ün gideceği hava*.

discussion, the migratory cycle and the area traversed establish the spatial limits of the analysis, much as they define the territory of primary field investigation.

The reasons for this are several, and should be made explicit at the onset. Among the Saçıkara (alternatively: Saçı Kara) and neighboring tribes, the migratory schedule is closely attuned to the agricultural cycles of the villages through which they pass, and from which they secure grazing lands. Studies of mountain nomadic pastoralism have emphasized the deterministic effects of seasonal changes in pastures, the needs and tolerances of livestock, and the character of approach routes to grasslands. However, in considering the Yörük adaptations which involve animal husbandry, careful attention must be paid to what might be termed the non-Yörük social environment, the villages which supply the nomads with grazing. Clearly the material or biological prerequisites of the herd delineate the extreme values of a number of essential variables, for example, the range of dates within which animals must be moved from one grazing zone to another in order to insure minimal acceptable rates of production. Nevertheless, upon examination, the actual order of migration, the residential pattern at any given time and, most importantly, pasture acquisition are conditioned by relations with the sedentary land owners whose economic interests are only partially identical to those of the nomads. The processes of negotiation and signing of formal contracts underlie the division of wealth within Yörük society and should be treated within a holistic framework. Furthermore, the Yörük rely on market-purchased foodstuffs. Therefore the price they obtain for the pastoral products they sell is the final determinant of the number of people that can be supported by this specialized means of production. If the price of grains and other products of sedentary life go up in relation to the market value of livestock and their by-products, it will take more animals to adequately maintain an individual in the nomadic pastoral system. Much of the dynamic interplay between specialized pastoral and agricultural populations derives from the nature of the exchange relationships. For example, the increased cost of grazing rights has substantially raised the number of animals it takes to support the "average" family, and hence selects for sedentarization. Probably the total number of animals owned by Yörük pastoralists is not greatly diminished in the last few years; however they are increasingly distributed among fewer and fewer families.

On another level, there are a number of particularistic grounds for defining the study broadly by the Yörük annual round

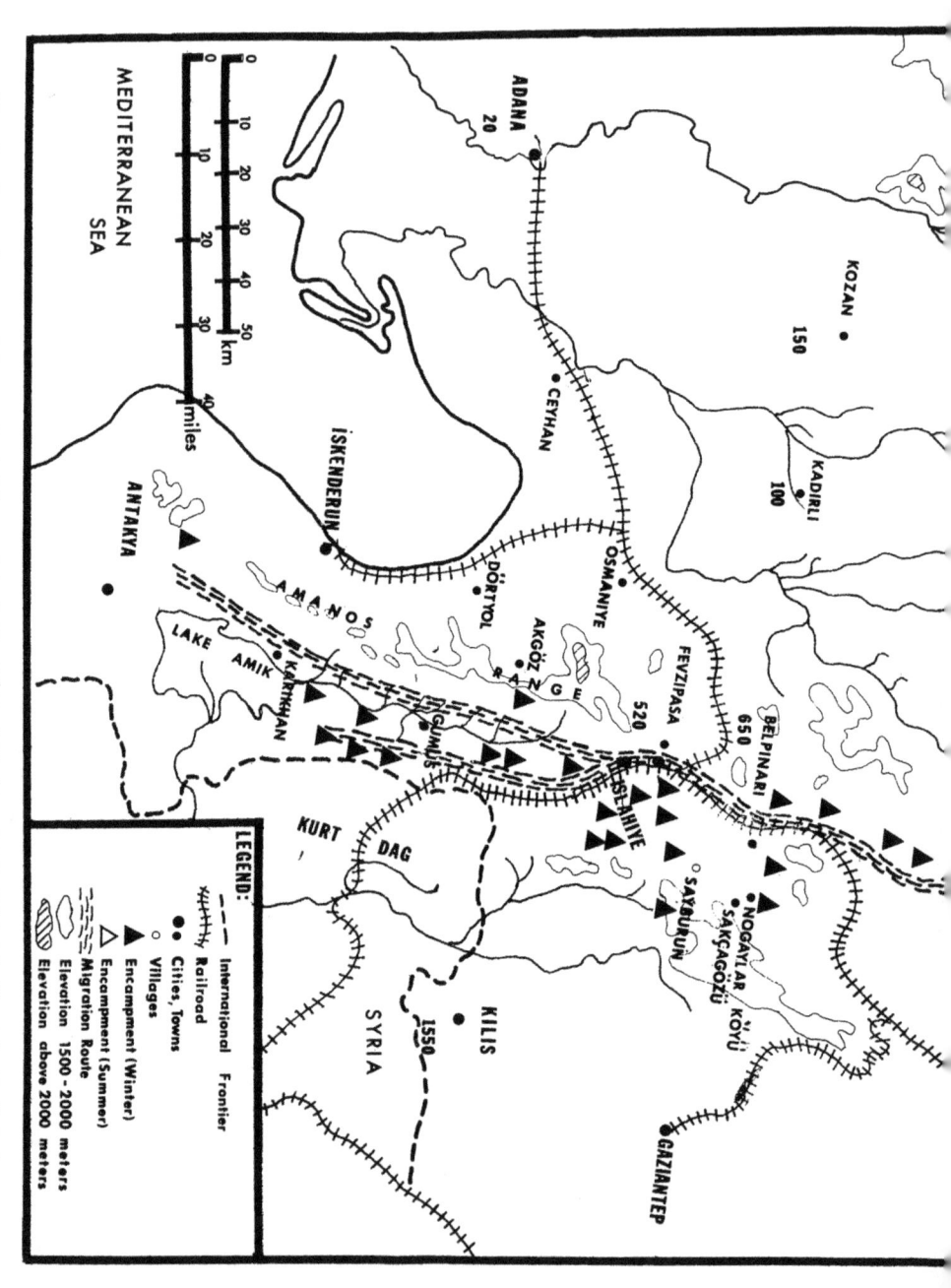

Fig. 2. Area of research (map adapted from plate 1-G; Atlas of Turkey, prepared by A. Tanoglu, S. Ering).

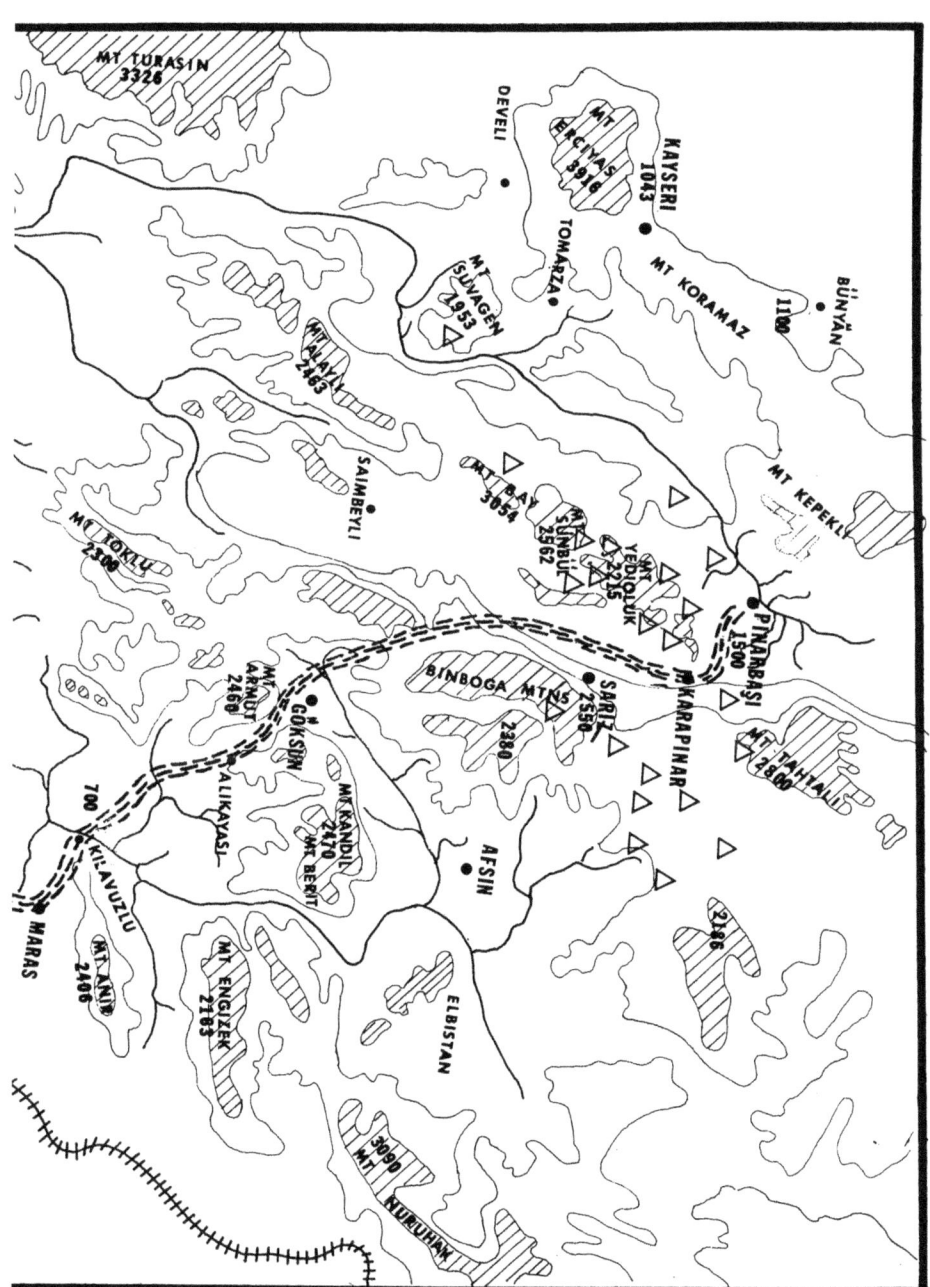

of migration rather than narrowly by tribe or community. As will be described in detail later, the Yörük tribes are not territorial in the usual sense; they are dispersed along much of Turkey's Mediterranean coast and highlands. In the area of investigation, a number of tribes or, better, a number of sections of dispersed tribes migrate in a similar fashion over a shared route and use a common set of alternative pastures. Furthermore, these localized segments of Yörük population possess a high degree of sociological coherence in the sense that a wide variety of social, economic, and political transactions occur within the Yörük community and are generated by it. The community is bounded by ethnic lines creating a sense of cultural identity which mitigates against those distinctions based on differing agnatic descent group membership and tribal divisions. Had a given tribe rather than a population been selected as the focus of the study, and many Saçıkara sections were visited by the ethnographer outside the area, it would have been difficult or misleading to speak of a pastoral nomadic adaptation and concomitant political economy. The highly dispersed original constituents of the tribes have little economic integration apart from that common to all participants in the Turkish national market economy.

THE GEOGRAPHIC DIMENSION

The area used by the Yörük nomadic pastoralists roughly cuts across four provinces of the Republic of Turkey. In the order that they are traversed as the pastoralists move from lowland plains and valley grazing upward to the central Anatolian plateau and adjacent mountain rim, these provinces (*vilayet*) are Hatay, Gaziantep, Maraş, and Kayseri (see Figs. 1 and 2).

From the vantage point of Yörük-defined patterns of land use, the region exploited by them is divided into three geographic areas or, temporally, according to the four migratory periods, each of which is associated with a specific physical environment (see Fig. 3). Geographically, one distinguishes lowland or plains pastures in the south (*kışlak*), the high mountain pastures to the northwest (*yayla*), and the rather more topographically variegated routes of access between them (*göç yolu*).

With respect to the seasonal cycle of land use, the herds are moved out in the spring from lowland plains grazing areas, taken on a one-and-a-half month trek to summer high mountain pastures, and returned again in fall to the winter quarters over the same

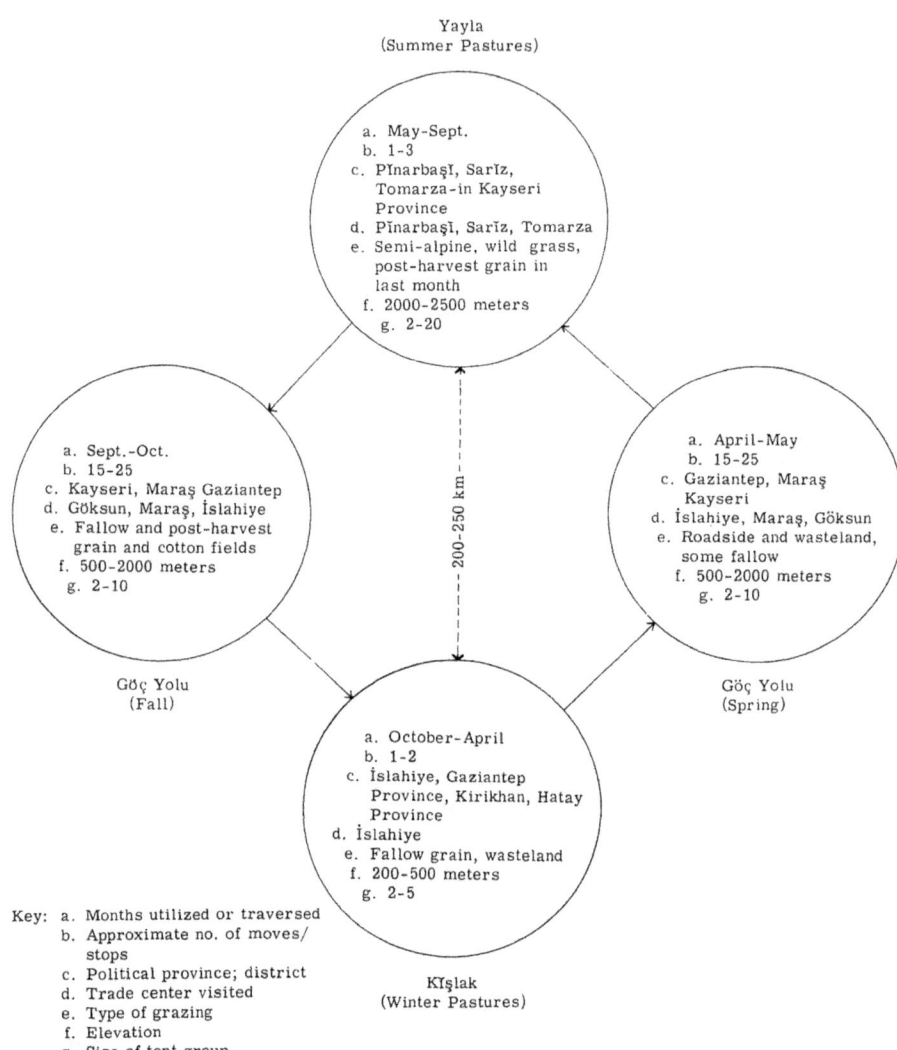

Fig. 3. Sequence of pastoral land use and movements of households.

route. Although the road (göç yolu) is the same both going to and returning from summer pastures (yayla), the conditions under which the trek is made are quite different, as are their importance for herd maintenance.

Kīşlak (Winter Pastures)

The term "winter pasture" is, perhaps, a misnomer made respectable only by the focus of the discussion on Yörük adaptation. The area is an extremely fertile and productive alluvial extension of the Amīk plain; one which supports a mechanized and market oriented agricultural economy. In this system the Yörük nomads are a more visible than important economic specialization. Keeping that in mind, the area defined by their winter encampments is largely contained between the Amanos range and Kurt Dağ, the former paralleling the southern Mediterranean coast with Kurt Dağ running in the same direction but farther inland. Kurt Dağ, in conjunction with the Kara Su River, forms a more-or-less natural border with Syria to the south. This border, which is closed to Yörük migration, together with the marshes and lakes of the Amīk constitutes the southern limits of Yörük grazing.

The Syrian-Turkish frontier restricts in an absolute way Yörük passage to grasslands in that direction. At the same time, military patrols and land mines offer sufficient problems for herd management that few families venture within three or four kilometers of the border, thus creating a rather wide buffer zone of good grazing lands. Special permits must be obtained from the government to camp within a 10 kilometer strip along the frontier and this deters many Yörük from camping along portions of the Kara Su near the border.

The valley, actually a series of interconnected plains of gently rising elevation, extends from Antakya, capital of the Hatay on the Asi River, north to Maraş covering a distance of some 170 kilometers. The area grazed by the Yörük herds runs somewhat more than half of this distance. The width of the valley varies from approximately 50 kilometers south of the Amīk to often less than 10 kilometers along the length of Kurt Dağ, narrowing to as little as three kilometers near Fevzipaşa to open in a funnel-shaped, irrigated plain around Türkoğlu (old name: Eloğlu), north to Maraş and Pazarcīk. The hill pass over Keferdiz (Sakçagözü) signals the point at which Kurt Dağ turns eastward in a sharp abutment.

The rich grasses and brilliant flowers characteristic of the higher Anti-Taurus mountains in Maraş and Kayseri, when the snow melts in the spring, are generally lacking in the parts of the Kurt Dağ range paralleling the Amanos. While deforestation by villagers in search of fuel goes on to the extent that the formerly extensive cover of deciduous trees is much restricted, there remain many wooded slopes.[2] These are primarily nettle trees on the lower reaches, while at 250 meters dense stands of Aleppo pine and black spruce give an unexpected sense of wilderness to what is a relatively densely inhabited region. The highest peak in the range (in İslahiye) is only 1,200 meters, rather low elevation for summer pasturage of any amount. It is used only by local non-Yörük villagers.

The Amanos range, as indicated above, forms a natural barrier stretching from the northeast near Maraş to the southwest, ending in Hīnzīr Burnu (ancient Rhosus) on the coast. Gavur Dağ, immediately northwest of İslahiye, the administrative center most visited by Yörük, is the range's most prominent peak. Its major pass, Arslanlī Beli, affords a natural route to Cilicia from Syria. Important highway connections across the often treacherous winter roads of Gavur Dağ (Mount Infidel) make its name of considerable antiquity sanctified by the daily imprecations of truck drivers.

The Ottoman rail network, expanded by the Germans in the late nineteenth century, reached this area in 1904, crossing by the repair facilities at Fevzipaşa and İslahiye, before passing along the valley to continue in one direction with the Baghdad line and in the other due south with the Aleppo and former Hedjaz routes. Although now made partially redundant by a first class highway system, the railroad was responsible for the early economic transformation of the region, culminating in the near complete mechanization of agriculture in the plains shortly after World War II (ca. 1949). As will be detailed later, these changes have had significant and continuing repercussions among the nomadic Yörük. The railway has also changed the appearance of the range itself. Whereas nineteenth century travellers remarked on the great stands of native cedar and pine (for example, Percy, 1901), now only scrub growth (*maquis*) and stony outcroppings remain over

---

[2] See Kolars (1966:passim) for an interesting discussion on the ecological impact of the goat in southwestern Anatolia, and for a demonstration that village woodcutting is more responsible for the extensive deforestation of the area than is small animal husbandry.

much of the Amanos, the trees having been cut for locomotive fuel during the coal scarcity of World War I.

The soil of the plain is extremely fertile, in marked contrast to that of the slopes of Kurt Dağ and those of the lower Amanos. Although the floral succession of the area is by no means clear, it is certain that the region has been a center of high agricultural production and population concentration since the Late Hittite Period (ca. 1300-700 B.C.) from which time numerous sites in the area are dated (Alkĭm, 1969:280-289). Following the historical development of settlements, and probably concomitant to the removal of virgin timber on the valley floor, great marshes have formed which have characterized the plain since prior to Turkish penetration in the tenth century A.D. These marshes are now largely drained and the resultant development of agriculture has vastly altered the nature of nomadic winter pastures. Irrigation is widespread on the valley floor. Rice and cotton, which date from the nineteenth century in the area of Maraş (Percy, 1901:99), now are primary cash crops throughout the area as far south as Antakya.

Double cropping or growing three crops in two years is common. Still there is considerable fallow land available in winter months, often on fields of wheat stubble (*firez*) which, after the fall harvest, remain empty until put to cotton in the spring. Whereas the valley floor is itself intensively cultivated, it is broken by frequent outcroppings of basalt-based rocky promontories. The slopes of these promontories are too irregular for intensive planting, and the wild grasses and scrub brush cover provide pasturage, as do the border zones between cultivated land and barren rock or forest along Kurt Dağ and the Amanos range. The remaining pine groves, although not choice for sheep, are suitable for goats. The government restricts access to most such stands. In the *sumak* (sumac) and thorn bushes of the Amanos herds of Yörük camels, collected from Yörük of all groups, graze and are cared for by several families of the Sarĭkeçili tribe (aşiret) who act as hired shepherds for tents camping under conditions optimal for sheep but not suitable for camels.[3]

Climatic conditions establish the zonal distribution of flora on which the Yörük livestock depend; but of more immediate concern are yearly variations in temperature and precipitation which affect

---

[3] Payment is in cash, and is calculated on a monthly basis per head of camel: roughly 20 to 30 T. Lira/month/camel ($1.00 = 12.00 T.L.).

pasture and animal mortality. In no portion of the nomadic pastoralist cycle is such variation more critical than in the kīşlak where the most time is spent, and where lambing takes place and the course of the year's milk production is set.

Altitude is the critical variable with respect to snowfall and temperature, although not with regard to precipitation in general. İslahiye, for which accurate figures are available, experiences an average of six days of snowfall a year, an annual mean precipitation of 856 millimeters, and a mean temperature of 16.7 C. Hoarfrost occurs 15 days a year, on the average, with 18.8 days of freezing weather (from *Gaziantep*, Köy İşleri Bakanlīğī, No. 64:18). Tables 1-5 summarize meteorological data from a local source (İslahiye) and indicate something of the variability which will later be referred to in discussions of herd management.

For the Yörük nomads, who use the region for five to six months in fall and winter, the critical climatic variable is the number of days of snowfall and freezing weather which can be

TABLE 1

VARIATIONS IN SNOWFALL DURING WINTER QUARTERS

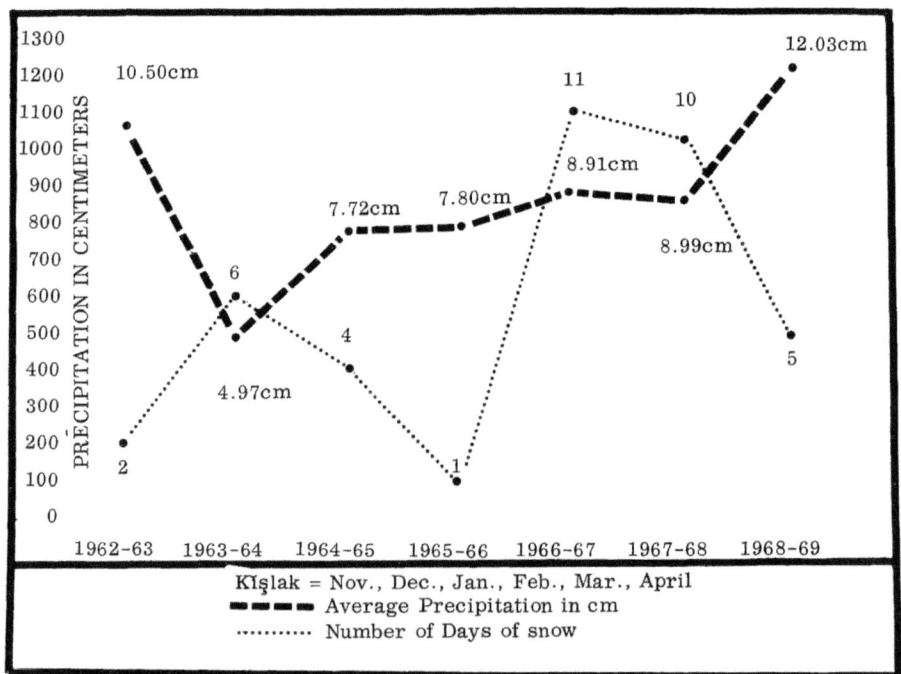

TABLE 2
TEMPERATURE VARIATIONS IN WINTER PASTURES*
(Kışlak)

(All temperatures in C°)

Kışlak Period	November High/Low	November Mean	December High/Low	December Mean	January High/Low	January Mean	February High/Low	February Mean	March High/Low	March Mean	April High/Low	April Mean	Mean per Kışlak
1962-63	28.3 / 7.0	16.8	20.5 / 2.4	8.5	15.0 / .8	8.0	16.8 / 1.3	8.7	21.2 / 2.0	8.5	25.7 / 7.0	14.9	9.4
1963-64	24.6 / 3.0	13.6	19.9 / -1.0	6.9	12.3 / -7.0	1.7	14.5 / -2.1	5.2	24.5 / -1.9	11.8	27.8 / 4.3	14.8	7.5
1964-65	26.6 / -0.5	13.0	16.8 / -1.5	7.5	13.7 / -2.5	5.8	15.4 / -1.2	5.6	23.4 / -0.2	11.5	24.3 / 0.0	13.4	9.5
1965-66	24.3 / 2.5	12.2	19.6 / -1.0	7.4	15.2 / 1.7	8.1	21.3 / 3.0	10.6	23.4 / 0.6	11.1	31.0 / 6.8	16.0	10.9
1966-67	29.8 / 6.6	15.6	17.0 / -0.2	8.0	14.3 / -2.0	5.3	16.0 / -2.6	3.4	19.0 / 0.6	8.4	28.4 / 2.8	13.8	9.4
1967-68	23.6 / -1.4	10.8	16.6 / -3.3	7.1	13.0 / -8.3	2.2	17.7 / 5.3	4.1	22.0 / -2.0	10.1	31.6 / 7.4	14.0	8.1
1968-69	23.2 / 5.3	12.3	16.6 / 2.4	7.6	14.8 / -1.5	5.0	15.4 / -4.0	6.1	22.0 / 3.2	11.6	28.2 / 1.8	13.3	9.3
Mean per month	29.8 / -1.4	13.47	20.5 / -3.3	7.57	15.0 / -8.3	5.15	17.7 / -5.3	6.53	24.8 / -2.0	10.3	31.6 / 0.0	14.71	7.71

*From local meteorological records (Devlet Meteoroloji İstasyonu İslahiye).

Key: High / Low, Mean

TABLE 3

MONTHLY TEMPERATURE VARIATIONS IN İSLAHIYE (C°)*

Mean monthly temperature (C°)

Year	I	II	III	IV	V	VI	VII	VIII	IX	X	XI	XII
1962	6.9	6.5	13.0	14.3	21.3	25.7	27.4	no data	26.0	20.3	16.8	8.5
1963	8.0	8.7	8.5	14.9	no data	24.4	27.2	28.7	25.1	20.3	13.6	6.9
1964	1.7	5.2	11.8	14.8	19.3	24.4	27.2	27.2	24.3	21.0	13.0	7.5
1965	5.8	5.6	11.5	13.4	19.3	25.9	27.7	27.7	25.7	15.9	12.2	7.4
1966	8.1	10.6	11.1	16.0	20.0	25.5	27.6	27.9	24.3	20.3	15.6	8.0
1967	5.3	3.4	8.4	13.8	18.9	23.3	26.7	27.0	24.4	18.6	10.8	7.1
1968	2.2	4.1	10.1	14	22.0	24.0	28.3	25.5	23.6	19.0	12.3	7.6
1969	5.0	6.4	11.6	13.3	21.2	25.1	26.2	27.6	25.5	18.5	12.1	7.6
Mean per month	5.37	6.31	10.50	14.31	20.29	24.69	27.12	27.37	24.86	19.20	13.30	7.57

*From local meteorological records (Devlet Meteoroloji İstasyonu, İslahiye)

TABLE 4
RAINFALL FOR YEARS RECORDED IN WINTER PASTURES*

Precipitation by month for İslahiye (cm)

Year	I	II	III	IV	V	VI	VII	VIII	IX	X	XI	XII	Total/Yr	Days of snow
1962	63.6	186.7	53.9	95.7	22.5	-	-	/	-	14.9	6.4	301.8	745.5†	2
1963	315.1	198.4	119.6	93.9	/	8.0	-	-	8.1	33.9	18.0	60.7	855.7†	2
1964	34.5	446.6	114.1	43.4	45.7	1.3	-	-	6.1	-	88.0	102.9	582.6	6
1965	132.0	224.6	127.2	93.6	3.7	5.9	-	0.1	-	42.1	58.6	211.4	899.2	5
1966	321.5	26.2	34.1	21.3	16.5	0.9	-	-	59.6	13.1	114.5	234.0	889.7	1
1967	129.0	135.3	130.1	94.7	48.4	1.1	0.6	-	0.3	67.5	125.7	108.1	840.8	12
1968	303.5	125.1	104.8	26.4	30.0	15.3	-	20.6	8.1	20.8	196.4	311.9	841.0	14
1969	220.1	139.3	159.4	59.5	95.9	20.3	-	-	-	19.9	39.5	139.8	893.7	4
Mean/mo. (cm)	191.16	147.77	111.65	66.06	37.52†	6.60	0.07	2.95†	10.27	26.52	80.12	183.82	864.51 average/year	5.8/year

*From local meteorological records (Devlet Meteoroloji İstasyonu, İslahiye)

/ = no record
- = no precipitation
† = incomplete data

TABLE 5

SUMMARY OF METEOROLOGICAL DATA FOR AREAS TRAVERSED BY YÖRÜK*

	Precipitation		Temperature (C°)			Freezing Weather		
	days	mean annual (mm)	maximum	minimum	mean	days	late frosts	early frosts
Yayla (summer pastures, Kayseri)	104	454	34.3	-28.5	6.9	141.0	April 1 to April 15	October 15 to November 1
Göç Yolu (migratory route, Maraş)	92.9	518.7	36.7	-29.5	9.6	102.0	early to mid-April	early October
Kışlak (winter pastures, Gaziantep)	83.5	855.5	43.2	-10.0	16.4	18.8	late February to early March	late November to early January

*Adapted from Table 4, Köy Isleri Bak (Yayinlar:64, 65, 96)

destructive to livestock. The quality of grazing, and the number of days of good grazing at any winter camp site, will vary according to a number of meteorological factors influencing floral growth. However, a number of successive freezing days or, worse, a heavy snowfall such as that of 1968, can drastically increase animal mortality. Pastures to the south of İslahiye, beginning roughly at Hassa, are appreciably warmer and rarely experience snowfall, although occasionally animal loss due to flooding is reported. These grazing lands are not sufficient to support the entire nomadic population, even should all wish to exchange the risks of cold weather for those of the border zone.

The upper reaches of the winter quarters, moving along the north-south axis of the valley, are both somewhat higher in altitude and more prone to heavy snowfall. While Maraş at the edge of the plain is relatively snow-free at ca. 700 meters elevation, immediately behind the city, where heavy snowfall is common, lies the beginning of the zone of mandatory stall feeding of domesticated livestock (ca. 1,000 meters). Although Yörük are found in winter encampments up to within one to 10 kilometers south of Maraş, most camp sites are below the Kümerler-Gaziantep highway (Figs. 1 and 2).

Göç Yolu (Migration Route)

The area lying between the southern extremes of the winter pastures and the nearest set of summer pastures around Sarïz, in Kayseri province, is strikingly different in climate and topography. Except as a migratory route for the Yörük, it seemingly has little geographic or ecological unity of its own. Whereas the range of winter pastures is basically framed within one long valley whose principal towns and villages are closely integrated in terms of economy and communications, the road north passes through a succession of mountain valleys which are economically dependent on the one main road, but which otherwise remain isolated from one another.

In general, the topographic relief is severe, with great variation in the floral cover and cultigens on which village production relies. Both are largely associated with elevation and relative compass orientations within each valley. While agriculture is the mainstay of all villages along the Yörük route, those higher in elevation tend to engage more in animal husbandry. Mountain villages of all types maintain more animals than do those of the İslahiye region because animal traction is more important in the highly fragmented field systems of the former area. Village-based small animal pastoralism (transhumance) is a common feature in the western Mediterranean and the Balkans, as well as in the Near East. One of the local consequences of this pattern in the Maraş-Göksun region is that most available mountain pasturage is utilized by village herds which need move only a few kilometers to gain them. Although some pastures are open or, at least rentable, they are not often used by Yörük of any tribe because they are so dispersed as to enable only a few tents to camp together. These tents would then be isolated from the main body of the tribe. Some individual tents from Kozan or Kadirli do use grazing lands around Göksun, but not an appreciable number. The groups studied here prefer to pasture in the less densely settled area to the north on the rim of the Anatolian plateau where, once situated, large numbers of families are within walking distance of one another.

Snowfall is heavy in the approaches to Göksun, beginning in mid-December and lasting on the ground through February. While the southern-most valley floors experience visibly milder climate with little lasting snow, all of the pastures associated with villages are snowbound until March and early April. The threat of a late blizzard along the route up to summer grazing (April or even May) is a factor which is considered in the decision to move from the kışlak.

Run-off irrigation is important in many villages not only for cereals but also for the grasses that supply animals through the long winter months. While wheat and barley are of primary economic importance, arboriculture, tobacco, and melons are a significant source of cash income. Timber is a highly salable resource, but is cut and sold by government monopoly.

From a Yörük perspective, the trek between the stable winter and summer encampments is more a set of obstacles than a productive period within the migratory schedule. This is because in spring it is difficult to secure adequate roadside forage and to avoid conflict with villagers over crop damage. Whereas the ambiance of domestic caravans walking at dawn along rushing mountain streams is a compelling reason for the ethnographer's presence, to the Yörük head of household, moving in this season is *rezillik* or misery (literally: vile).

The road itself rises sharply outside Maraş, and then again after passing through the Ali Kayasï gorge, following a laterally positioned series of valley confines upward in stages until reaching the highest pass, Ayer Bel (2,500 meters), just before Göksun, which is midway.

PASTURES, ROUTES, SOCIAL LANDSCAPE

Larger portions of the road below Göksun lead through state owned or regulated pine forests where sheep, but not goats, are permitted. In general while grazing varies from valley to valley, it is poor in the spring when roadside fields are green with winter wheat and other grain, forcing the sheep to be moved long distances to find even scanty tracts of wild grass. Fall is quite different: post-harvest grain fields provide much grazing with little danger of crop damage, and the downward trek is correspondingly easier and of longer duration.

For nomadic Yörük, annual climatic variation is important during the month-long migration to yayla and, to a lesser extent, during the two-month return trip. In the winter quarters such variation affects rates of animal kill-off and spontaneous abortion (bırakma), to be discussed later.

Yayla (Summer Pastures)

High summer pastures (yayla) are still snow covered in part when the Yörük herds arrive in May and, with the exception of the ice fields themselves, rich expanses of flowering Alpine and semi-Alpine plants offer welcome relief to the flocks exhausted by the migration. The quality of this early grazing is less subject to yearly fluctuations in rain and snowfall, as even the mildest winter suffices for the initial period of lush vegetation. However, summer rain and, in particular, late showers can extend the yayla season by weeks. By early August desiccation greatly reduces available grassland, and water sources (both small springs and wells) are so depleted that some pastures become unusable for that reason alone. Not all yayla tracts suffer from limitations of drinking water for animals. In general it is the lack of fresh grass rather than the coming of cold weather that marks the end of the season in the fall. As pastures give out, with the highest ones in Dumanlı holding on the longest, tent groups begin to gather along the road where they often camp for a week or so in stream-side clusters prior to setting out for kışlak.

The pasture lands themselves are deforested and the dead root systems of large pines attest to the correctness of the Yörük assertion that until 10 to 15 years ago substantial wooded tracts were common. As elsewhere, the trees were cut for village fuel. The Yörük use the dead roots for cooking fires, supplemented by thorn and evergreen shrubs. The mountain villages below the pastures are distinguished by dense groves of poplars which are planted and maintained along sources of water for use in village house construction. The villages which own the pastures used by the Yörük are generally remote from the nomad camps; indeed, it is rare that one is visible from the tents.

As in the area of winter quarters, all pasture is owned by non-Yörük villagers, either as village commons (*mer'a*) or, less often, as private property held by individuals. While in the winter pastures fallow and post-harvest crop land is much utilized by nomad animals, in the yayla only land which is not under cultivation is available.

Village herds in the Türkmen and Çerkes communities visited averaged about 25 sheep and goats (mixed) per household, with some herds of more than 100. Men already fairly wealthy in land also tended to own the most sheep. Some cattle are kept in addition to the pair of oxen vital to the self-sufficiency of the village household. Again, cattle like sheep are held in larger numbers by land owning families. This is because domesticated grasses must be collected and stored for the long winter period.

Village herds in summer are taken up to high yayla pastures by members of their owner's household. All of the animals of a village make this move on the same day and for the duration of the stay the villages are largely deserted except for men working the fields. But by July most animals are again brought to tracts closer to the village proper, often to graze on harvested hay fields. These pastures are not, of course, rented to the Yörük as there would be insufficient good grazing for both. However, once the village animals are removed Yörük sometimes do bring their sheep onto them for a few weeks prior to decamping in the fall. Often they do not have to pay for this temporary occupancy.

Most arable land is restricted to narrow valley-bottom or stream-side plots which reflect the irregular contours of the topography. Much of the field production is not amenable to mechanization and, when compared with the İslahiye area, agriculture can justly be termed strongly subsistence oriented. Run-off irrigation is used on the more level valley floors, with streams being diverted through canalization for this purpose. There is little attempt to terrace hillsides to increase the amount of cultivable land. The soil on the slopes is generally so poor, due, no doubt, to erosion which has followed deforestation, that should terracing be attempted, it would necessitate a laborious process of enrichment.

The villages are very dispersed and those not situated on the Göksun-Sarız-Pınarbaşı road are often not accessible by motor

PASTURES, ROUTES, SOCIAL LANDSCAPE

transport. Although the settlement pattern and history of occupation are not entirely clear, it is apparent that during and after World War I depopulation occurred, and that for the remaining (and new) villages, land shortage was not a significant problem (cf. Stirling, 1965:134 ff). This has now changed and a number of inter-village legal and extra-legal contests are underway to determine mer'a boundaries which will assume more and more importance as pressure on land of all sorts increases with the growth of population.

All of the villages in which the Yörük yayla pastures are located are administratively connected with either Pinarbaşĭ, Sarĭz, or Tomarza district (*kaza*) centers in Kayseri province (see Fig. 2). Most are found in Pinarbaşĭ and as that town is also the largest, it serves as the market and meeting place for Yörük of all tribes during the summer months.

THE SOCIAL LANDSCAPE

In the opening pages, ethnic heterogeneity as well as geographic diversity was alluded to as characteristic of the area. While ethnic variety contributes to the dynamics of the regional system of land use, the distribution of ethnic groups does not correlate with any set of strictly environmental features. More directly it reflects past politics and, in particular, the differing ways in which ethnically defined populations articulated with the former Ottoman government of Turkey and its Republican successors. For example, the Circassian (Çerkes) immigrants to Anatolia were granted right of settlement and land in the middle and late nineteenth century. Türkmen and nomadic Kurdish tribes were settled by force in 1865. Then, as now, no ethnic group could claim a monopoly of the techniques of any specialized mode of production. This meant that the territorial expression of any population was not limited by a commitment to a narrow range of resources or by a political economy dependent on one mode or level of production. Few of the ethnic groups presently encountered along the Yörük schedule of migration have occupied their contemporary positions within the larger regional settlement pattern for any substantial period of time. The Yörük pastoral nomadic tribes themselves are among the most recent arrivals to the area. Several populations of significance 50 years ago are no longer found, and others have drastically altered their basic means of land use in response to both changing technology and a highly variable political milieu.

Before presenting a brief resume of the social landscape essential to an understanding of the contemporary pattern of nomadic pastoral land use, a number of conceptual questions must be considered. This may enable us to avoid the confusion that often attends studies of nomadic pastoralism. Foremost, perhaps, is the way in which such terms as "nomad," "true nomad," "semi-nomad," and "transhumant" are employed. Too much concern has been directed toward the elaboration of taxonomies and too little toward their usefulness or logical consistency. This problem will not be pursued here except to mention that there is no necessary relationship between the amount of regular movement of residence and the degree of dependence on livestock production. Rather, both should be treated as independent variables: one does not necessarily involve the other. Furthermore, distinctions are often made according to a typology based on migratory patterns without questioning the assumption that migration is a determining, or even an important, factor in shaping the social and economic system under consideration.

In addition, nomadism is sometimes treated as a "culture type": nomadic peoples are held to differ perforce in their political and social organization from sedentary societies. Often, however, the same tribe is found to encompass both far-ranging nomadic pastoralist and sedentary agricultural segments. By classifying societies for general comparison according to only one dimension of their adaptation, here movement of residence or animal husbandry, oversimplification results which can obscure considerable variation in social and political organization. The present discussion focuses on a specific nomadic pastoralist economy and how this system of production is integrated into a larger, regional pattern of land use involving a number of different community-level political economies.

The literature on the Near East is replete with references to the antipathy felt by nomads for peasants. Occasionally these references are misleading and probably result from the confusion of ethnicity with specific modes of production. This is understandable for two reasons. In many areas of the Near East, particularly in desert zones, nomadic pastoralism is often pursued by a single ethnic group and as a consequence this mode of production locally acquires an ethnic coloration (see Barth, 1969:19-20; Haaland, 1969:54-55). Furthermore, there are economic reasons in many areas for conflict between sedentary agricultural and nomadic pastoralist communities in that they are in direct competition for land under certain circumstances. However, such conflict is not inherent in the modes of production, and, despite possible hostility or a lack of warm social relations, exchanges between pastoral nomadic and other specializations is important.

The Yörük, for example, view their social environment through eyes conditioned by their own ethnic experience. Accordingly, they emphasize a number of cultural, linguistic, and religious distinctions when speaking of their neighbors, all Turkish citizens but locally identified, as traditionally is the case, by ethnic ascription, and within each such rubric, by such increasingly finer criteria as religion, tribal segment, and locality of residence. The attitudes Yörük hold toward other ethnic groups, sometimes negative or condescending, should not be considered the response of "nomad" to "peasant," but simply that of one excluding social entity toward another. The attitude of the Saçıkara Yörük toward farming is largely a neutral one, but it varies among individuals according to how each views his own self-interest. While there is a close association in the minds of the Yörük between nomadic pastoralism and their ethnic identity, informants are all agreed that Yörük identity would not be lost with settlement.

Nomadism, or the regular movement of residence, is represented in the area by two ethnically defined populations apart from the Yörük: the so-called *Arabacı* who are purportedly East European Gypsies, and indigenous Anatolian Gypsies (*Çingene*). These two populations, insignificant in actual numbers, husband few animals and range far afield each spring and summer to central and eastern Anatolia working as musicians, dentists, circumcisers, fortune tellers, traders in hides, and performing a number of other traditionally little esteemed services. These tribes raise animals, if at all, primarily for their own transport; the Arabacı own oxen and horses to pull their gaily colored wagons, while the poorer-appearing Çingene use donkeys to carry their possessions and characteristic white tents. Both of these winter around İslahiye, in the Hatay region, and along the coast. They are a common sight along the road throughout the area of study. Like Yörük, Gypsies have settled in many of the major towns of the southeast, as well as in a number of villages on government-granted land.

There is little direct competition between Yörük and the Gypsies as there is no overlap in the resources used. In fact such contact as does exist results from the occasional engaging of Gypsy services for cash payment. These services (especially dental work and circumcision) are usually those customarily reserved for such practitioners in the Near East because they are defined by Islamic ideology as unclean. Nevertheless, no direct ties of a patron-client nature develop between Yörük and Gypsy and the services provided by the Gypsies give them no economic or other influence in the affairs of the people who engage them.

A significant, perhaps predominant, cultural identification in the area of winter pastures is that provided by Kurdish ethnicity. This is less true of the other areas traversed or used by the Yörük tribes studied here, although there are several Kurdish villages of the Alevi sect in Pınarbaşı and Tomarza. Refering now only to the tribes settled in and around the İslahiye district, local tradition puts their entry into the area following the 1517 Baghdad campaign of Selim II, who reputedly rewarded a leader of the Çellikanlı Kurdish tribe (Sunni) with grazing rights in return for tribal military levies in Iraq. Two other locally important Kurdish tribes are the Bellikanlı and the Mellikanlı, likewise formerly nomadic but now settled. They are said to have entered the region under the same circumstances as the Çellikanlı.

It is probably impossible to arrive at an accurate figure for the Kurdish population in the area of study. Virtually all of the villages on whose land Yörük camped were Kurdish, belonging to one of the three tribal designations mentioned above. Probably over half of the present inhabitants of the district of İslahiye are of Kurdish ancestry. Kurdish is often heard spoken in the streets of İslahiye, although most, if not all, men appeared to be bilingual. The extent to which Kurdish tribal identity is important politically or economically is a matter for empirical determination and is beyond the scope of this study. However, it is safe to venture that it is likely to prove of considerable significance in most communities, including İslahiye proper, where political factions seem often to be coterminous with tribal divisions.

Kurdish villages in the lowlands are generally of two types, irrespective of tribal identity. Most common is the large landlord-dominated village of tenant farmers or sharecroppers, many of whom supplement their income by providing paid agricultural labor during the cotton and rice planting and harvesting seasons. Less prevalent are the villages where small farmers maintain their own fields without falling under the complete economic hegemony of any one family or tribal leader. Such distinctions, while important for a description of the region generally, do not directly affect how the Yörük nomads obtain their land for grazing. Even though most such pasture is rented from the large land owners, the rent paid in any event is largely uninfluenced by the nature of field ownership.

Ethnicity is important in another respect and thus does directly impinge on the nomadic Yörük economy. Because most of the agricultural land is owned by Kurds, and as residence is in nucleated villages, it is difficult for wealthy Yörük simply to purchase land should they wish to settle. While it would not be difficult to find a seller, it would be difficult for the Yörük buyer to exercise ownership completely. Yörük who have settled as single households in this manner have not been successful due, it is said, to a lack of cooperation on the part of the dominant cultural group.

Ninety-two households of Yörük are settled in two villages studied by the ethnographer (Sayburun and Nogaylar) and 81 households have settled in İslahiye, also included in the study. Sayburun was settled in 1949 by Kurds of the Çellikanlı tribe and two Yörük lineages on free land granted by the government. It is predominately a community of small landholders, with two or three families from each group owning enough to be considered economically influential in the village. Among the Yörük these families are headed by men regarded as leaders of named descent groups, and their positions of wealth owe largely to the fact that, being owners of extensive herds before settlement, they could augment the land granted by the state with that sold to them by their Kurdish and Yörük neighbors. The Yörük and Kurdish settlers form two compact settlements at a distance of several kilometers from each other, although they share a common formal political organization with respect to the offices defined by Turkish law for village administration.

Nogaylar, to be discussed later, is somewhat different. Here land was granted Yörük in a pre-existing Nogay Turk or Çerkes village which was then dominated by one landowning family. This family was occupying village lands which had originally been granted to some 100 households that had established the village in 1856-1865, upon their arrival from the Nogay River basin region of the Caucasuses. After malarial epidemics in the late nineteenth century, most of the original landowners died or moved to upland communities in Kayseri province, leaving their land in the hands of the remaining family. Legally this land reverted to the state. In 1949, upon petition by 27 families from the Saçıkara tribe, part of it was parceled among the Yörük and the landless workers of the Nogay.

While village Yörük households are socially not distinguished from their nomadic relatives, their presence has little overall effect on pasture acquisition in the lowlands. What pasturage is found within village borders is either utilized by villager-owned animals, or by a few close patrilineal kinsmen of Yörük residents.[4] Both the leading Yörük landowner of Nogaylar and the two of Sayburun have useful connections with officials and merchants in İslahiye, and often intercede as intermediaries on behalf of members of their own lineages, or clients, whether nomadic or sedentary. In this respect, the leading families from among those settled in İslahiye are more important. İslahiye is the administrative center for most of the area of winter pastures, and is the principal trading town for the region. Approximately 25 to 30 shops and businesses are owned by sedentary Yörük. These include the town's newspaper, several furniture and clothing stores, shoe stores, cotton gins (*çırçır*), brokers in grain and commodities on a wholesale basis, and numerous small groceries (*bakkal*). Of these, only a few grocery and dry goods stores can claim a clientele drawn exclusively from the Yörük community, although most of the businesses draw heavily on members of their descent group for regular patronage.

It is interesting to note parenthetically that many of the Yörük who settled out of poverty or failure as herders 20 years ago are now well-established merchants. In many ways it is possible to view the system of animal husbandry practiced by the Yörük as a good preparation for sedentary commercial life. Nomadic members of the tribe are continually entering into partnerships for marketing, etc.; credit is widely extended with complicated arrangements for interest, and animals are bought on speculation for sale with the hope of taking advantage of short-term fluctuations in price in regional markets. One nomadic lineage leader (*ağa*) told the researcher that business was the best profession, better even than an official position with the government.

Most nomadic households have settled patrilineal relatives in the grocery and dry goods business and most such supplies are purchased from shops which grant credit through the winter months. While credit does not invariably move along lines established by patrilineal kinship—and some shops seem to extend

---

[4] Ironically, the nomadic lineages most likely to continue profitable animal husbandry are those which have lineage members in the two villages of settled Yörük as they have cheap or free use of village commons (mer'a).

credit to virtually anyone who requires it—it was found in observing such transactions over a year and a half that the great majority of creditor-debtor dyads involved members from the same descent group (*kabile*), normally close agnates.[5]

What is relevant to the present discussion is that the sedentary Yörük community is a major component of the social landscape of its nomadic kinsmen. Further, there is no social discontinuity separating nomadic from sedentary households. Marriage and social intercourse form patterns or exhibit statistical characteristics largely undeflected by this dichotomy. Until now very little sense of "urban" or "village" identity has visibly developed among sedentary families, and the primary referent remains rooted in tribe or descent groups.

As there are only four or five families of settled Yörük in the Pĭnarbaşĭ area, the intensity of social and economic transactions among sedentary and nomadic families of the tribe is greatest during the period of winter camps and while the tents are moving within the plain below Maraş. Nevertheless, even during summer months men return by bus or truck from Pĭnarbaşĭ to İslahiye on business, for social visits, or to appear before government officials in the district where they are legally resident. Thus while the *type* of residence, sedentary or nomadic, is immaterial to many social processes, locality or sheer distance does have an influence. While serious matters will draw Yörük to their kinsmen from great distances, as does the desire to see relatives whom one has not seen for a long period, day-to-day purchases of flour and other staples are necessarily made with non-kin in the closest market town. Credit, however, is rarely available under these circumstances. Furthermore, the two villages mentioned earlier are somewhat less in contact with nomadic families outside the descent groupings represented in the settlements for the same reason of geographic separation.

Although no estimate of population size or of demographic processes has been presented so far for non-Yörük communities,

---

[5] The researcher's field assistant from the tribe established a small grocery with money from the sale of his herd. He purchased much of his stock on credit from non-Yörük wholesalers, and most of his sales were for credit to Yörük. However, he gave credit to many individuals with whom he had had no previous dealings and who were not related. While perhaps only in part due to this, he experienced extreme difficulty in collecting and was on the verge of failure at the end of the study.

this information was collected in a detailed and systematic manner for the Yörük of all residence types.⁶ The accompanying graphs (Figs. 4-7) describe the distribution of population, households and age-sex parameters over the four communities studied: İslahiye, Nogaylar, Sayburun, and the nomadic pastoralists. One point is worth drawing the reader's attention to. Numerous writers concerned with either Yörük history or their pastoral nomadic adaptation have quite correctly noted that nomadic pastoralism is rapidly declining as a viable pattern (for example, Kolars, 1963; Johnson, 1969:23-23; Planhol and İnandik, 1959:375-389). However, it should be stressed that in the region of study, Yörük pastoralism, whatever its long-term ability to maintain itself may be, demographically is still very much represented by a sizeable and growing population. This is clear from the population pyramids (see Figs. 4-7) which indicate that the factors affecting sedentarization are not specific to any segment of the population as defined by age, sex, or marital status. It is possible, however, to see the demographic effects of mass settlement 20 years ago. It is likely that this is the last remaining viable *nomadic* Yörük population in Turkey.

The description of the social landscape will be complete with mention of two other ethnic groups with which the Yörük nomads have regular contact in the summer pastures: the Çerkes and Türkmen. There are only two or three villages of Çerkes in the İslahiye region. In the words of the local inhabitants, they have become "Turkified" (*Türkleştirildiler*), meaning that they speak only Turkish, practice few, if any, uniquely Çerkes social customs, and no longer observe the prohibition against marrying kin within seven ascending or descending generations (*göbek*). While this latter custom was probably, if the Crimean Tartars are analogous, limited in practice to local group or named descent group exogamy, nevertheless the adoption of Turkish forms of close cousin marriage is a realistic indication of their adjustment to a new cultural milieu.

There are 15 to 20 Çerkes villages in the Pinarbaşi-Sariz area of summer pastures that own yayla pastures which they rent to Yörük nomads. Here the Çerkes maintain a strong sense of ethnic and cultural identity, evidenced not only in the villages but

---

[6] Dr. Frederic Shorter provided substantial assistance in preparing the questionnaire schedule for the demographic data, and also contributed many suggestions for its analysis.

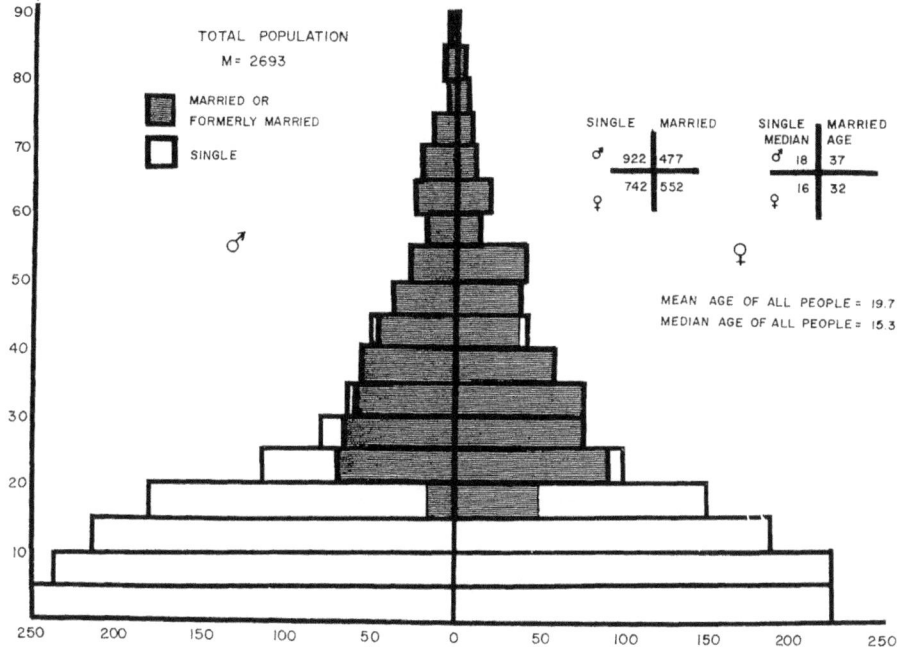

Fig. 4. Population pyramid for total population under study, nomad and sedentarized Yörük populations.

also in Pĭnarbaşĭ itself where they own numerous businesses. Percy (1901:84-92) travelling in the 1890's, comments on the settlement of Çerkes in the vicinity of Sarĭz. Sümer, a noted Turkish historian of tribal peoples in Anatolia, writes that this involved granting them formerly Avşar Türkmen-owned grazing lands (1967a:195-96). Certainly conflict continues over actual ownership of some tracts which were divided among the two populations in 1865. The ethnographer witnessed a land dispute between Avşar and Çerkes villagers in 1969.

The Yörük come into contact with Türkmen families of several tribes along their migratory route, but most frequently they have to deal with Avşar Türkmen in the summer pastures. The Avşar are a major branch of the Anatolian Oğhuz Türkmen (Sümer, 1967a: passim; see 206-08 for diagram of descent lines). As mentioned previously, the Avşar control many of the yayla pastures rented by the Yörük. The Avşar are held by the Yörük to be

30   THE YÖRÜK OF SOUTHEASTERN TURKEY

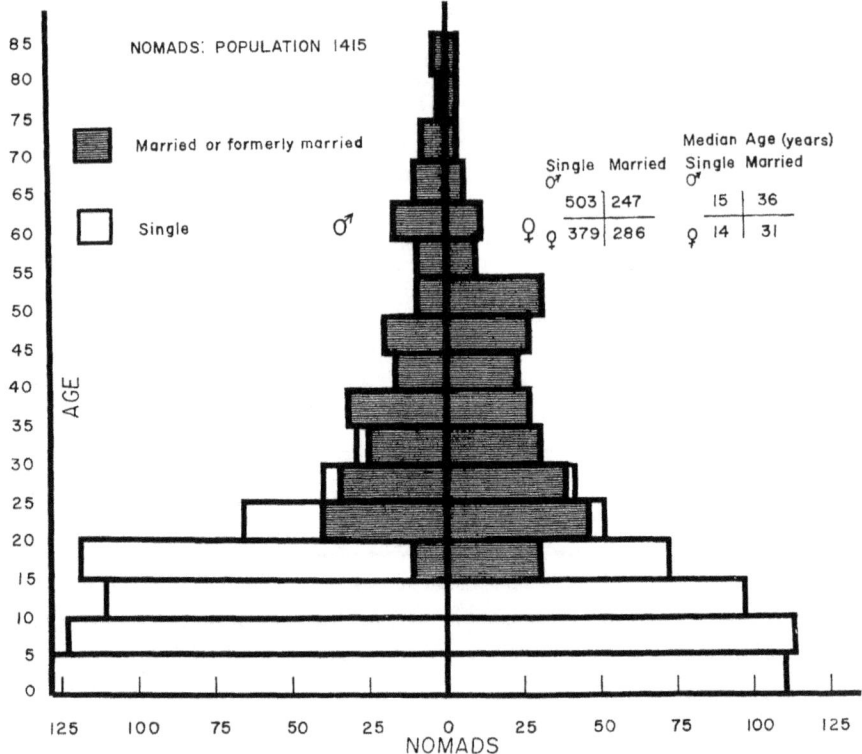

Fig. 5. Population pyramid for Yörük nomad population.

remotely from the same ethnic stock ($kök$).[7] They are, of course, Turkish speakers. Most Yörük informants declare the Avşar to be "untrustworthy neighbors," even though there is a vague recognition of common ancestry and a shared origin in Central Asia. *Khorasan* is almost invariably cited as the ancient homeland of the Yörük. This presumed common descent has not led to rates of intermarriage that are more frequent than obtain with non-Turkish ethnic groups. The total number of women of non-Yörük origin constitutes less than two percent of total married women, and most of these are married to village Yörük (Fig. 6).

---

[7] See Sümer (1967a:277-78) for a list of Türkmen villages in Sariz and Pinarbaşi. All of the Avşar encountered by the ethnographer stated that they were Sunni Moslems and were so regarded by the Sunni Yörük. Percy (1901) mentions an Avşar village (Yalak) which he says is Kizilbaş. These are not, for rural Anatolia, mutually exclusive identifications.

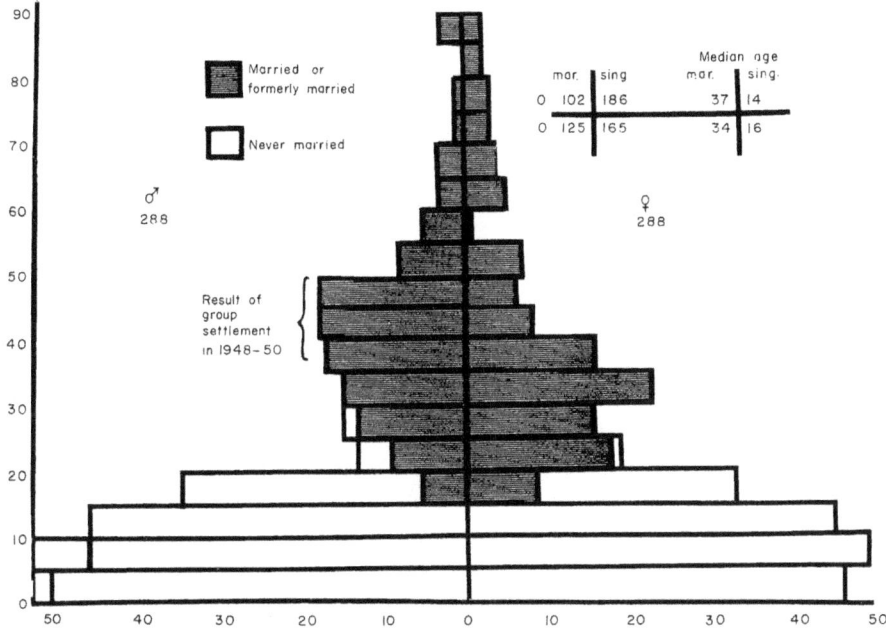

Fig. 6. Population pyramid for İslahiye (population: 576).

During the summer months animal theft is a major concern of the herders, and from their own accounts is a significant source of loss. The Yörük themselves regard sheep stealing with considerable disapproval, and not only declare it contemptible, but an act which no man would commit against an enemy even in a blood feud. The Avşar are widely held by the Yörük to be sheep thieves, and there can be little doubt that village youths, if not their elders, take advantage of straying animals in difficult herding country to furnish a mountaintop banquet if the opportunity arises. Both the Çerkes and the Alevi Kurdish communities are better regarded by the Yörük in this respect.[8]

---

[8] The Kurds are regarded as particularly honest (*söz sahibi*). The Yörük have warmer personal relations with their Kurdish neighbors in the winter pastures despite problems of crop damage than they do with any of the groups or communities encountered in the yayla areas. This is because of the longer stay in kışlak, and better communications networks in general. Long months of rainy weather encourage Yörük and Kurd alike to seek out neighbors with whom to pass the time.

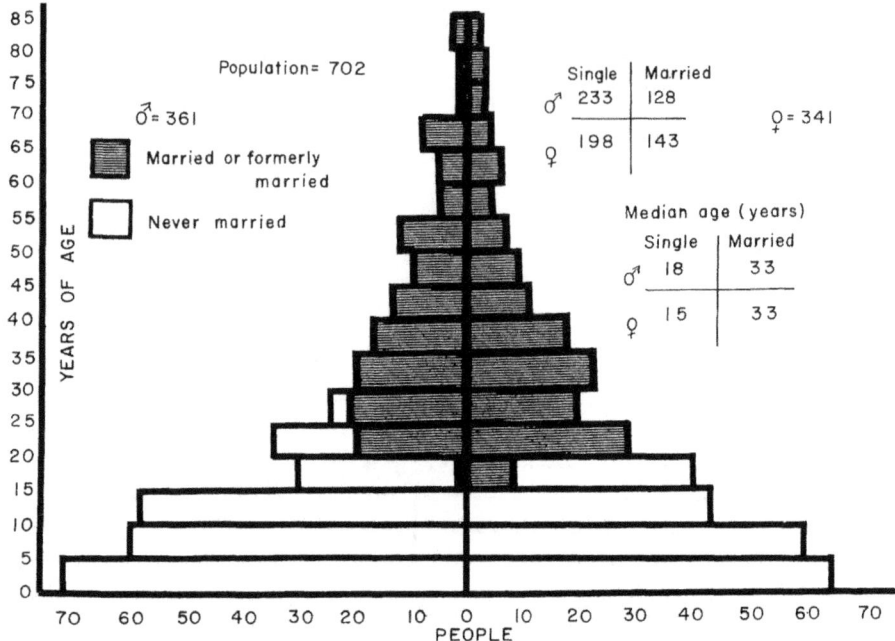

Fig. 7. Population pyramid for Yörük in sedentarized villages of Nogaylar and Sayburun.

Such ethnic stereotypes do not greatly affect the quality of the transactions that take place between Yörük and non-Yörük. First, the Yörük have no option but to deal with whatever community owns the grazing land on as amicable a basis as possible. Secondly, actual rental of pasture does not entail any transfer of personal services or prolonged face-to-face contact. The villages are remote from the yayla in most cases. The rental is done on a cash basis with the terms of the contract specified in writing and approved by the district's assistant governor (*kaymakam*). This latter practice is instigated by a desire on the government's part to prevent the misappropriation of rental fees by the elected village officials.

During the period of study no serious conflicts were observed in the yayla between Yörük and non-Yörük; however, just prior to the ethnographer's arrival in the fall of the previous season one family was robbed by armed villagers along the route of migration. Other cases of violence were reported to have occurred in the past but do not seem to have disrupted camping patterns for families not directly involved.

Conflict or the threat of violence is a feature of Yörük life, although perhaps not one that is disproportionate to their numbers when compared with rural southeastern Anatolia in general. Every tent or village home has its shotgun, often even an illegal pistol. Among the nomads, shepherds tend their flocks armed and are ever wary of thieves. During the 18 months of field research one head of a nomadic household was shot and killed in winter pastures by a farmer who had found him grazing his sheep in a field of winter wheat. While it was not possible to learn what action or vengeance might be taken in return (the incident occurred in the last week of the study), it seemed unlikely to develop into a large-scale feud involving many people. While close patrilineal relatives of the victim were concerned about revenge, more distant patrilineal relatives of the man's kabile were equally adamant that he had paid for an obvious folly, and that they would not like to be involved. Without describing the principles of vengeance (*intikam*) at this juncture, it is noteworthy that violence or conflict with non-Yörük is not automatic cause for a group response. Instead, it is treated like violence which has taken place within the tribe and revenge, while felt very strongly to be a duty, is seen to be the responsibility of those immediate patri-kin who would carry it out if the perpetrator had been a Yörük.

In another case of potential violence which occurred during the study, a Yörük man was invited by an Avşar village to camp without payment on disputed pastures along the boundary which separated that village from a neighboring Çerkes one. The Çerkes had traditionally claimed and received rental fees for the grazing in question. In the heated conflict that ensued, the Yörük received no encouragement from his kinsmen, who regarded his action as foolhardy. Had he been wounded or killed it is not certain, his relatives said, that anybody would have concerned themselves with revenge as he had clearly intruded into a violence-ridden situation for his own gain, and against the advice of his lineage mates.

Yörük interaction with their ethnically distinct neighbors is best viewed as an adjustment to the demands of a dominant non-Yörük economic and political structure. The pastoral nomadic niche which they presently exploit is one created by government forces which, in 1865, settled the hitherto nomadic Türkmen and Kurdish tribes, but later allowed Yörük nomads from the southwest to enter the area as they offered no threat to the political stability of the region.⁹

A strong ideology of patrilineality is supported in the close cooperation of kinsmen so related and by the frequency of marriage among close patrilateral relatives. However, the kin-based cooperation most evidenced is not that of the raiding party or paramilitary force. It is the cooperation of the marketplace; the extension of credit by the grocer or the grain broker for food for man and flock. All transactions, social or economic, take place against a backdrop formed by the political paramountcy of the Turkish state and its governing institutions. Force rather than being a useful tool in the acquiring of access to resources is detrimental to this purpose. The following chapter will detail how the tribal structure of the Yörük is an expression of this reality. Just as the natural landscape requires the regular concentration and dispersion of herds and tents, so does the social landscape dictate patterns of unity and fragmentation.

⁹ The Ottoman government in 1865-66 sent a military expedition, *Fïrka-i İslahiye* (hence the town's name), to the inner Taurus and Amanos mountains to destroy the power of the *derebey* families, and to settle the Kurdish and Türkmen tribes (Lewis:445).

This force was led by Derviş Paşa and Cevdet Paşa and was the successful culmination of repeated government attempts to break the power of these tribes (see Refik [1930] and Orhonlu [1969] for good accounts of earlier efforts). Nogay Tatars from the Crimea and Turkish settlers from Crete and Salonika were given land around Adana, Ceyhan, and in the valley below Maraş. See Eberhard (1953a:32-49) for an excellent description of the settlement pattern. At the same time Yörük tribes, among them the tribes studied here, entered the area and began to use the pastures vacated by the Türkmen and Kurdish nomads. The Yörük, while perhaps not altogether unacquainted with brigandage, were a highly fragmented population lacking strong leadership, and in no way threatened the authority of the state. Andrew Gould of UCLA is presently preparing a doctoral dissertation on the pacification and settlement of tribes in this area in the 19th century.

II
THE IDEOLOGY OF AGNATIC DESCENT, DESCENT GROUPS, AND SEGMENTATION

THE term "Yörük" denotes membership by virtue of patrilineal descent in one of a number of tribes. In the area studied the appellation has also acquired certain ethnic and occupational connotations, and is occasionally used as verbal noun *yörükcülük*, or "the Yörük way," implying pastoral nomadism. The fact of tribal or Yörük identity has nothing to do with whether members live in a village or migrate as sheep herders. As noted previously, the Yörük of southwestern and southeastern Turkey are distributed through towns and villages, as well as nomadic encampments. Tribal and lineage identities are usually maintained and continue to carry important social burdens in the daily ordering of the activities of these people.

Although many aspects of Yörük tribal organization, both among sedentary and nomadic sections, will be taken up in detail later, it is appropriate to address the question of what constitutes the Yörük tribe as a political structure and to outline the principles along which it is organized. The discussion that follows will focus chiefly on the ideology of descent and descent groupings, on how these are defined in the contemporary political context.

Of the several Yörük tribes or tribal segments encountered during the investigation (usually treated as one population in the analysis), by far the largest is the Saçıkara tribe. The Saçıkara, who number 139 nomadic households, (of the 171 nomadic tents studied), took up their present pattern of movement and pasture utilization 60 to 70 years ago when families representing most of the present lineages broke off from the main body of the tribe which had traditionally wintered at Aydın on the southwestern coast (see

Fig. 1). Apart from a change in territory and climatic conditions, this emigration entailed a shift from a primary reliance on long-haired black goats (hence their name Saçıkara, or the "Black Haired Ones") to sheep pastoralism. Few Saçıkara remain nomadic in the Aydın district and the most significant present-day concentration of Yörük nomads of any tribe in Turkey is in the region of study.

Oral accounts of the Saçıkara mention conflict with other tribes over leadership (*beylik*) of a confederation of tribes which was recognized administratively by the Ottoman government. This is called by them the "time of the beys" (*bey zamanı*) and reasonably dates to the latter half of the nineteenth century. True *bey* local leaders (*Derebeyler*) were actually eliminated by government fiat and force prior to this period (Sümer 1967a:195). But important tribal leaders were nevertheless recognized for tax collection and one wealthy, now settled member of the Saçıkara in Finike district stated that he was regarded by the Republican government as a nomadic equivalent to a village headman (*muhtar*) until 1949, and that he had used an official seal of office. In any event, neither that individual nor any other recently prominent member of the tribe has held power as a political functionary rivaling those of the state. Other Saçıkara accounts of their history cite conflict among Yörük brigands for supremacy in the mountains above Aydın and Afyon (Boz Dağ), with segments of the Saçıkara losing and being forced to flee. This has a ring of truth about it, as it is mentioned by numerous informants. Ahmet Refik, a Turkish historian, writes of court records which deal with conflict among Yörük tribes in the area in the latter part of the nineteenth century (1930: 118-53).

Most of the Saçıkara did not move directly to the southeast, but rather made the shift in stages. The entire process lasted two adult generations. The various places through which the Yörük spread later will be shown to coincide roughly with the formation of named descent segments.

In the initial move, families forced out of their winter base in Aydın simply shifted to locations along the coast between Fethiye and Antalya, while continuing to migrate to familiar summer pastures above Denizli and Afyon. Of these, those in the Finike district of Antalya established a pattern of movement taking them to yayla grazing in the mountains around Elmalı. Approximately 45 to 48 households of Yörük from Saçıkara have settled in a coastal village there (Tekke Köy), while a small number of tents continue to go to the Elmalı pastures.

Shortly before and during World War I a number of developments stimulated the Yörük in the west again to seek new grazing, ultimately pushing them into the region studied by the ethnographer. This eastward drift of nomadic peoples parallels the expansion of lowland plains agriculture and the population increases among sedentary communities as a result of the eradication of malaria (Planhol 1958:123 ff.; Kolars 1963:50 ff.). Today nomadic pastoralism is not a viable economic strategy in the west and southwest due to the lack of access to winter pastures (Kolars, *ibid.*) and the high cost of rental for those scattered ones that are still available.

Concomitant to the increase in sedentary population during that period, (well summarized by Johnson, 1969:22-23) was the increased effectiveness of governmental administration. Saçıkara Yörük cite as a strong inducement to leave the fact that the animal tax was being collected much more effectively than previously. More onerous, they say, was the fact that military conscription was extended to include the Yörük, who were made to register for this purpose. At this outrage, many sections moved to the southeast in order to winter around Ceyhan and Osmaniye, to visit yaylas in Maraş and Kayseri provinces which were less accessible to government officials.

Other families took their herds to the Black Sea coast to use pastures in the Pontic range, with some settling on land granted by government in Yozgat (Abdurrahman köy). This was an area that had not known Yörük tribes until then (see Planhol, 1965:passim). Their move in that direction was not successful, and those who settled as well as those who remained nomadic joined their kin who, in the meantime, had come to winter in the plains around İslahiye. Some went to İslahiye to settle, while others, formerly settled during the 20-year stay in Yozgat, again took up nomadic animal husbandry.

Thus the Yörük, like other ethnically defined populations in Anatolia, have a general distribution more determined by political than by strictly economic processes. Much as Irons (1969*b*) describes for the Yomut Türkmen of Iran, the Yörük of Turkey have changed many of their fundamental patterns of migration and land use in response to pressure by the government. In the majority of cases they have done so in reaction to demands of the state felt by them to infringe on their way of life, such as taxation or conscription. More recently, they have acted to avail themselves of such services as education and health care provided by the national authorities. Presently more Yörük are settled on government-granted land than are still nomadic.

Military conscription is now, and has been for the last 15 years, an unavoidable fact of life for Yörük males upon reaching age 18. Young men of the present generation placidly accept, even anticipate, what their fathers energetically sought to avoid. The animal tax, collected in all parts of the country under the successor governments to the Ottomans, was, in every practical sense, abolished in 1950. The Yörük are now in the enviable position of not paying any taxes but those imposed on finished goods bought in the bazaars. However, the rising prices of pasture rights, quite like the taxes and military duties of the last generation, exert pressure on nomadic families to move still farther east where land is available for grazing at less cost. As this involves establishing sites for winter and summer grazing alongside nomadic Kurdish tribes, and living in districts where there are no other Yörük, eastward movement remains slow. One family of the tribe has recently returned to İslahiye after being in Diyabakir province for several years; they cite conflict with the Kurds as a reason for their return. Another tent left for that area during the study period (leaving substantial debts behind). Settlement for most families is a more attractive alternative than abandoning a familiar environment.

TRIBE AND LINEAGE CONCEPTIONS

While the Yörük of Turkey feel themselves related by virtue of shared patrilineal descent, there exists no common genealogy purporting to show the segmentation implied by the numerous tribes subsumed under that identity. Furthermore, among tribes visited by the researcher, no apical ancestor was cited by any informant for the Yörük in general. No attempt to fashion one overall descent framework embracing *all* tribes or named tribal segments could be elicited, even from those individuals most interested in speculating on Yörük history.

Nevertheless, the principle of agnatic descent is the rationale for all proper-named, non-dyadic social units in nomadic Yörük society. In sedentary Yörük communities, the fact of co-residence and a territorial commitment may generate other named social identities (for example, village quarters or factions), but descent-defined statuses are important even where actual utilization of the ties formed in this way is conditioned by other social processes. Table 6 lists descent groupings, the number of households in each, and the number of members affiliated. Women are counted, for this purpose, as members of their natal groupings as they do not lose this identity with marriage. No attempt is made to present the internal segmentary relationships uniting many of these descent groups.

Similar to many Near Eastern tribal societies, Yörük descent groupings may be characterized as forming a sequence or hierarchy of named segments of increasing genealogic inclusiveness when seen from the level most immediate to any member of Yörük society. In general, the application of agnatic criteria to determine membership in such named segments becomes less rigid or strict as the range of inclusiveness broadens.

Before pursuing the question of membership and the processes underlying segmentation, it should be mentioned that the Yörük refer to descent groupings in two ways. These approaches to their own social system are relevant to an understanding of the dynamics of lineage organization. First, Yörük employ generic designators for recognized levels of segmentation—terms which like *aşiret*, *kabile*, *sülâle*, and *aile* are usually best glossed as "tribe," "maximal lineage," "lineage," and "family," according to the context.[1] There are, among the nomads, no *named* residence groups, such as those transiently formed by clusters of tents which migrate or camp together. Secondly, and most commonly heard in conversation, the proper names of segments are used for segments and to describe one's membership or the lack of it.

---

[1] Among the Sacïkara, and other Yörük in the area, the words "kabile" and "mahalle" are often interchangeable, although kabile refers to a patrilineal descent group (tribe or lineage here), and *mahalle* in standard Turkish means simply a ward or quarter of a village or town (from Arabic "place"). Mahalle is possibly a recent verbal acquisition; its use by the nomads is strictly for a group of patri-kin: a named lineage or group of related lineages less than the total tribe, with *no* territorial connotation. The Sacïkara do not use *oymak*, but know its meaning as aşiret among the Türkmen. They use *oba* rarely as a synonym for sülâle or kabile, but more commonly to refer to a group of tents of *unknown* or foreign origin. It is never applied to one's own camp group or descent group. *Yurt* is frequently used with reference to a camp site or cluster of tents among the nomads, for example a fresh, hitherto unvisited and thus preferred camp site is called an *acar yurt* or "new yurt." It is not a social group designator, and people do not become associated with given ones. Obviously, aşiret, kabile, sülâle, mahalle, and, in some cases, oba overlap a great deal in practice, although they can also indicate segments or different levels of inclusion within a patrilineal descent system.

TABLE 6
NAMED DESCENT GROUPS AT THE KABILE LEVEL
(h = household   p = people)

	İslahiye		Nomads		Nogaylar		Sayburun		Total	
	h	p	h	p	h	p	h	p	h	p
Göğebakanlar	16	93	44	352					60	445
Çavuçlu	10	77	14	107			15	118	39	302
Sadïkoğullari (Satïlar)	6	42	11	91					17	133
Hayta			3	20	1	7	18	104	22	131
Arabalïlar	5	41	28	208					33	249
Kölemen	13	96	2	16			4	39	19	151
Kelebekli	11	84	11	105	4	25	1	8	27	222
Karataş	5	36							5	36
Köleli		3								3
Sümenli	14	83							14	83
Hacïkaracili	2	8							2	8
Cücü/Sermaye			3	28					3	28
İzmirli	1	4	3	20					4	24
Haciçiller (İsmirli)			2	23	34	330			36	353
Kabaklar (İzmirli)			2	13					2	13
Horzumlu							2	8	2	8
Dazkirli			10	84					10	84
Tirtar			2	16	1	5	3	16	6	37
Arïklï					2	10			2	10
Koçbïyïk							1	6	1	6
Çakmak							2	19	2	19
Sarïkeçili			26	232					26	232
Tekeli			1	10					1	10
Osmanlï			8	83					8	83
Other Yörük and non-Yörük women	1	12		4			2	7	3	23
	84	579	170	1412	42	377	48	325	344	2693

Bacon (1958:123-34) usefully calls such units "fixed lineages," in contrast to "sliding lineages," which are egocentric such as, for example, those which could be described by the kinsmen obligated in vengeance by the *degree* of relationship. While the "fixed lineage" has a membership that does not, in theory, change when viewed by different individuals of that type of group, it also does not preclude ambiguity: although each member conceives of the named group as a fixed entity, different members may have different, even mutually contradictory, opinions on what constitutes the total membership. Further, even though the principle of patrilineal descent, as expressed by the Yörük, does not incorporate residence criteria in determining membership, co-residence and a shared locality are important in conditioning segmentation. Residence patterns, or the regular interaction of individuals, affect both the membership of named fixed lineages and, by extension, descent lines themselves.

In the present situation of dispersed tribal sections, the larger descent category (aşiret) is so constituted that the internal connections among all households or all maximal lineage segments are not genealogically demonstrable or even asserted. Membership is more a matter of desire to affiliate on the part of the would-be Yörük joiners than of reciprocal "contract" with established sections. A number of individual tents as well as several "alien" descent groups, lacking any wider agnatic descent linkages in the area, have attached themselves to the locally dominant tribe, the Saçıkara. The apparent ease with which this is accomplished is striking, as is the obvious lack of concern shown by historically established sections in tracing even putative genealogical lines among kabile.

In the case where a number of related tents claim affiliation in the larger tribe (aşiret) no substantial problems are posed by either a well known, pre-existing genealogic reference system or by any economic or political corporateness at that level. The tribe in its most general expression is presently limited with respect to corporateness to the sharing of a common name and cultural heritage. It is only within the lineages and lineage sections that significant rights and obligations arise from the fact of common descent, and rights to real property, the ownership of capital, and the means of production, are vested only in the household, notably in its head.

Where individual tents for any reason are separated or estranged from their natal lineage for a long time, whether from within or outside the Saçıkara, their affiliation to a new descent group is rather different from the above. This reflects the fact that within lineages (kabile or mahalle) genealogies are known, or putatively known. Even more important is the fact that the greater intensity of kinship ties among patri-kin in any small descent group, and the importance of these ties in framing future marriages, means that the "alien" status of a household coming from the outside cannot be ignored.

In practice, most households that claim membership in this way do not assert possible remote patrilineal ties as the basis for calling themselves members of the new section, but rather matrilineal kinship ties which usually have existed earlier. Of 171 tents counted in the area of study, approximately 20 are clearly "passing" as members of lineage or section level descent groups to which they have no close agnatic ties; all but two (who derive from a Kurdish child adopted in the previous generation) have matrilineal connections which they utilize. "Membership," then, is used advisedly in reference to such households as it is only when genealogic merging is achieved that their foreign status is completely obscured. It is significant that there is no common Yörük term connoting lineage membership in the abstract; but rather one usually either "follows" (*takip etmek*) a lineage to which it is clear that one does not have descent lines, or one is "from" it (e.g., *İzmirliler'den*) if there is no question that one was born into it.

An example illustrating a number of the points just made is appropriate. Three brothers each the head of his own household (tent), have associated themselves with the Satılar kabile (17 households) of the Saçıkara tribe, although by agnation they belong to another tribe (aşiret) found in the region, the Sarıkeçili. This was, they say, occasioned by disagreements with close patri-kin, and as they had matrilineal ties of kinship with the wealthiest and most respected member of the Satılar (mother's brother's son), they came to camp regularly with the groups with which that individual migrated and rented pastures. They also came to rely on settled members of the Satılar lineage in İslahiye who supply them with store goods on credit. The oldest of the three brothers gave a daughter in marriage to the son of the lineage leader mentioned above. When asked, the Sarıkeçili brothers state that while they are Sarıkeçili, they "follow" (takip etmek) the Satılar from preference. When Satılar members are asked to recount the heads of households in the lineage they almost invariably list the names of the three brothers, as well as that of another recent joiner who similarly has matrilineal ties.

However, there are two differences concerning their position in the lineage which have to do with descent status, unaffected by the fact that all three are personally highly regarded. First, although marriages between their children and those of the Satılar are regarded good matches between close matri-kin, they cannot expect or demand brides from the Satılar as they might from close, "true" patri-kin.[2] Secondly, it is very unlikely that the obligation of support or vengeance would be felt to devolve on any member of the Satılar; they would remain the duty of their Sarıkeçili patri-kin. Vengeance (intikam) is an important and strongly held obligation which rests with males falling within the first ascending and descending two degrees of patrilineal relationship (brothers, father, father's brothers and their sons, sons of brothers, and one's own sons), but which is not rigidly defined to limit the participation of more distantly related patri-kin, all of whom share in the shame if vengeance is not exacted when called for. The object of vengeance is a similarly defined close patrilineal male kinsman of the man who perpetrated the act of violence calling for vengeance, if not the aggressor himself. The three Sarıkeçili brothers just prior to the time of the study had avenged the killing of their father's brother's son by a member of another lineage of the Saçıkara tribe. One of them was indicted by the provincial court for the return murder of the killer's brother, the killer being himself in prison. Members of the Satılar lineage did not feel any direct involvement in this matter, nor did they fear that they would be included in possible return killings. This neutrality would be impossible if any natal member of that small a lineage, no matter how distantly related by traceable descent, were involved.

This neutrality, too, has another side which is of equal interest here. In this case, as is typical among the Yörük, the fact that the

[2] Marriage will be described later, but it is relevant to note that the Yörük have a strongly expressed ideology favoring father's brother's daughter marriage—and the classificatory extensions of this—which are reinforced by a practice they call *emmi hakkı* or "uncle's right." In brief, this grants the father's brother (or other close patrilateral relatives) first rights to claim his brother's daughter as a bride for his son. Bride price, in any event, is paid and is high regardless. But if the father's brother is ignored or slighted in this respect he often causes conflict and claims (successfully in most cases) a cash fine from the girl's father. Kabile "members" who do not demonstrate close patrilineal connections are thus somewhat handicapped in marrying, although this is not an overly severe disability. See also Barth's (1953:164-71) discussion of a similar practice among Kurdish tribes of Iraq.

three Sarıkeçili brothers were embroiled in a conflict with members of one Saçıkara lineage does not affect their relations with other lineages of the latter tribe such as the Satılar. Thus, while external opposition elicits a response which unites agnatically related individuals, it rarely (if ever) brings together descent groupings that are not from one kabile. This serves, in the absence of any formal rules for making peace following a killing or other violence, to prevent conflict from spreading widely. Given the high potential for violence between Yörük and the non-Yörük villagers with whom they have to negotiate passage and grazing rights, it is undoubtedly advantageous that disputes be contained within fairly narrow limits. Furthermore, should conflict automatically ramify to the extreme limits of descent ideology, when involving families from two tribes, it would greatly restrict flexibility in local camp group composition[3] and the relative ease with which households could temporarily attach themselves to another kabile.

Returning to the question of descent and the groupings rationalized by such criteria, it has been noted that the Saçıkara tribe, like other Yörük tribes, is territorially dispersed, and that it lacks corporateness with respect to common access to resources, or any set of binding rights and obligation inherent in tribal membership. As one would expect, given this, there is no formal political hierarchy or pan-tribal office. Clearly certain individuals exercise more influence than others in the day-to-day decisions of small groups of families to move and camp together, and in numerous economic affairs. Of these men, some come to be regarded as lineage leaders (*ağa*), but they hold no formal office and their status is an achieved one. This will be treated in more depth later, and is mentioned here to point out again the restricted sense in which the term "tribe" is used.

The tribe, the maximum unit of presumed common agnatic descent, consists of a number of descent lines, each named for an ancestor from whom all members claim, but sometimes cannot demonstrate, descent. Within each of these lineages (kabile or mahalle), depending on its size, there are often named units of lesser genealogical inclusiveness (*sülâle*) within which members are all able to trace not only descent to the third or fourth generation ancestor after which it is named, but also to specify accu-

---

[3] This will be described in Chapter IV. It is important to bear in mind here that it is *not* coterminous with the descent group.

rately many other affinal and uterine ties of kinship among all co-members.

Saçĭkara ideology states that there are 12 major descent lines (kabile). In practice, however, it is rare that any two informants, even if from the same sülâle or kabile lineage, would agree on which are "legitimate" of the *more* than 12 kabile claiming Saçĭkara affiliation. Informants' attempts to find a solution to this apparent contradiction are usually of two kinds. First, a common approach is to distinguish the *köklü* or "rooted" from the presumably recently affiliated *köksüz* or "rootless" sections. While confusion and the contradictory use of discriminatory criteria surround most attempts by Yörük to set apart the köklü from the köksüz, the most commonly given basis for making such a distinction is whether a kabile was a named segment of the Saçĭkara when it still had a political function in the nineteenth century, as expressed in the tribal bey. Since there are no Yörük-owned records and only the most tenuous of oral traditions relating to this period, there is little agreement among informants from different lineages as to which kabile are köklü and which köksüz. This distinction, therefore, amounts neither to a moiety system nor to any hierarchical political structure. What it seems to accomplish is to distinguish temporarily, relative to the speaker's lineage, new tribal accretions from older ones, or from those originating in fission, and thus to reinforce the Saçĭkara ideology of 12 lineages in an embarrassing logical confrontation with social reality.

The second means by which the 12 ideal sections of the tribe are arrived at is, expectedly, by lumping present-day segments under the names of their supposedly antecedent lineages, of which there are fewer. The actual oral process by which this is done is informative, although it does not always inspire confidence in the historical results. The considerable debate occasioned by attempts to group lineages and the often contradictory suggestions made by the interested discussants are realistic indicators of the structural ambiguity that surrounds all aspects of descent above the lineage level.

In terms of social process, the kabile and sülâle lineages are more important than the tribe (asiret), as is suggested by the fact that the descent lines become increasingly ambiguous above those levels. Further, there is no important difference between purportedly older lineages and the more recent kabile accretions, and regardless of the well-developed Yörük faculty for disparaging other descent groups, all of the lineages are essentially equal in status. If a Yörük informant is asked directly, he will invariably assert that all of the locally found descent lines, both within and outside of his own tribe, share equally in the Yörük heritage, a common Turkic origin in Central Asia, and are of equal suitability with respect to marriage. This is not seen to contradict the common ascription by individuals of negative social attributes to other descent groups, for example proclivities for theft, bride stealing, etc.; such views are not uniformly held within any lineage, let alone within a tribe. Thus they do not form a coherent system of stereotypes which would rank lineages. The ascription of less esteemed social traits to other lineages is much akin to the also frequent habit of Yörük men to denigrate privately their own close relatives, often those with whom they camp and carry on close social and economic transactions. Nevertheless, within lineages, no household is considered to be superior (or inferior) by birthright.

The history of any descent group's segmentation must necessarily include social incidents unique in context and cause. This, however, does not imply that regularities are lacking in the general dynamics of Yörük lineage formation. Foremost among these is the predictable way in which the passage of time acts on the genealogical charter through a variety of structural amnesia which cuts genealogies at the fifth generation. Second are the effects of social processes which precipitate, or select for, differing levels of descent group inclusiveness. As the Yörük lineages do not collectively own any wealth and since access to resources does not depend on kabile or sülâle membership, there are no inexorable demographic pressures for conflict and segmentation arising from a limited amount of property to be allocated among increasing numbers of claimants. They have little in common in this respect with Arab *mush'a* villages of the Hatay, where descent group membership carries with it rights to collectively owned land (see Aswad, 1968 and 1972:passim). Localization of Yörük families related by descent and the regular interaction of these in social and economic transactions is important in determining the segmentary junctures which are culturally recognized and enshrined in the names of kabiles. Although members of all kabile lineages are able to trace ancestors through four or five generations in the patriline, not all named kabiles are of the same segmentary depth as expressed in genealogies. Some lead to the ancestor who provided their kabile name (all are named after individuals) in two generations, some in five. While there are no pressures for segmentation arising from land rights, conflict can and does instigate splitting at a shallow level. It should not be thought that differential size of collateral lines or the distance between collaterals alone determine segmentation. Since property rights are not gained or lost in this way, there is no immediate economic penalty to groups of close agnates for stressing their separate identity when faced with known collateral groups of a larger size.

A sharp limit to the scope of genealogies is seen in informant efforts to recite their patrilineal ancestry. A point is reached below which every male can place most of his patrilineal relatives, but above which even elderly males of a higher generation cannot pass. This is not a feature unique to Yörük segmentary lineages: Irons notes a strikingly similar pattern of "limited recall" among the Yomut Turkmen (1969b:58-65). His explanation is that the Yomut obscure their genealogies above a certain point in order to avoid the risk of being included in vengeance killings or feuds which through remote linkages of agnatic kinship might be held to define them as objects of revenge. Vengeance among the Yörük, as noted earlier, is an obligation which falls to close patri-kin of the victim of murder, but without clearly defined outer limits of either involvement or responsibility. Thus, Iron's suggestion might have validity here in that genealogical amnesia likewise serves this function. Further, we have indicated that it is advantageous to isolate the effects of violence which originate from outside the Yörük population. Structural amnesia facilitates the narrow containment of hostilities in the face of a descent ideology which stresses the unity and mutual support of all patrilineal kinsmen. Another positive aspect of this is that flexibility in descent group restructuring is enhanced, a feature that will be shown to be well suited to highly variable camp groups.

The process by which descent group restructuring is achieved is that as genealogic depth increases with each maturing generation, the apical referent either drops one generation or is lost. With each successive shift, sons of the apical named figure gain importance and one of them ultimately emerges as the highest named person to whom descent can actually be traced without gaps. Genealogies consistently extend, in detail, through four or, at most, five generations from the present generation of living adults, and rarely go farther back. This would indicate that descendants of households who have joined descent groups through co-residence

three or more generations previously are fully absorbed in the
intervening period, and that the name of the initial newcomer is by
then regarded in the same way as other remembered males of his
generation: as the head of a shallow lineage (sülâle) presumed to
be closely related agnatically to other such lines in the lineage
(kabile). Beyond four or five generations, most remembered males
in a Yörük genealogy are *ipse dixit* considered brothers, or the
sons of brothers.

Furthermore, the phenomenon of by-names or nicknames
(*lakab*) among males contributes to the ambiguity of descent lines
and genealogies as relationships are traced through progressively
ascending generations.[4] Yörük use both given names, surnames
and lakab by-names according to the social context. The use of
family names is a recent innovation resulting from the 1932 law
promulgated by Kemal Atatürk. At that time all Turkish citizens
were formally required to take last names which were to appear
on all official documents. For the most part, Yörük adopted last
names which indicated either tribal or kabile identity; however,
many chose, or were assigned, whimsical names or names which
they found personally pleasing.[5] Such names are used only in
formal, usually bureaucratic, situations and rarely in normal
discourse.

In face-to-face conversation, or with reference to an absent
person while speaking with a close kinsman or friend, given names
are employed with an honorific "bey." Such names are almost
invariably selected from a limited number of Islamic religious
figures, or from among names which carry a religious meaning.
The contemporary urban middle class pattern of assigning pre-
Islamic Turkic or non-religious names is vehemently eschewed.
The names in use are relatively few in number and, if used without
context, are of little use in distinguishing individuals.

The Yörük use by-names to refer to a person who is not in the
speakers' presence. These are either the unique property of the
person referred to, or are specific to one person when employed

---

[4] See Dorian (1970:303 ff.) for a description of by-names in the Scottish Highland, which, like those used by the Yörük, are considered rude when used in direct conversation. Structurally more analogous to their function in Yörük society is the system of teknonymy in Bali which Hildred and Clifford Geertz (1964:94-108) analytically relate to "genealogical amnesia."

[5] Many brothers bear different last names, as do fathers and sons. One family is even divided by a typographical error. Four brothers decided to take the last name "Güzel"; however one, and his offspring, is registered as "Güzek."

together with his given name. Generally, lakab names are derogatory or, at least, slightly derisive. It is considered rude to address a man by his lakab; but in indirect reference, the lakab is almost invariably used. By-names range from the simple (and relatively innocuous) addition of a color term—"black," "purple," "blue," or "yellow" (*kara, mor, gök, sarī*)—before the given name to highly unflattering ones. Often lakabs derive from physical deformities or distinguishing characteristics—*golak* ("one-armed"), *topal* ("lame"), *deli* ("crazy") for the impetuous, and so on.

What is particularly interesting is that while these names very accurately specify every individual in the society, when genealogical reckoning is attempted lakabs paradoxically act to obscure descent lines. This is because with time individuals in the genealogy may become remembered in some instances by lakab and by given name separately. Most of the kabile bear names which, while purportedly are those of their apical ancestor, are actually lakab by-names. This is undoubtedly a factor in cutting off known genealogies at a fairly low level, and in creating the structural confusion which attends historical reconstruction. Also, it makes it possible for a newly fissioned (or geographically separated) group of agnates to both claim and believe that they possess a deeper-reaching genealogical charter validating their particular line: the lakab of the apical ancestor is followed in some cases by what seems, to the ethnographer, to be his given name cited as his own lineal descendant.

A point of interest concerning most genealogies collected in the field is that the distinction commonly made between putative and demonstrated portions of genealogies does not apply readily to the Yörük. It is true that we have characterized certain descent relationships as "putative," but only where this corresponds with native statements of doubts concerning the descent line; it is not a distinction imposed by the ethnographer. The relationships and descent group segmentation Yörük cite for their own kabile lineages seem to be historically accurate up to the point where they admit a lack of knowledge. When they claim common membership with other Yörük in descent categories beyond this and ultimately, for example, at the aşiret or pan-Yörük level, they are admittedly reasoning by induction. Sedentary Türkmen (Avşar) in the region of study, by contrast, are extremely interested in theorizing on their descent connections beyond the limits of what they accept as demonstrable, and invariably would list all ascending generations without gaps in the patriline until the local group was articulated into one of the major branches of the Oğhuz Türkmen (to which the Yomut studied by Irons also belong). The Yörük simply assert that connections exist, without attempting historical reconstruction of this sort.

Concomitant to the "forgetting" of the upper-most figure to whom descent is traced is the importance gained as a referent by a male of the following generation or, if a split occurs, by more than one. This is a function of how many people, both within and outside of the descent group, use a particular name to describe individual statuses or related congeries of people vis-à-vis others.

The Yörük, like all Turkish speakers, distinguish between the eldest and subsequent brothers, as well as between the sons of first and subsequent wives. The kinship terminology ascribes the term *ağabey* or *ece* to the eldest brother, although it does not distinguish among other kin by criteria of relative age. The distinction among sons of different mothers but of the same father is not part of the kinship terminology; it is considered "unbrotherly" to place much emphasis on this. In practice, there are differences in social interaction along such uterine lines, but these are not openly reflected in genealogies unless specifically elicited. One does not always know if one's patrilateral grandfather and one's father's father's brothers are the sons of which wife even if it is known that the great-grandfather had more than one.

However, the relative age of brothers is remembered and commented upon whenever male siblings appear in the genealogy. This ranking is not merely a linguistic phenomenon; it has considerable importance in interpersonal relations among siblings.[6] What is relevant here with respect to segmentation is that the eldest of the brothers is held to be senior to all younger, irrespective of wealth, in situations of formal etiquette; he serves as spokesman when brothers act in concert. After the father's death, he is obliged, more than the father in his lifetime, to provide for his single brothers, and to assist them in time of trouble. While beyond the scope of the present discussion, it might be observed that the economic responsibilities of this trust are not always fulfilled and brothers are often on cool terms for long periods. Although inheritance favors the younger brothers, as will be discussed in a later chapter, marriage takes place in order of

---

[6] Turkish has a parallel term for older sister, *abla*, which is rarely used among the Yörük, except occasionally by small children to refer to their father's second wife (co-wife).

IDEOLOGY OF AGNATIC DESCENT

birth, which again sets the order of household fissioning to form new ones as younger sons marry and bring their brides into the tent. This, of course, gives older brothers in any generation an earlier start in the production of progeny to further their name. The Satılar, for example, claim that their most distant, directly traced, patrilineal male ancestor was the eldest of three brothers, as was Sadık, their namesake. Not all lineages, however, claim their namesakes as the eldest of several brothers and the potential for ranking collateral names lineages by this criterion is not seized upon in practice. Among the contemporary named kabile lineages in the area of study where a number of brothers head their own households, the eldest is always considered the most significant in the relations of the brothers to outsiders; and one would suspect that, "other things being equal," senior brothers would have a somewhat better chance of being cited as the namesake of a later descent group.

However, just as the point of segmentation does not depend entirely on genealogical depth, neither does the relative seniority of brothers escape the impact of political and residential fact in determining which of several will provide the name under which the group passes.

The Satılar state that while they are of the Saçıkara tribe and one of its 12 major constituent kabiles, they are related to another maximal lineage, the Hayta (whose meaning in Turkish—"out of hand" or "hooligan"—does not escape invidious commentary). They say that the name "Hayta" predates their own Satılar (*Sadıkoğluları*) and that both the contemporary descent group called Hayta and their own are the descendants of three brothers, two of whose offspring are contained within the Hayta and continue that name, while the third has produced the Satılar. There has been no recent intermarriage between these lines. Informants from both mention this patrilineal relationship, but the Satılar do not attempt to trace their genealogies directly, without gaps, to one of the three putative founding brothers. Rather, they state that these brothers lived "two or three generations" before the highest male directly traced without generational gaps.

The genealogy given by Satılar informants offers a diagram of the history of segmentation, including their estimation of the number of generations separating the various collateral descent lines. However, it is not obvious from this just when the named segments acquired their separate identities. The sequence of named groups roughly parallels the process of tribal dispersion described at the onset of this chapter. If one accepts the Yörük hypothesis that the contemporary segment named Hayta is simply a continuation of a group appellation in use at the time of the grandsons of the individual by that name, there would be rather close agreement between the development of the collateral lines and the movement of populations during World War I.

A Satılar male ego of the most recent adult generation can cite two major named descent groupings to which he belongs by virtue of his direct agnatic ancestors. These are major groupings because nearly all informants determine the same groups and because they are widely known beyond the limits of the Satılar among Yörük.

At the immediate level is, of course, the Satılar kabile, whose households are all either migrating in the same pattern between İslahiye and Pınarbaşı or else settled in İslahiye (in the same quarter of town). A collateral grouping of the same generational span is found in Finike, called the Güzeller, corresponding to the movement of a number of families there just before World War I. Both the Satılar and the Güzeller are aware of the existence of the other's line and some visiting takes place. Separation dates from 1905 (1323 H.) when the sons of Sadık moved to the Black Sea and then on to İslahiye, while the sons of Sadık's brother remained on the coast. While it is only possible to speculate, it seems likely that had all of the group remained together, economic and political advantage from somewhat greater numbers might have delayed segmentation. There is little to be gained from dispersed descent group unity under present political circumstances—state bureaucratic control which grants tribal leaders no power to tax or to administer formally—but there are advantages to close relations among members of the descent line if they are in a position to interact regularly in credit transactions for sheep and pasture rights. Such close relations are often reflected in the shared identity of members as expressed in a common name. This is not, of course, by any means a foregone conclusion as at least one lineage has fragmented through conflict into named, rival descent groups of a lower order of genealogical inclusiveness than that which defines the Satılar as a whole.

At the second level of inclusiveness with respect to named descent groups is the division formed by the three sons of Hayta (see Fig. 8). At this level the descendants of two or these sons carry the name "Hayta," while the descendants of the third

IDEOLOGY OF AGNATIC DESCENT

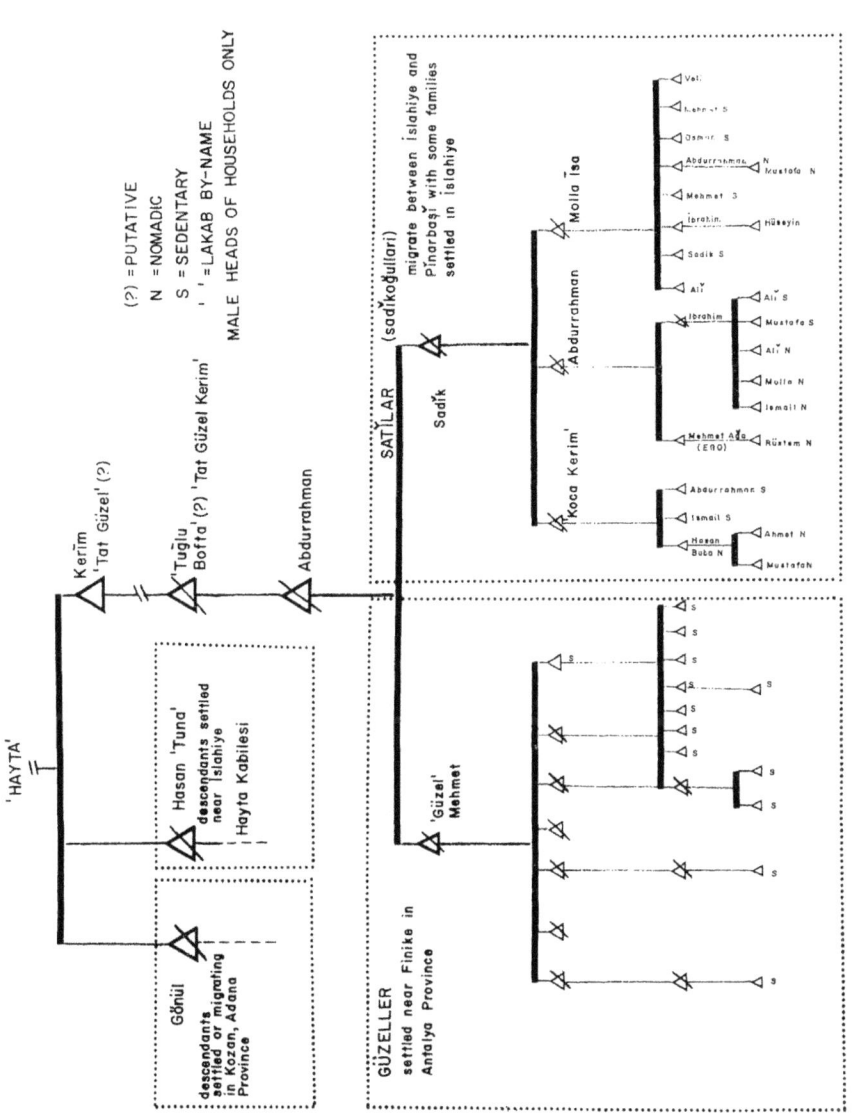

Fig. 8. Diagram of Satılar descent groups.

(Satĭlar) claim a collateral status, even though they do not employ any name of that generation as a descent group name. Among the Güzeller and Satĭlar, their ancestor Kerim, the eldest (they say) of the three brothers, is sometimes cited as the source of an archaic (*eski*) name for themselves (Kerimliler), while Hayta is never employed or referred to in this way. The basic differentiation between those who maintain their Hayta identity and the Satĭlar who do not is, as noted before, the basis for distinguishing the two related kabile. It is noteworthy with respect to the time limits of genealogical recall that at least two fewer generations are seen to separate the contemporary adult members of the Hayta kabile from their namesake than separate the contemporary Satĭlar from the eldest of the three brothers who are said to be the forerunners common to both kabiles.

The limits of the named segmentary groups expressed in the genealogies of informants are not an outcome of the descent ideology but, like more recent segmentation, derive from shifts in locality and migratory patterns which occurred in the late nineteenth century. At the same time that segments of the tribe began leaving Aydĭn and some of the Saçĭkara moved to the Antalya region, others began to winter on the Muğla coastal plain. Later some of these sections moved to Kozan and Osmaniye on the seaward side of Gavur Dağ where they wintered while migrating to summer pastures near Göksun and Tomarza. The descendants of Gönül and Tuna Hasan were among these. The migratory schedule and subsequent political events effectively separated the two branches. Many of the Gönüllü and Tuna members of the Hayta settled on government-granted land in mountain villages in Kozan district. The Satĭlar branch, while later moving to the southeastern region of Turkey, established a pattern of marketing in towns not visited by the Hayta. Because their migratory routes did not cross, most effective contact was cut off. In recent years, after World War II, a number of Hayta of the Tuna section have started to move along the same route as the groups described earlier. However, little interaction arises by virtue of common descent so distantly defined. About 20 households of the Hayta lineage moved into the İslahiye district in 1949 in order to settle on land granted to them in a Kurdish village. The nomadic members of the Hayta kabile winter in that village and seem to have little to do with the more numerous and richer Satĭlar. They do not enter into joint economic ventures with the Satĭlar. Neither do they intermarry, choosing instead to intermarry with several other similarly poorly represented lineage sections and with another settled kabile of the Saçıkara, the Çavuşlular.

The processes of segmentation recounted here correspond closely with histories taken from other Yörük lineages. The tribe or the Yörük population at large is made up of a number of autonomous named groups claiming and demonstrating the common agnatic descent of localized members. The kabile level descent group is highly endogamous with approximately 60 percent of all marriages taking place within it. The intensity of social process working on, or in some cases in spite of, the descent ideology largely determines the boundaries of named groups. The tribe as a whole is made up of kabile lineages, some of which while claiming affiliation by descent must be considered recent accretions; in any event, they pass under different tribal colors in other parts of the country.

Another dimension of Yörük tribal structure pertains to how Yörük society is viewed from the outside, by non-Yörük, and how, in response, Yörük individuals present their identity to outsiders. Yörük in the area of this study, whether sedentary or nomadic and of all tribes and lineages, are called Aydınlı (from Aydın) or, collectively, the "Aydınlı Aşireti." The Yörük regard this as a lakab or nickname, which if used by itself is a synonym for "Yörük." Non-Yörük, however, understand it as a tribal designation and generally assume that all Yörük partake of the same social structure. This tends to obscure to outsiders differences not only among Yörük tribes, but also among less inclusive descent lines, such as the named kabile lineages.

The Yörük in no way regard this lakab as a derogatory expression, and foster its use by regularly applying it to Yörük in general and to characteristics of Yörük culture in conversation with non-Yörük. For example, as the ethnographer was returning from a market visit by truck to the point where the road intersected the trail up to a summer camp, a fist fight was seen ahead on the outskirts of a Çerkes village. As the driver slowed and stopped, Yörük fellow passengers saw that two young men from another tribe were involved, and, shouting "Aydınlı," jumped from the vehicle. Without attempting to join the fight, they quickly separated the Yörük protagonists from the villagers, holding them by force so that their pride was somewhat salved as they left a fight they had come out of second best (and which they had brought upon themselves). The point here is that despite the lack of demonstrable common descent, they articulated a common Yörük identity in a way that was readily understandable to the non-Yörük villagers. At the same time, this minor incident illustrates the selective manner in which support is given and to whom it is held due. While the Yörük often speak of the need for patri-kinsmen to support kin, and for Yörük to support Yörük in disputes with others, such aid, if given, is not provided indiscriminantly. In this case, the men entered the foray to break it up, not automatically to lend assistance to the Yörük involved. Indeed, they are very wary of entering any dispute unless it involves a close patri-kin or unless a fellow Yörük is obviously the victim of unwarranted assault, such as robbery.

The use of Aydınlı by Yörük is perhaps best thought of as a partial attempt to present a unified front to outsiders; but it also shows a feeling that divisions internal to Yörük society are irrelevant in dealing with non-Yörük.

The use of Aydınlı has two effects significant to an understanding of Yörük social structure as expressed in the region of study. First, it undoubtedly contributes to the structural dichotomy between tribe (aşiret) and lineage (kabile). Identification beyond the level where common descent can reasonably (by Yörük criteria) be demonstrated in the kabile is rapidly diffused to the largest body of people among whom common descent is claimed: the Yörük population in general. Second, although taken from a place name (Aydın), the term has come to imply locally an ethnic identity which draws together Yörük from diverse descent lines and defines them collectively, even vis-à-vis other native Turkish speakers. At the same time it signals this emergent ethnicity in a euphemism acceptable in a state dominated political milieu which stresses national homogeneity. The Yörük are able to achieve in the eyes of non-Yörük populations an external visage of tribal unity that obscures a near total lack of pan-Yörük political integration and the fragmentation of descent groupings at relatively low levels of agnatic inclusiveness.

The appearance of unity is useful in maintaining the "cultural self-respect" of the Yörük population in general. Local Gypsies, for example, are not thought to have any such unifying tribal structure. More important is the unity reflected in economic cooperation in the form of credit extension, and the greater integrity of economic transactions among Yörük and non-Yörük. However, actual unity in situations of inter-ethnic conflict or disputes would be dysfunctional in that the tribe, no matter what degree of solidarity it achieved, could not rival the power of the State. It is fair to say that if the Yörük had the political organization often attributed to them by non-Yörük, even government officials, they would have long ago been economically destroyed by forced settlement and dispersion as an intolerable rival to the national system.[7]

[7] Members of the non-Yörük sedentary population, including officials, often refer to certain Yoruk men as *aşiret reisi* or "tribal chief." Such an expression is only used in banter among Yörük as there is no such office.

III
YÖRÜK NORMATIVE AND ALTERNATIVE SYSTEMS OF MARRIAGE

THE second chapter has shown that the Yörük of all residence categories possess a well-defined ideology of agnatic descent, and that they have named descent groups arranged within a segmentary structure which ultimately relates all Yörük to all others. They speak of tribe, of lineage, and of the larger familial groups which are defined by descent statuses passed in the patriline. In spite of the obvious emphasis on descent in the ideological structuring of Yörük society, a large portion of social and economic transactions occur along non-agnatic lines of kinship, and are phrased in terms of consanguinity and affinity.

The analysis has developed the thesis that in a political environment of firm state control, the rigid application of rules calling for vengeance and supportive action along descent lines would be dysfunctional. Nevertheless, it is the case that Yörük economic adaptations, sedentary and nomadic, call for the close cooperation of numbers of people beyond the level of household. Kinship and kin-type linkages are important in many of the credit, marketing, and production activities as well as in the patterns of residence that will be described in the following chapters. These ties are important whether they parallel lines of agnation or cut across them.

Kinship ties and such kin-type relationships formed by the marriages of near affines are shaped by the system of marriage. The following discussion will outline Yörük preferences in marriage and the statistical outcome of marriage choices. The social and economic effects of the relations created in this manner will emerge in subsequent portions of the study, particularly with respect to relations among households.

The formalized rules of marriage among Yörük of all types of residence (sedentary or nomadic) seemingly contribute to the concentration and redundancy of kinship and kin-type ties within the narrowest of extra-household descent group confines. Statistically, marriage patterns are highly endogamous at all levels of descent segmentation (see Table 7). There are, however, a number of factors which serve to mitigate the concentration of kin ties within the narrow range implied by culturally stipulated preferences. The high incidence of marriage arising from kidnapping (*kız kaçırma*), and the fact that marriages outside the narrow range of preferred ones ultimately create the possibility of future approved matches work to disperse kinship ties among descent lines.

It should be mentioned that the Yörük do not strongly express a sentiment for lineage-specific marriages within Yörük society at large. Also, as in most Near Eastern societies, women from outside the ethnic group, if accompanied by conversion where religious differences obtain, are acceptable. They are not ideal mates. It is degrading to give women beyond the limits of the Yörük tribal community, particularly to a non-co-religionist. No case of a Yörük woman marrying a non-Sunni Muslim, or even a non-Yörük was discovered during the study.[1] Thus lineage endogamy is best considered a statistical by-product of other features of the marriage system, not itself a primary determinant of the kinship nexus.

CULTURALLY STIPULATED PREFERENCES OF MARRIAGE

Yörük of all tribes studied here state a strong preference for close cousin marriages. All first cousins are considered good matches; of the four types possible, matings with the patrilateral parallel cousin (father's brother daughter-son) are the most esteemed. Given this clear favoring of marriage with true or

---

[1] Some marriages of Yörük women to non-Yörük may have occurred but are suppressed in the genealogies. It is likely that arranged, recognized marriages of Yörük women to non-Yörük Sunni Moslems will take place in the near future. Three families in Sayburun village have taken brides from their Kurdish and Arab immediate neighbors in arranged marriages. They, or their children, will be called upon to reciprocate. Until these matches took place, most women taken from non-Yörük were kidnapped.

classificatory father's brother's daughter it is obvious, should actual practice follow belief, that marriages of the other three cousin types would be also within the definition of remote patrilateral parallel cousin marriages, e.g., within the agnatic descent group. This follows from the fact that if ego's parents are related as father's brother's son and father's brother's daughter to each other (e.g., the children of brothers), any true MBD whom cousin ego might marry would also be an agnatic kinsman.

Furthermore, the likelihood that FZD's (father's sister's daughters) and MZD's will be close agnatic kinsmen is high, the exact rate being determined by the incidence of FBD marriages in previous generations. The inherent tendency for marriages to be more frequent within the lineage, or other descent groups, and the structural consequences of the preference for FBD matches is much commented upon in the literature of Near Eastern kinship (for example, Barth, 1954; Ayoub, 1959; Randolph and Coult, 1968; Patai, 1965; Murphy and Kasden, 1959 and 1967; and Aswad, 1968 and 1972).

The tendency for patrilateral parallel cousin marriage, true or classificatory, is much reinforced by a custom known as "father's brother's right" (*emmi hakkı*).[2] This custom, in essence, gives every man the "right" to claim the daughter of his brother in marriage for his son, should he have one of marriageable age. In practice this is extended so that a man might well feel that he has claim on the daughter of his father's brother's son, and so on. It is held to apply in extension only among agnates and does not obviate payment of bride price (*başlık* or *kalın parası*), which is on the average no less for an agnatic kin than any other (see Tables 8 and 11).

It is not possible to say how many marriages between agnates occur because of the application of this rule. But in a number of cases where men did not marry their daughters to a close agnates who wanted them, conflict and disagreement lasted long after the marriages. One case involved a family with whom the ethnographer was staying in the field. In that instance, a marriage was arranged between a girl who was mother's brother's son's daughter (MBSD) and her father's father's sister's son (FFZS). Both were of the same lineage and could trace more distant ties of kinship patrilineally (FFBSSD-FFFBSS). The man who claimed

---

[2] Barth (1954:164-71) describes "father's brother right" among the Kurds of northern Iraq.

TABLE 7

ORIGIN BY DESCENT GROUP OF PRESENTLY MARRIED WOMEN AS COMPARED WITH THE DESCENT GROUP OF HUSBAND

	Nomads	(SEDENTARY)			Total	%
		İslahiye	Nogaylar	Sayburun		
Non-Yörük	4	7	0	7	18	3.2
Outside the Tribe (but Yörük)	31	2	1	3	37	6.7
Outside Kabile (but within tribe)	98	37	15	22	172	31.0
Within Kabile	190	58	47	33	328	59.1
Total	323	104	63	65	555	100.0

Note: 90.1% of all marriages occur within the tribe, and less than 4% occur with non-Yörük.

TABLE 8

BRIDE PRICE AND THE DEGREE OF CONSANGUINAL KINSHIP OF WIFE TO PRESENT HUSBAND: NOMAD WOMEN

Bride Price in T.L.	True and Classificatory Relationship to Husband				
	FBD	MBD	FZD	MZD	Total
First Quartile 0-999.00 T.L.	15	13	6	8	43
Second Quartile 1,000-3,999 T.L.	25	14	4	2	45
Third Quartile 4,000-8,999 T.L.	25	16	4	6	51
Fourth Quartile 9,000-30,000 T.L.	27	6	9	3	45
Total	93	49	23	19	184

Note: Close agnates pay more bride price than other consanguinal kinsmen

Chi square $x^2 = 15.1$
d.f. = 9
p = 0.10

that his rights were ignored in the marriage, and who later tried to kill or wound the groom's brother, was related to the girl's father as father's brother's son. He claimed a portion of the 3,000 T.L. bride price (which was small by Yörük standards) from the girl's father, and was given it. This indemnity was called "coffee money" (*kahve parası*). When he received no money from the groom's family, he encouraged one of his sons to waylay the groom's brother with a shotgun. His son was himself later beaten up when this was unsuccessful. The hard feelings generated are likely to persist because of the incidence of physical violence.

This custom encourages marriages within the lineage among close agnates, particularly where this is applied to cases where the girl is not the daughter of one's true brother. Also, the father of the girl (or brother if he is her guardian after her father's death) is held liable even if the girl elopes with or is kidnapped by a non-agnate. One man's sister was kidnapped by a boy from another lineage. He received a bride price some time later from the boy's father, but his father's brother, who had expected the girl for his son, took the opportunity to renounce a substantial debt in animals which he had owed his nephew whose father had died a few years earlier.

The preference for FBD (or FBS) marriage has another structural effect that should be noted, one which is logically the converse of lineage encystation.[3] That is, where classificatory FBD marriages (e.g., FFBD, FBSD, etc.) occur with any regularity, it would be difficult for a culture to ignore or sanction against any of the remaining three types of cousin marriage: MBD, MZD, and FZD.

Among the Yörük when one recounts ties of kinship between closely related spouses or other individuals, those passing through the fewest segments or genealogic junctions are mentioned first regardless of laterality. Simply put, lines of kinship traced through the first ascending, but no higher, generation are invariably detailed correctly without lineal bias, even if it involves

---

[3] Aswad usefully introduces this term in her detailed analysis of marriage over three generations in an Arab Turkish village (1968:61-95). Encystation is the logical outcome of repeated FBD marriage in a society possessing patrilineal descent groups. Aswad's diachronic analysis of marriage suggests that polygyny is a means of achieving alliance in a marriage system which would formally hinder outreaching marriages. The Yörük marriage system would show a similar pattern if analyzed in this fashion, with kidnapping serving to further disperse marriage-formed affinal ties.

following the line through a number of descending generations. Thus, for example, a true mother's brother's son's son would always be described that way even when the speaker could refer to him in patrilineal—but more distant—terms. If the closest kinship connections can be described only through the second or higher ascending generation there is a definite bias for patrilineal, selective recall. For example, a man might describe his mother's mother's brother's son's son (MMBSS) by an equally distant patrilateral term, should such a relationship exist. The point is that when marriages cut across lineage lines or tribal identities, the emergent linkages of close consanguinity are not systematically obscured by more distant or putative relationships through common agnatic descent.

Prohibitions on marriage do not affect rates of endogamy, nor in any way disfavor extra-lineage matches. The forbidden marriages are those set by Islamic jurisprudence (see Levy, 1954:104 ff.) of the Hanefi code. These will not be recapitulated here except to note that two "bad" marriages were found during the study: one involved the taking of a wife forbidden by religious law, while the other was considered ambiguous. The first, and most flagrant, violation occurred when a man eloped with or kidnapped his wife's sister, and brought her home as second wife. This was exacerbated by the fact that she was already married. Shortly after this he was forced by public opinion to divorce the first one, although both women, people say, were content in their new domestic arrangements. Needless to say, this is not an everyday occurrence, and most informants say that the only reason the aggrieved husband of the stolen bride did not attempt action against the kidnapper was that he had "no relatives."

The second ambiguous marriage involved a man who married the widow of his deceased father's brother. This was seen by the man and his family as a form of the levirate while others said that it was a prohibited marriage. There was no pressure to break it up, and it does not occasion much negative commentary.

OBSERVED MARRIAGE FREQUENCIES

Actual marriage distributions do not contradict but rather agree with the stipulated cultural norms. True father's brother's daughter marriages take place at a frequency as high as could be expected considering the probability that such individuals will fall into the proper age categories (see Ayoub [1959:270 ff.] for a discussion of this problem). True father's brother's daughter (or *öz emmi kïzï*) marriages occur at the 20 percent level in all residential types, with no statistically significant differences in frequency when grouped by that criterion (see Table 9). Next favored are marriages between true mother's brother's daughter and mother's brother's son which occur at an overall frequency of nearly 11 percent (see Table 9). The remaining two cousin types are less frequent, neither taking place at a rate of more than 5 percent when all residence categories are averaged (see Table 9). All true first cousin marriages amount to 40.7 percent.

Classificatory cousin marriages parallel true ones in the order of frequency, and are themselves culturally distinguished by the term *uşak*. While "uşak" literally means "male child," it is most commonly used for close kin who are one or two generations removed from the "true" (öz) kin-type. For example, true FBS is usually called *emmi oğlu* while FFBS or FBSS are most often called *emmi uşağï*. To be emphatic that a relationship is precisely described, it is often modified with the word "öz" or true (see Table 9). Classificatory cousin marriages amount to 21.0 percent of the total. Classificatory and true (öz) first cousin marriages constitute 61.7 percent of all the ones contracted. Of these, true and classificatory cousin type matches attain a rate of 38.5 percent in the present population.

Second marriages are not analyzed here but they would show a markedly lower frequency of first cousin marriages. Second marriages, whether to acquire a second wife or to replace one who has died, do not invoke the rule of father's brother's right (emmi hakkï), and by informant accounts are not particularly directed to near kin. Men are reluctant to give a virgin daughter to widowers or to men who already have another wife. Bride price is accordingly higher, and few men are able to secure a virgin second wife. Most men who marry for the second time marry widows or divorcées, unless they kidnap a bride. The bride price will be high for kidnap marriages, but not for divorcées or widows.

Again looking at Table 9, it is clear that there are no substantial differences among members of different residence types (village, İslahiye, and nomadic) for most of the categories of marriage defined by degree of kinship of wife to husband. In two areas, however, there are significant discrepancies between the sedentary and nomadic groups. Among the nomads it is seen that

TABLE 9
MARRIAGE TYPES BY DEGREE OF KINSHIP OF WIFE TO PRESENT HUSBAND
(living women only, 473 cases)

Kinship of Wife to Husband	(SEDENTARY)						Nomad		Total	
	İslahiye		Nogaylar		Sayburun					
	f.	%	f.	%	f.	%	f.	%	f.	%
FBD (true or öz)	14	20.0	17	24.6	11	16.7	60	22.4	102	21.6
MBD (true or öz)	8	11.4	7	10.1	3	4.5	33	12.3	51	10.8
FZD (true or öz)	2	2.8	4	5.8	0	0.0	17	6.4	23	4.9
MZD (true or öz)	1	1.4	4	5.8	1	1.5	10	3.7	16	3.4
Classificatory* FBD or emmi uşāgï	6	8.5	11	15.9	14	16.2	36	13.4	67	14.2
Classificatory* MBD	1	1.4	4	5.8	6	9.1	8	3.0	19	4.0
Classificatory* FZD	0	0.0	2	2.9	0	0.0	3	1.1	5	1.1
Classificatory* MZD	0	0.0	3	4.4	2	3.0	3	1.1	8	1.7
Non-kin within the lineage	3	4.3	3	4.4	1	1.5	7	2.6	14	3.0
Non-kin from same Yörük tribe, different lineage	26	37.2	13	18.8	18	27.3	56	20.9	113	23.9
Non-kin from another tribe	2	2.8	1	1.4	3	4.5	31	11.6	37	7.8
Non-kin, non-Yörük	7	10.0	0	0.0	7	10.6	4	1.5	18	3.8
Total	70	100	69	100	66	100	268	100	473	100

*Classificatory kin types are calculated through two ascending or descending generations, e.g., FFBD, FBSD, FFBSD.

f. = frequency

women who are non-kin and from outside their husbands' tribes are married at a rate much higher than is evidenced among the sedentary populations. This is somewhat counter-intuitive: one would expect, on the basis of stereotypes of tribal society in the literature, that tribal distinctions would become less important after settlement. However in the area of study, Yörük who have settled have done so in the proximity of other close kin. Thus the fact of fixed residence in many cases puts individuals in closer and more frequent contact with their kinsmen, especially agnates, than previously was the case. The nomadic population is highly flexible in residence patterns with each temporary camp group representing a social concensus rather than the only residential option open to a head of household (see Chapters IV, V). This undoubtedly has an effect on marriage choices. Further, the nomadic population contains a number of families who have affiliated themselves with other descent groups and tribes. Although they have not yet lost their descent identity, their near-incorporation in the groups they "follow" makes intermarriage a logical step for them.

The second point with reference to marriage differences among sedentary and nomadic groups is that İslahiye and Sayburun Yörük residents have intermarried (but not yet given daughters) with non-Yörük families, while the nomadic and Nogaylar Yörük have not done so. It is likely that rates for such marriages will increase with time among sedentary Yörük as the entire community benefits from the increased security and mutual aid which results. Such intermarriages are still not considered "good" matches, and they are framed most often by poorer individuals. In Sayburun seven women are from outside of the Yörük community, and while these are poor families, the relationships established are widely called into play by people from the wife's kin group and from the groom's group. In Nogaylar village no such marriage has taken place, although it was proposed several years ago by the leader of the Yörük village population that such a marriage be arranged with between the ağa's son and a Çerkes girl. Other villagers opposed such a match; however, the opposition centered on an already existing conflict and ill-will, and not on the fact that the girl was Çerkes. Since that date violence has occurred which precludes intermarriage for the time being. The Yörük do not believe in marriage as a means of settlement in situations of bloodshed, and often comment on such Türkmen and Arab practices very negatively.

The low rate of inter-ethnic group marriage among the nomads is probably the result of not only their preferences for Yörük brides because of their known "purity" (also true of the settled Yörük), but too because they have little to gain from such marriage arrangements. The Yörük move over a wide area in which there are a variety of ethnic groups. They utilize pastures and camp sites in numerous villages and trade in several towns. It is clear that close affines from among the Yörük population, either nomadic or sedentary, would be more advantageous and could potentially figure in a wider variety of transactions.

BRIDE PRICE AND KIDNAPPING

Two further aspects of Yörük marriage practices remain to be dealt with here: bride price and bride stealing. Before proceeding to these, it should be mentioned that this section does not purport to exhaust all avenues of analysis of Yörük marriage. It is meant only to set the backdrop for subsequent discussions of residence and domestic economic processes.

Bride price and kidnapping are two closely associated aspects of the general problem of acquiring a bride in Yörük society among both sedentary and nomadic populations. They are, as it were, symbolic of the two strategies by which a man takes a wife. Bride price (başlık) is the money paid in cash by agreement with the family of the bride-to-be. It is money paid by the groom's family, usually his father, to the girl's guardian, normally her father. It is the culmination of inter-family negotiations, carried out at first fugitively by female intermediaries, and later solemnized by a direct meeting of the two heads of households. Quite apart from the financial effects of the often large payment of cash, the tendering and acceptance of başlık money signifies the beginning of a social alliance between the family of the groom and the family of the bride. It represents, from the boy's point of view, the successful conclusion of his efforts to find a bride in the culturally acceptable manner.

Kidnapping a bride is an alternative to the process of acquiring one by inter-family agreement, negotiation, and a formal wedding ceremony (düğün).[4] Whereas başlık in its usual sense

[4] A formal wedding is perhaps the most important social occasion in Yörük society, particularly when there is time to arrange for Gypsy entertainment and for guests to come from distant groups. However, due to the number of murders which have attended large wedding celebrations in the past 10 years, by general agreement none have been recently organized among the nomads. Instead, the marriage festivities are performed without fanfare and without dancing on short notice. Since an

represents agreement between families to establish social relations on the basis of affinity, the kidnapping of a girl by a member of one family from another household marks the onset of bad relations, or at best an indeterminant period of no social relations. Bride price taken for a daughter given in the proper manner is a sign of the bridegroom's family's respect for the house which gave them a bride. In situations where a girl is taken by kidnapping, başlık is again paid, after the fact, but is viewed as an indemnity. It is paid as an alternative to violence, and is exacted with bitterness on the part of the girl's father or brothers. It does not in itself symbolize the resumption of normal relations between the two households, let alone the beginning of the special affinal relationship.

The Yörük (and standard Turkish) term for kidnapping a bride is *kız kaçırma*, distinguished by an infix -*ır*- from the reciprocal -*ış*- which would denote elopement (*kaçışma*). This latter term is never employed by the Yörük for the reason that it is socially immaterial whether the girl is abducted by force or is enticed to run away. In both instances parental approval is lacking, and it is the familial nature of the marriage arrangement which is crucial to its definition as an approved match.

This stems from the fact that one of the most stringently observed moral codes is that of single female chastity, and the faithfulness of married women. Yörük informants have stated that should one witness a case of pre-marital intercourse, or adultery, it would be the obligation of the witness immediately to kill the woman. This is, no doubt, unlikely to happen, but suspicion of adultery or pre-marital intercourse is grounds for the killing of the errant wife or girl. It is the duty of the girl's brother, even in the case of married women, to secure family honor by punishing the transgressor. One such case was known to the ethnographer to have been settled with such drastic action. In that case a teen-age boy killed his father's second wife upon determining that she was committing adultery. Such matters are not, understandably, much discussed but it is unlikely that sexual access among persons not married to each other is very common.

important part of the festive atmosphere is the wild firing of guns, accidental death, suspected murder, and murder seem to accompany large weddings. The ethnographer witnessed one large village Yörük wedding and two small, unannounced weddings. The potential for violence is clear, and the government sent two *jandarma* to the village to supervise the three days of festivities.

It is this moral code that, quite apart from the overt flouting of social amenities, makes kidnapping a serious offense against the family of the girl. Marriage contracted in the approved fashion involves the legal uniting of husband and wife (or their representatives) and the public celebration of the nuptial rites. It is customary for an old woman (often an *ebe* or midwife) to determine that the consumation of the marriage is completed and that the bride is a virgin. If she is not, or if the groom cannot perform his husbandly services, the marriage is annulled.

Kïz kaçïrma is the antithesis of the proper marriage. It is, in fact, no marriage at all until a *hoca* can be found to perform in private the rites that are by definition public, and then only after sexual intercourse has taken place. While it is possible to view kïz kaçïrma as an alternative way in which to secure a bride, it is not without its dangers. From the girl's family's perspective it is considered an assault on their honor and property, and should they apprehend the kidnapper soon afterwards, their first impulse would be to kill him. Several deaths were determined in genealogies to have been caused during kidnapping attempts.

Further, it is not invariably a cheaper way to obtain a wife as bride price may well be higher once it is possible to arrange its payment. If the girl is under 18 years of age, the abductor can be brought to law and tried for statutory or actual rape. The threat of this is almost always used by the girl's family, and the large number of men under sentence for this crime in Turkish prisons attests to the fact that it is not always an idle threat.[5] One known Yörük man is presently under a 15-year sentence for kïz kaçïrma in Finike. There are many known cases where the father of the girl had instigated court proceedings before being persuaded to accept a cash settlement.

There are two basic types of kidnapping. In the first, perhaps the most common, the girl is contacted by an intermediary of the boy and an agreement is made to elope together at a given time. Neither the girl's nor the boy's parents will have knowledge of the plans although it is possible that women in the girl's tent will know what is going on. Particularly, the wives of the girl's brothers are apt to be a party to the elopement, but never the girl's own brothers. The boy's younger brothers are sometimes included in

---

[5] Several deaths occasioned by kidnapping appeared in genealogies. In several cases the girl's father had demanded legal action and the abductor was tried and sentenced.

his part of the conspiracy, but not older brothers, particularly unmarried older brothers who might well be losing bride wealth that would be used to bring home a bride for them in the legitimate fashion. The boy usually is accompanied by a friend to assist in getting away.

The second variety, only slightly less common than the first, is the taking of a girl against her will or without her prior consent. Men sometimes say that they had not arranged an elopement with their wives, but that once captured, they offered no resistance. Others state that they took their wives captive bound and kicking.

On the fourth day of the ethnographer's stay in the tribe a girl was kidnapped from the tent in which he was staying. Her abductor had made his arrangements earlier and the girl left voluntarily. The boy and girl were close patrilineal kin (FFBD-FFBS) and the marriage type was a "good one." However, the girl was tentatively promised to another, equally close patrilineal relative and considerable disruption of social relations resulted.

When the elopement was discovered during the night, a great chase began, involving everyone in the tent, to catch the couple who were heard running in the bushes along a river bank. Shots were fired in their direction. One brother of the girl later recounted that while hunting for the fleeing couple, he encountered the boy's older brother tending sheep, unaware of what had taken place. Pointing his gun at him, he questioned him about his brother's whereabouts. If, he said, the boy's brother had shown any knowledge of what had taken place he would have shot him.

The father's initial reaction was to take the matter to the court and to prefer criminal charges, saying that he did not want a settlement but only to gain the return of his daughter and the punishment of the culprit. Within three days, a tentative settlement was agreed to by respected intermediaries, and a cash başlık of a substantial sum paid (13,000 T.L.). Apart from a symbolic meeting which took place without food between the two fathers, they had no further social contact known to the ethnographer during the following two years. Also, none of the brothers of the girl, nor men of the tent to which she would have gone, maintained further social relations with the boy's tent.

In this case, settlement was relatively quick and without violence, perhaps because the tents were close kin. The girl's father agreed to accept başlık without prolonged attempts for revenge. He may have been motivated by the fact that the abductor's father was the richest man in the lineage, and one of the richest in the tribe. It would not be correct, however, to infer that a status differential is inevitably important in determining the frequency of kidnapping and the social direction kidnapped girls move in. Often kidnapping is generated by pressures arising from the domestic circumstances of the boy who seeks a bride. He is not as motivated by questions of relative social status as would be his father in arranging a marriage, although differences in wealth may obstruct some matches.

In another case, two men, both single and distantly related, kidnapped a young girl who was unrelated to either of them. They took her forcibly to a remote spot and gave her the choice of accepting one of them, but not the choice of rejecting both. She was then raped by the man she chose, and shortly thereafter was married to him. In this case it was some time before a cash settlement of başlık was agreed upon, and although relations are cool between her husband of 20 years and her brothers, he enjoys good terms with her other close kinsmen (MBS, FFBS) who often visit their tent and with whom they sometimes camp.

An interesting aspect of the first kidnapping described is that gossip among the women has it that the girl's stepmother (her mother's co-wife) arranged the elopement to spite her husband. She herself had been kidnapped unwillingly as a 14-year-old girl and taken as a second wife. The settlement in that case had involved the man giving up his entire herd in payment of başlık, some 45 sheep. Over half of all the polygynous marriages presently intact (for which information is available) involve the kidnapping of the second wife (seven out of 12).

It is possible to isolate the structural consequences of kidnapping from the motivations of the participants who carry it out. From an individual perspective, kidnapping is a means of forcing one's father's hand in getting a bride. It can be that the youth wishes to marry out of birth order as well, although this is regarded as particularly bad behavior due to the sibling conflict it can engender. Few such cases were observed in the total recorded. It is a sign of the young man's bravery (*yiğitlik*) and undoubtedly some kidnapping is instigated from a desire to demonstrate boldness and independence. For a period after a kidnapping, the successful young man is the focus of much admiration by his younger peers, and even adults not directly involved in the consequences speak of the deed in half-amused terms.

SYSTEMS OF MARRIAGE 73

What is interesting from a social structural vantage point is that kĭz kaçĭrma constitutes an alternative marriage strategy. Yörük, as individuals, are all aware of the occurrence of kidnapping, but because of the negative way it is defined, do not regard it as anything but an aberration. It is usually described as something which takes place among other groups, not the speaker's own, and is not thought to have a pattern of its own. It is not considered a regular feature of their marriage system.

However, any consideration of Yörük marriage would be inadequate without detailing patterns of kidnapping as by actual direct census count of present marriages, a full 19.8 percent (72 of 364)[6] of them arose through kĭz kaçĭrma (see Table 10). Genealogical data covering several generations exhibit a similarly high frequency (over 20 percent).

TABLE 10

ARRANGED AND KIDNAP MARRIAGES BY RELATIONSHIP OF WIFE TO HUSBAND (364 cases)

Marriage Type by Kinship	Arranged Marriage f.	%	Kidnapped Marriage f.	%	Total per Kin Type	Percent of Kin Kidnapped
FBD*	121	41.4	19	26.3	140	13.6
MBD*	42	14.4	10	13.9	52	19.2
FZD*	23	7.9	2	2.8	25	8.0
MZD*	19	6.5	3	4.1	22	13.6
Other in lineage	6	2.1	2	2.8	8	25.0
Other outside lineage	81	27.7	36	50.1	117	30.8
TOTAL	292	100	72	100	(364)	(19.8)

*classificatory included, i.e., FBSD and FFBD.

[6] It should be pointed out that different tables regarding marriage and residence often involve differing numbers of cases. This variation is due to the fact that unsatisfactory data are omitted. Most of these tables are based on census information which is felt to be more accurate than genealogical data. A more detailed analysis of kidnapping and Yörük social structure is in preparation.

Furthermore, kidnapping is not random in its occurrence with respect to categories of kinship or in the frequency with which kidnap marriages are contracted in each category (see Tables 10 and 13).

The problem can be approached on two levels. First is the question of which features of Yörük society generate high rates of theoretically disapproved, socially disruptive behavior in an area as closely regulated as is marriage. This involves a consideration of the motivation of individuals, and the immediate circumstances which surround a kidnapping.

Second is the problem of analyzing the general structural effects of kidnapping in Yörük society, and how it affects consanguinal kinship networks.

THE CONTEXTS AND CAUSES OF KIDNAPPING

The two main responses of Yörük informants to the query of why one would kidnap a bride are that the boy "fell in love" (*kïz takïldï*) or that he was impatient and could not wait for his family to find him a bride in the prescribed manner. As for the first reason, "romantic love" is a paramount theme in Yörük oral narrative (*destan*), but it is explicitly denied a role in the arranging of marriages. Elopement or kidnapping are, then, often solutions to a problem that needs no further clarification here. The second category of explanation regarding impatience is a statement about an important set of constraints imposed by the normative system on the individual. Each person in a sibling set must marry in order of birth. Because bride prices are often high (see Table 11), long-term economic planning is necessary to accumulate sufficient capital for marriage where more than one son is involved. This is often contrary to the immediate self-interest of the single male since the society also restricts full adult status to those who are married. Sons therefore may wish to force their father's hands, or (rarely) to marry out of turn before a still single older brother.

When men who have kidnapped are questioned, they usually stress their disinclination to wait for their father to make the arrangements. Bride price is frequently brought up as featuring in decisions to kidnap or elope. It is likely a major immediate cause of kidnapping.

SYSTEMS OF MARRIAGE 75

TABLE 11

HISTOGRAM OF BRIDE PRICES PAID FOR PRESENTLY MARRIED
YÖRÜK WOMEN OVER THE LAST 55 YEARS (15 intervals)
(273 observations*)

```
                      I---------+---------+---------+---------+
          1.0000000   +
                   56 I***************************
         15.000000   +
                   29 I**************
         29.000000   +
                   46 I**********************
         43.000000   +
                   26 I*************
         57.000000   +
                   24 I************
(Bride Price in 100's of T.L.)
         71.000000   +
                   15 I********
         85.000000   +
                   13 I*******
         99.000000   +
                   17 I*********
        113.00000    +
                   12 I*******
        127.00000    +
                   10 I******
        141.00000    +
                   14 I********
        155.00000    +
                    4 I***
        159.00000    +
                    4 I**
        183.00000    +
                    1 I
        197.00000    +
                    2 I*
        211.00000    +
                      I---------+---------+---------+---------+
                      0        20        40        60        80
```

*31 cases of *no* bride price are omitted.
12 cases of *no* bride price are kidnap marriages.
Overall mean bride price paid, excluding those cases where none was
paid = 5,976 T.L.

Although the outlay of bride price money is a substantial expense for the would-be groom's family, it is said that the boy's father is never a party to the efforts of his son to kidnap a wife. This is because not only are his existing relations with the girl's family threatened, but also he is responsible for any indemnity that might be paid after the act. Even though a majority of men who kidnapped their wives stated that they did so in order to marry either when they did not have enough money or when their father would not agree to put it up, as many families paid substantial indemnities as got away with no payment or a nominal one. Table 12 indicates the nature of bride price payments for kidnap marriages: 35 (or 48 percent) of the 73 kidnap marriages involved a bride price payment of less than a 1,000 T.L., which is nominal, while 11 (15 percent) entailed a payment well above the median. Twelve (16 percent) of the kidnap matches occurred with no indemnity, while relatively fewer of the arranged marriages took place without the transfer of bride wealth (7 percent or 20 out of 263). The arranged marriages were, in fact, all instances where daughters were ex-

TABLE 12

ARRANGED AND KIDNAP MARRIAGES BY QUARTILE OF
BRIDE PRICE: 336 cases
($1.00 = 12.00 T.L.)

Bride Price in Quartiles of T.L. Paid in Cash	Mode of Marriage				Total Row	% Row Kidnapped
	Arranged		Kidnapped			
	f.	(%)	f.	(%)		
First Quartile (0-999)	69	(26.2)	35	(47.9)	104	33.7
Second Quartile (1,000-3,999)	66	(25.1)	10	(13.7)	76	13.3
Third Quartile (4,000-8,999)	66	(25.1)	17	(23.3)	83	20.5
Fourth Quartile (9,000-21,000)	62	(23.6)	11	(15.1)	73	13.7
Totals	263	(100.0)	73	(100.0)	336	---

f. = frequency

changed (değiş) thus nullifying the bride price payment for both parties.

One aspect of bride price and marriage is that there are families with marriageable sons that cannot afford any real payment or not one large enough to acquire a virgin bride.[7] Only two cases were found in which a man married a divorced or widowed woman as his first wife, and both were of poor (landless, sedentary) families. It is not an esteemed type of match and reflects poorly on the character of a young man and of the family that consents to it. Marriage to the widow of one's older brother, of course, is not thought of in the same light—such a match perpetuates an already existing relationship.

For a family to be so poor as not to be able to afford başlık, it must have no marriageable daughters whose bride price might be used to secure women for their brothers. It is, however, an economic hardship in many cases. Poverty, when başlık and marriage, are concerned should be measured by the number of sons who have to be married, and the number of daughters who can bring cash into the household when given out in marriage (see Irons [1969b:265 ff.] for a good discussion of bride price and economic mobility).

Direct daughter exchanges (değiş) are not highly favored, and if they occur, it is taken for granted that one of the families involved is getting a "poor deal." For example, one of the richest men of the tribe arranged to exchange his highly regarded daughter with a poor family for a bride for his feeble-minded son. The girl they received was not an outstandingly attractive mate by Yörük standards, but she would not have been given in marriage to a handicapped youth except under such circumstances. In this case the poorer family did come out quite well, but the stigma attached to değiş with its clear implication of the deficiency of one or more of the parties makes it difficult to arrange.

Sons in families with limited capital and no marriageable sisters are confronted with the likely prospect of late marriage.

---

[7] Nomadic Yörük do not give large dowries (cehiz) although village Yörük follow local, non-Yörük custom and do give them. Among the nomads a father customarily provides his daughter with gold coins, perhaps up to a tenth of the value of the başlık. Sometimes a radio, sewing machine, or other expensive household item is provided, but usually it is not a significant portion of the bride price. The bride does bring sheets and bedding, as well as camel bags (çul) and rugs which she has made herself.

Kaçïrma is a solution for the poor in that if the boy's father has little or no capital, the family of the girl can do little to secure an indemnity. Thus, those at the lower end of the wealth spectrum seem to reduce their effective bride price requirements through kidnapping, even though this is not a deliberate strategy on the part of the boy's parents. A disproportionate number of the kidnap marriages where little or no bride price was paid are found among families who were in the lowest quartile of wealth (30 out of 35).

Conversely, the son of a family of median or above holdings in animals is placing his own advantage before the seemingly optimal economic course that his father would pursue. He acquires a bride, and a certain amount of bravado status among the young men of the tribe, but forces his father's hand with respect to making an immediate payment of bride price. Wealthy men are more apt to pay large indemnities.

In this way, kidnapping might be interpreted as mitigating the unequal impact that high cash payments of bride price would have on families in different categories of wealth. Admittedly this hypothesis needs refinement before it can be properly tested, but the available indicators seem to confirm it. Even though the average bride price paid for all kidnap marriages is virtually the same as for normative ones, there are relatively more cases where no payment or only a nominal payment was made. These cases occur in the lower category of herd size.

Kaçïrma is also related to the problem of multiple "claimants" for the same girl. Generally it is clear which of a girl's several FB's has a son of marriageable age. The fact that older brothers marry first, and that women ideally should be younger than their husbands, means that older brothers are more likely to get brides for their sons from younger brothers. This is not a stipulated rule or even preferred arrangement. Where two brothers have marriageable sons, and a third has a suitable daughter, it is rare that they do not agree on the priority of the older brother's "claim." True father's brother right (emmi hakkï) is not a source of conflict. What does happen with considerable regularity is that, lacking a true FBS, a man will negotiate a marriage for his daughter with a more distant agnate or consanguine. If he "passes over" the claims or advice of more closely related agnates, animosity may result. This was observed in the field and was noted as the source of several disputes. We will return to this at a later point in the discussion. As a result, marriages are negotiated in considerable secrecy and are contracted rapidly. A boy may attempt to abduct or elope with a girl whom he had hoped to marry in the normative fashion. His father, it should be noted, will not likely be a partner to this since he is responsible for the indemnity and because of the social disruption to the descent group caused by kidnapping.

In summary, then, the immediate causes and contexts of kidnapping are rooted in the rigidity of the normative system of arranged matches and in the requirements of large cash bride price payments. Elopement gives the girl freedom of choice otherwise denied her in this area, and the boy the ability to bypass the often deliberate and time-consuming plans of his household. An apparent immediate function of the practice is to facilitate the marriage of poorer men faced with raising cash payments in a market economy, thus leveling potential distinctions of wealth in this vital area of behavior. A possible consequence of the high incidence of kidnapping is that normative marriages take place shortly after puberty for girls, and without any period of betrothal. The threat of kidnapping makes it difficult to keep a marriageable daughter at home too long, and once a bride price payment is made, marriage takes place immediately.

KIDNAPPING AND THE DISPERSION OF KINSHIP TIES

The concentrating effect of the preferences for father's brother's daughter marriage has been noted. Kidnap and elopement marriages parallel the order of preferences for the categories of close kin; that is, FBD is favored over other cousins and all other kinsmen display similar rates of marriage (see Table 10 for the relative frequencies for both modes of marriage by kinship type). Despite the common preference for kinsmen in the two marriage strategies, significantly different frequencies of marriages in the non-kin categories have the *net effect* of dispersing marriages beyond the circle of consanguinal mates favored strongly in practice in arranged marriages. Moreover, those FBD kidnap marriages which seemingly "reflect" the normative ideology in terms of kinship, as do the cases of cousin kidnapping, nevertheless have quite different structural implications.

In comparing kidnap and the culturally approved marriages, the two striking differences are the relatively fewer marriages with FBD (Table 10) and the relatively greater number of kidnap marriages with non-consanguinal kin outside the lineage (Table 13). Furthermore, looking at Table 10, which shows the percentage of each kin-type marriage which is kidnap in origin, it is clear that a significant amount of all extra-lineage, non-kin marriages occur through kidnapping (30.7 percent). Also, over half of all non-close consanguinal marriages, 55.7 percent regardless of lineality, arise from kidnapping (Table 13).

The dispersal effects of kidnapping can be shown to be statistically significant (Table 13). If one assumes that kidnap marriages with non-kin occurred in place of arranged marriages with kin, one can say that over 30 percent (40 of 131) of all such "out marriages" were caused by kaçǐrma. Even if this assumption is only approximated in reality, kidnapping would generate a noticeable number of new extra-lineage kinship ties. This is of some importance in itself, given the fact that the normative ideology of the Yörük, like most Near Eastern tribes, accords marriage small scope for such alliance functions: preferred matches occur within the lower-level units of political segmentation.

Although the net effect of kidnapping is to disperse kin ties in a structural framework which concentrates affinal and cognate relationships within pre-existing circles of close consanguinity, it is reasonable to question the extent to which such ties are usable

TABLE 13

KIDNAPPING AND EXOGAMY: 382 cases

Relation of Wife to Husband	Arranged		Kidnapped		Total
	f	(%)	f	(%)	
All consanguinal kin, and lineage mates	215	(70.3)	36	(47.4)	251
All non-kin, outside lineage or tribe	91	(29.7)	40	(52.6)	131
Total	306	(100.0)	76	(100.00)	382

Chi square x^2 = 14.3
    d.f. = 1
    p. = .001

Note: Actual rates of lineage exogamy are somewhat higher than indicated here since consanguinal kin of all types are lumped together.

f. = frequency

in social transactions. Further, it is necessary to examine the effects of kidnappings that occur both outside and within the lineage against the larger political environment of the Yörük nomadic pastoralists.

Marriages in general do not create "alliances" in the usual anthropological sense, as lineages do not enter into a special relationship with one another upon the intermarriage of any of their members. Any features that resemble an alliance possessed by the Yörük marriage systems remain at the household level. Ties of patrilineal kinship and even those of close consanguinity usually take precedence over simple materialistic considerations in arranging marriage, particularly since it is known that the relative economic positions of families are highly variable during the lifetimes of their members. Primarily, of course, a family with a marriageable daughter has to take into consideration the opinions of the close agnates who culturally are recognized as having a claim on the girl, or a say in her disposal. After all, it is their agnates who will be asked to supply their own sons with brides on some future occasion. Moreover, not to heed the claims of agnates would (and does) cause conflict.

The Yörük are aware that affinal ties can, under some circumstances, supplant agnatic ones, and that to acquire a daughter from outside the circle of pre-existing close kin might lead to their "losing a son." They have a saying that expresses this awareness well: "Don't take a bride's scarf from strangers, they'll take the groom and go," (*Iyad elden alma düveyi, çeker gider güveyi*). A man is particularly apt to camp with affines if he is on bad terms with his brothers or other close agnates. Normally, however, it is not thought well of a man to be too close with the tent of the wife's father, particularly if the father-in-law is wealthy. This would imply a dependence which is seen as degrading. However, men often camp with close kinsmen of their wife, particularly with her brothers. This further selects for endogamous marriages.

Against this cultural backdrop, kidnapping and elopement could broaden the *effective* kinship nexus of a family, provided that relations are normalized or that the children of such a marriage are able to interact normally with all of their cognatic relatives. The first condition is met with enough regularity so that a sizable number of long-married kaçĭrma couples were observed interacting closely with the bride's kinsmen. This outcome, however, cannot be predicted at the onset of events, and the desire to gain affines does not motivate men to kidnap. The second condition is satisfied entirely. Children are not tainted by the mode of marriage of their parents, as long as they were born in wedlock and not repudiated by their father.

Following a kidnapping, relations between the households involved are extremely poor, and they remain so for a long period. Even though a bride price settlement may be paid shortly after the incident, there will be very little social or economic contact. The risk of violence is great under these circumstances and has been known to flare up even at reconciliation meetings several years later. The primary threat of violence emanates from two sources: the brothers of the girl and the household into which she likely would have been married if a normative arrangement had been in the planning stages at the time of kidnap. If physical confrontation is avoided during the initial days following the event, the families will usually follow a pattern of complete mutual avoidance. This is a recognized method of preventing the near-certain escalation of conflict. Another control limiting potential violence is the fact that the affair is regarded as deviant behavior and all direct participants are morally somewhat suspect. This ensures that the girl's agnatic kinsmen do not usually attempt revenge or direct action against the groom's family, as they would do in cases of personal assault. If physical violence is prevented and if an indemnity is paid, time may lead to a true reconciliation. Such a conclusion is not predictable in any given instance, and furthermore will not occur soon enough to benefit the boy's father who paid the bride price. In cases where the girl is kidnapped by an already married or older man, it is unlikely that normalization of relations will take place at all.

On balance, ties of affinity can be termed tenuous at best, and the direct alliance significance of kaçïrma might seem to lie more in how the practice deflects inter-lineage cooperation and restricts social movement through avoidance. A conclusion of this nature, albeit negative, would nevertheless ascribe considerable structural significance to kidnapping in as much as it would be then serving to isolate minimal named descent groups. However, this is not the interpretation which best fits the information at hand. The concluding discussion will show that kidnap-created ties of kinship can be activated to carry integrative social burdens, and that the dispersal of kin ties is ultimately important in much the same way that inter-group marriage is in any society where kinship is relevant in the political economy. It increases the options available to households plotting survival strategies in a complex system of land use.

    The Yörük, as stated before, operate in the context of firm state political control and in a market economy. Grazing rights must be negotiated for seasonal usage since all pasturage of consequence is owned by non-Yörük villagers. The social unit which contracts for grazing rights for the spring highland pastures (yayla) and for winter lowland fallow grain fields (kīşlak) is the camp group (see Chapter V). This consists of families who contract to share the cost of rental prorated by the number of mature sheep owned per household. These groups vary in size from two to 20 tents, and are generally formed around a core of male agnates. Further, it is common for the tents of a group to sell their milk—the source of cash for rental fees—to a cheese-maker from the same lineage segment. Some of these men have recently acquired considerable economic power and provide *de facto* leadership functions although they hold no customary office. As will be described elsewhere, the need for pasture rental money and the sale of milk to agnates tends to regularize camp group composition. At the same time it contributes to the stabilization of the wealth of a few households in an otherwise extremely fluid political economy. This encourages other members of the descent group to camp near them because of their superior ability to negotiate for good grazing.

    Despite such selective forces, no tent is required to camp with any specific group in order to rent pastures, and indeed this would be impossible. There is great fluctuation in the amount and distribution of grazing tracts available each year. No segment of the population—however defined—returns year after year to the same pasture tract in the summer or winter areas. Camp groups have to adjust to this variability in the resource base by regularly altering their composition. The optimal strategy for any Yörük tent is to camp with a sufficient number of other families to fully graze (but not over-graze) the land rented in a single tract. Without here going into how a family pursues such a course, there is continual movement of tents among fluid camp groups as they adjust to the grasslands available each season. Also, the effective cost of grazing is not fixed; it will differ from pasture to pasture according to a number of variables: amount of water, closeness to roads, safety, altitude, etc. For example, some families will camp in areas where the risk of conflict with villagers is greater but the cash cost of grazing is lower. During a month-long period prior to renting for the subsequent season, there is intense negotiation not only between Yörük and village representatives, but also among Yörük men as tents attempt to join others or to put together camp groups. Almost always in this process, tents will join groups in which they have at least one kinsman or close affine. Usually (and ideally) these will be close agnates and the overall patrilineal coloration of the groups is clear.

However, on occasion every tent camps with groups in which the only kinsmen are affines or cognatic relatives outside the descent group. This constellation is sometimes dictated by the amount and configuration of pasturage available, but more often it is in order to lower grazing costs. Conflict within the descent group is likewise significant in decisions to camp apart from agnates. Of the 11 tents of a medium-sized lineage closely observed in the field, eight camped for extended periods with groups in which the most direct ties among men were affinal or extra-lineage cognate ones. In four of these cases there were also more distant agnates in the group joined, but the decision to camp was generated by interaction with the nearer kinsmen. In the remaining four cases, the only kin-type ties were affinal or cognate. These decisions involved both economic and social objectives, the latter stemming from disagreements with male agnates. In one tent's decision to camp regularly with affines outside the head of household's descent group, these ties were originally created by the forced abduction of the wife. Here normal affinal relations had gradually been developed in the 20 years that had elapsed. The major reason that this tent chose (during the investigation) to camp with the wife's mother's brother was disagreement over the marriage of a classificatory father's brother's daughter of the head of house which took place without his being consulted. Since he had a marriageable—but rather dim—son, he felt that his rights had been ignored. He later received a portion of the bride price as compensation, but still camped apart from male agnates for several seasons. Ironically, the ultimate cause of the altercation was the kidnapping of another girl in the descent group by a close agnate, an event which upset tentative plans for the boy's marriage. This kidnapping, described earlier, caused considerable and bitter disagreement within the descent group, and resulted in a number of social and residential realignments.

Affinal and cognatic ties beyond the descent group are utilized in camping and acquiring pasture, in spite of the ideology which stresses the patrilineal composition of residential groupings. In a number of instances observed in the field, the cognatic linkages used to join camp groups, for social visiting or mutual assistance, were created by kidnap marriages in the previous generation. Although whether or not a kaçırma marriage will lead to useful affinal ties is never certain, and the object of kidnapping is never to gain useful ties, it is the case that children born of such matches will be able to interact normally with matrilateral kin. In particular the relationship of a man to his mother's brother is expected to be a warm and mutually supportive one.

A concluding paradox: one factor which serves to further disperse *actual* patterns of interaction is the high (relative to other kin types) incidence of kidnapping that takes place within the descent group. This generates conflict precisely within the circle of kinsmen where mutuality of interest is most heavily stressed in ideology. This contradiction follows logically from the cultural model of marriage which emphasizes descent group endogamy through a preference for father's brother's daughter matches. As families realign socially in response to social disruption—such as caused by marriage by capture—they often make use of uterine kinsmen. Approximately 20 percent of such realignments based on uterine kinship ties are ultimately from kidnap-created marriages. Moreover, of all the marriages that take place outside the named descent groups, one-third are formed by kaçırma.

SUMMARY AND FINAL REMARKS ON MARRIAGE

The preceding discussion has carefully eschewed any closely formulated hypothesis that kidnapping is adaptive in the sense that it contributes to the survival potential of the Yörük population in a nomadic pastoral system of land use. It is possible that a case could be made for such a hypothesis, but the evidence is refractory and amenable to varying interpretations. There are, however, a number of statements that can be made regarding the significance of kidnapping in Yörük society.

First, it is clear that any adequate consideration of Yörük social structure will have to treat alternative modes of marriage as well as the normative ones. If one were to do simply an analysis of how Yörük marriages statistically conformed by kin-type to the ideology of marriage, one would derive a limited picture of the actual system. Ideology calls for closely endogamous marriages and stresses the primacy of patrilineal ties in innumerable ways. On the face of it, the high frequency of marriages within the sub-tribal named descent groups would indicate that the ideology approximated behavior. Yörük informants would heartily endorse such a conclusion. The Yörük cultural model of their own marriage system defines kaçirma as an aberration. Native interpretation of actual marriage practices tends to regard kaçirma as infrequent and random with respect to who kidnaps whom. Analysis shows, contrary to this, that it is quite common in all descent groups and that it is non-random: 26 percent of the women kidnapped are true or classificatory father's brother's daughter to their kidnappers. Although relatively more kidnap marriages are outside the descent group, the emphasis on patrilateral parallel cousin clearly reflects that of the normative model. However, when the normative ideology is "acted out" in a kidnap marriage, the social consequences are quite different. Rather than strengthening ties among agnates, kidnapping disperses actual patterns of interaction. Kidnapping, in general, tends to impel both patterns of social interaction and lines of kinship outward from named patrilineal descent groups.

Second, the high incidence of kidnapping in Yörük society is unrelated to any possible appreciation the Yörük might have regarding the utility of dispersed lines of kinship. Instead it is generated by such features of the culture as high bride price, the common inability of individuals to choose their own mates, the conflicting claims of agnates, and the fact that a man must be married to enjoy adult status. One of the immediate functions of kidnapping is that it levels the impact of wealth differentials among families regarding marriage opportunities. The threat of kidnapping makes long betrothal periods impossible, and may well contribute to earlier marriage for women. This latter problem, and the demographic implications raised by it, was not treated in the analysis; but further research seems indicated. In any event, there is little doubt that kaçirma is a significant factor in both the age structure of mating and the socioeconomic structure of marriage.

IV
RESIDENCE AND THE FORMATION OF NEW HOUSEHOLDS THROUGH SEPARATION AND INHERITANCE

RESIDENCE is central to any consideration of social processes within a society. This is particularly true of nomadic Yörük adaptations where the portable nature of the basic residence unit, the tent (*çadır*), makes the settlement pattern at any given point a document of contemporary social relations. Although post-marital residence arrangements are more easily reduced to a limited number of alternative forms, they, too, represent a domestic consensus as the alternative of separation into smaller units is completely feasible. Further, the spatial distributions of people among households, and of households in groups, are visible expressions of that community's integration into a wider environment. Just as political relations among lineages display great flexibility in a milieu where force and pan-tribal unity are dysfunctional, actual patterns of personal interaction in residence are more varied than would be suggested by the formal primacy of agnatic kinsmen. An important expression of social transactions and economic cooperation is how people arrange themselves in voluntary or contractual relations with others. In a nomadic society residence implies such a social contract, however transitory it may be.

Unlike lineage and tribal identity, residence defies simple characterization. For example, the Yörük can be termed patrilocal with respect to the post-marriage ideal according to which residence is with, or in the proximity of, the bridegroom's father. Actual patterns, however, are more complex. The rules and al-

ternatives of post-marital residence do not speak to the problem
of tents camping in proximity of one another, nor do they explicate
the nature of camp groups themselves. It is not sufficient to regard
co-residence with, or residence in the proximity of, a kinsman as
expressions of the same social and ideological realities. Residence
in the same domicile among the Yörük, as in most societies, implies a relationship of close interdependency. Residence defined by
proximity need carry with it no such implication, and is rather the
exercise of choice by the heads of independent domestic units.

Given the importance of residence, however considered, in
Yörük nomadic pastoral society where the population regularly experiences periods of concentration and dispersion, it is necessary
to isolate as many as possible of the factors which determine
household and group composition.

Further, in every society in which individual residence within a
domicile is described in relation to other members of the same
living quarters, it is obvious that no single designation will suffice
to indicate how changing household composition alone serves to put
the individual in different types of residence. In analyzing residence in a nomadic society, this complexity is amplified by the fact
that there is no necessary congruence between the type of residence
formed by people living in an unpartitioned tent and the emergent
social units formed by tents camping together in shifting patterns.

The discussion will proceed from a consideration of individual
preferences and the cultural norms of post-marital residence to
treat the social factors which influence decisions to employ various
options of co-residence. Secondly, patterns of residence involving
tents camping in the proximity of each other will be analyzed as
distinct from the problem of post-marital co-residence. The camp
groups themselves will be treated in Chapter V, together with the
economic processes which underlie them.

RULES OF POST-MARRIAGE CO-RESIDENCE
AND STATED PREFERENCES

The only cultural norm of co-residence so emphatically
stated as to constitute a near jural rule of behavior is that governing post-marriage residence; the new bride and groom take up
residence in the groom's natal tent and become part of his father's
household. It is considered abnormal and shameful (*ayip*) for a son
to establish a neolocal residence immediately upon marriage, even

if he remains in the proximity of his father's tent. To reside in one's wife's natal tent (*iç güveylik*) is virtually ruled out by cultural sanctions as a feasible course of action. A man should not normally work for his wife's father immediately upon marriage. To live with one's father-in-law would be an admission of the boy's poverty and his family's inability to provide for him. No such case was found among nomads during the study; it occurs only rarely, when a family lacking sons arranges for a son-in-law to take up residence.

Tables 14, 15, and 16 summarize the expression of the ideology in practice with respect to the composition of the çadĭr (tent) domicile. The tent is the fundamental unit of shared consumption and production. It utilizes one hearth (*ocak*) and its inhabitants sleep in one physically unpartitioned living quarter. A separate tent invariably implies a separate ocak and independently held wealth in animals. From Table 15 it is clear that patrilocality when defined as residence in father's tent is fairly closely adhered to in practice. Of the 113 married men who have living fathers, 78 (69 percent) reside with them. The remaining 35 (31 percent) represent households in which residence is neolocal although the husband's father is living. They (the 31 percent) do not flagrantly contravene the rule if separation took place after a period of co-residence with the groom's father. One exception, well known to the ethnographer during the study, involved a newly married man leaving his father's tent after one year of co-residence because of a disagreement with his father. This was thought to be very poor behavior on the son's part as, even though he had remained in the tent some time following marriage, he left long before any of his younger brothers were of marriageable age and while the family's herd was depleted because of the bride price (başlĭk) paid on his behalf.

Actually, the behavior of this person in separating differed only by degrees from the actions taken by all men who leave their natal tents prior to their father's death. Nevertheless, it seemed to be regarded as distinctly unfilial behavior by the population at large. The reasons why this is so pertain to how certain processes generated by the practice of bride price and the passage of time, measured egocentrically, affect the interpretation of the rule of patrilocality.

Bride price paid by the groom's father to the bride's father (or nearest agnates in the absence of these) is an important factor

TABLE 14

DISTRIBUTION OF DOMESTIC STATUSES AS DEFINED BY DOMICILE
AND RELATIONSHIP TO HEAD OF HOUSEHOLD
(nomads only; 171 households)

Residence-defined domestic status	Number of individuals
head of household[a]	171 (all)
senior wife of head	158
co-wives of head	15
son of head[b]	474
son's wife[c]	87
son's son	85
son's daughter	66
daughter of head	297
brother of head	15
sister of head	3
brother's wife	4
brother's son	9
brother's daughter	6
mother of head	10
son's second wife[d]	1
father's second wife (stepmother of head)	1
other kin (shepherd)	4
non-kin (shepherd)	9
Total nomadic population	1,415

[a] includes 11 widows
[b] includes 78 married sons
[c] includes 9 widows of sons, not remarried
[d] brother's widow

TABLE 15

POST-MARITAL RESIDENCE FOR PRESENTLY MARRIED NOMAD MALES

(245 cases)

	In Natal Tent		Outside Natal Tent		Totals
	Patrilocal	Fratrilocal	Other	Neolocal	
Father Alive	78			35	113
Father Dead		4	3	118	125
No Data				7	7
Row Totals	78	4	3	1600	245

TABLE 16

POST-MARITAL RESIDENCE FOR PRESENTLY MARRIED NOMAD FEMALES

(260 cases)

	Neolocal	Within Husband's Natal Tent	Total
Non-polygynous	163	81	244
Polygynous	15	1	16
Row totals	178	82	260

in the final interpretation of the ideal of patrilocality. It is because of the known immediate adverse effects of bride price payments on the giver's domestic herd that the case just mentioned was defined by Yörük as a violation of the norm. Bride price represents an investment of the family's capital for the future growth of the property-owning unit. It brings in a new member who, apart from her labor, will bear children. Separation (*ayrīlmak*), on the other hand, marks a stage in the dissolution of the household and the break up of its capital in animals. Whereas başlık payments and the marriage which follows are widely heralded, and the expenses not openly grudged, the departure of a son and his wife from the household is treated as an unfortunate occurrence, the severity of which depends on the circumstances surrounding it.

The relevance of başlık to the present discussion is in how it affects the interpretation of residence rules. However, it should be noted that this does not exhaust the problem of başlık in Yörük society. For example, any institution which regularly transfers wealth and personnel among households in a society can be viewed as a part of that society's political economy. It may affect the overall distribution of wealth in the society and the social mobility associated with it.[1]

What is pertinent here is that whoever supplies the bride price, particularly in the majority of cases where it is the bridegroom's father, does so with the expectation the bride (*gelin*, from *gelen*, "one who comes") will contribute to the household labor force. If a Yörük were to describe an ideal household, it would include at least one married son and his bride. The status of gelin or bride remains with the girl regardless of whether she has borne children, until she is established in her own tent with her husband, or until she has resided so long in her father-in-law's tent that younger brothers of her husband have brought in their own brides. Brides are distinguished by dress, particularly by their cloth headdress, gold headband, and the locks of hair allowed to hand in front of her ears (unlike a virgin's).

Within the household, the bride is more at the disposal of her husband's parents than at her husband's, in all but sexual access. He, in fact, does not publicly address her during the first year of marriage, a period during which she performs *el öpme* (literally: hand kissing). She is expected (during the first few weeks at least) to kiss the hand of any person entering the tent for the first time since her marriage, and is to avoid speaking in public except as needed for the performance of her duties. These are considerable, and include all of the more onerous tasks such as collecting firewood, carrying water, going out in the rain to adjust the tent ropes, and the like. Divorce can occur during this period; but it is very

---

[1] Irons (1966:265 ff.) shows how bride price among the Yomut can be an institution which equalizes or levels economic differences in a society by compensating those families that have deficiencies in male labor with money. It likely serves the same function in Yörük society.

degrading for both the bride and her family if she is sent back to her natal tent. The bride price is supposed to be returned if cause for divorce is shown, but in many instances this does not occur. Eleven (4.6 percent) of the presently married males and seven (2.8 percent) of the presently married females from the nomadic population have been divorced. Seven percent of those women formerly married but now single are divorced. This is not a high rate and bears out the Yörük contention that divorce is rare. They are not, however, particularly hesitant to speak of it if asked directly (see Table 17 for a statement of marriage stability).

The bride is referred to by those in her new home as *"bizim gelin,"* or "our bride," and by the younger siblings of the girl's husband, frequently as *"babamın gelini,"* or "my father's bride." Her relations with her husband's father are restrained with respect to social interaction, and she is expected to pay him considerable deference, waiting on him as much as he wishes. The gelin is thought by the Yörük to be the main source of personal service to the middle-aged head of house. If he is sick, the gelin, more often than his own wife, will wait on him, arrange his clothes, and prepare his meals. It seemed from observation that relatively little conflict or even muted disagreement transpires between husband's father and son's wife. Her relations with the siblings of her husband are generally warm, often joking, although any brother of the husband is able to (and does) order her to perform household tasks. Gelin were infrequently seen struck by brothers of their husbands, and by their husbands, although it is not considered appropriate action except for outrageous disobedience. The mother-in-law and the wives or the husband's older brothers are senior to the bride, as the women of a household are socially ranked in a parallel fashion to their husbands.

The gelin's status in her new home is one of inherent contradictions, and these set the ground rules for the eventual conflict which marks her departure and the formation of an autonomous tent. The prestige which she brings her new home is considerable, as is the understated pride which her affines display in frequently letting friends hear (outside her hearing) how well she is serving their household. While the tent migrates, the "fresh" (*taze*) bride, dressed in her best clothes and gold, leads the household's string of camels which are otherwise led by a virgin daughter.

However, as long as she resides with her husband's mother or the wives of his older brothers, she enjoys a distinctly inferior

TABLE 17
MARRIAGE STABILITY AMONG NOMADIC YÖRÜK

		Number of Marriages Contracted	Married Males		Married Females		Formerly Married	
			f.	%	f.	%	f.	%
	Times Married	1	199	83.6	239	94.5	21	78.0
		2	32	13.5	13	5.1	6	22.0
		3	5	2.1				
		4	1	.4				
		6	1	.4				
		Totals	238	100.0	252	100.0	27	100.0
Times Marriage was Dissolved	By Divorce	0	227	94.5	245	97.2	25	92.6
		1	10	4.2	7	2.8	2	7.4
		2	1	.4				
		Totals	238	100.0	252	100.0	27	100.0
	By Death of Spouse	0	218	91.6	247	97.2	1	3.6
		1	15	6.3	5	2.8	24	89.3
		2	4	1.7			2	7.1
		3	1	.4				
		Totals	238	100.0	252	100.0	27	100.0

status in the domestic unit. She is continually at the command of these women, quite apart from the males of the house, and these women view with abhorrence the sight of an idle hand. When tea is served the new bride is likely not to drink at all, and as long as she remains a gelin she will drink and eat only after all other members of the household are finished. On many occasions it appeared as if she went without tea altogether because by the time the smallest child (perhaps even her own) had finished, there would be none left. Since neither brides nor other women smoke, tea is literally their only visible indulgence. Senior women are never excluded from tea drinking unless it is an extremely formal occasion, although often they accept it only after the men have each had one glass.

The new bride is under considerable strain as she adjusts to her new home and to the demands of her affines; however, she is also much reinforced by the knowledge that the initial period is one of proving her character and her natal family's reputation. With the passage of time and with the coming of her own children she is no longer regarded as a new bride. While the demands of her services remain great, she is no longer the prized new member of the household. The potential for conflict, particularly with her husband's mother, increases with time and as the tent physically becomes more crowded with children.

The fact of domestic conflict, whether between son and his family or between his bride and her co-resident affines, is most commonly the overt reason for the establishment of a new tent household and a separate hearth. However, even though domestic squabbles are frequent in almost all cases, should the son decide to leave during the period of el öpme, or before his father is able to use the labor of a younger brother in herding, it is considered a violation of the norms of filial behavior.

EXTENDED PATRILOCALITY: FRATRILOCALITY

An extension of the norm of patrilocal residence is the coresidence of married brothers still in the natal tent following their father's death. When asked about "ideal" residence, Yörük informants do not differentiate between the post-marital residence of sons in their father's tent, or the residence of sons of a deceased father in one domicile. Just as sons are expected to stay with and closely assist their fathers, brothers are similarly expected to work and reside together. This ideal, unlike that of patrilocality, is rarely achieved in practice (see Table 14).

Fratrilocality is not a viable residence form for a number of reasons, even though structurally it is locally regarded as an extension of the highly prevalent patrilocal ideal. While 78 (69 percent) of married sons with living fathers live with them, only four (4.4 percent) married men out of the some 90 who have living married brothers, actually reside with them in the undivided natal tent after father's death.

Paradoxically, there are relatively many cases where more than one married son reside together in a household where the father is still alive and in authority; 60 households in the nomadic society have one or more co-resident married sons. Forty-five of these tents have one married son and his wife; 15 households (25 percent) have more than one married son (see Table 18). That is, 35 married men are living with one or more married brothers in their father's tent. This amounts to 43.7 percent of all dependent married men who are not heads of their own households or 35 out of 80. Of the 15 households in which they live, all but one are in the upper two quartiles of wealth, owning animals in excess of 249 head of sheep. The fourth quartile of wealth (350 or more sheep) alone accounts for 11 of the 15 households (73.3 percent) with more than one married son resident in the same domicile.

It is apparent therefore that while a large percentage of married sons do remain in their father's tent until a junior brother is also married, the final dissolution of the natal tent proceeds very rapidly once the father is dead. This is despite the fact that there is a high correlation (r) between the number of people co-resident in a household and the wealth in sheep of that domestic unit (see Table 19). The relationship between size of the domestic unit in people and the number of sheep owned can be demonstrated to be a strong one. Table 19 shows that, using a linear measure of the

TABLE 18

POST-MARRIAGE RESIDENCE OF DEPENDENT
SONS BY HOUSEHOLD

(nomads only)

Number of Co-resident Married Sons	Number of Households	Total Number of Married Sons
1	45	45
2	12 ⎫	24 ⎫
3	1 ⎬ 15	3 ⎬ 35
4	2 ⎭	8 ⎭
Total	60	80

Note: 171 households considered; 111 households have no co-resident married son

TABLE 19

RELATIONSHIP OF THE NUMBER OF PEOPLE CO-RESIDENT
IN THE HOUSEHOLD AND WEALTH IN SHEEP

(168 households)

N (cases)	Statistic	Values	Significance
168 Households	Chi-square	$x^2 = 54.8$	P = .001
168 Households	Pearson's r (cor.)	r = 0.49	P = 0.000
168 Households	ETA² (coeffic. det.)	$\eta^2 = 0.57$	P = .01

Note: ETA^2 independent variable: people; dependent variable: sheep

coefficient of determination, r^2, 24 percent of variation in wealth is "explained" by the size of the family. The ETA^2 coefficient of determination, curvilinear, is strikingly higher, which indicates the nature of the distribution.[2] Chapter VI will treat this in a more detailed analysis. Here it is sufficient to keep in mind that efficiency in herd management is seemingly not always maximized through the co-residence of even those individuals for whom the stated cultural rules dictate a shared household.

The problem of wealth, labor, and household formation is a subject for later treatment. But, it should be noted that the apparently inherent instability of fratrilocal residence limits the nature of a large household to those headed by men whose dependents are offspring, not siblings. The major source of fratrilocal instability and attendant economic penalties, regardless of the apparent impetus given fratrilocal residence by ideology, is probably the negative or dependent way in which members of a household are culturally defined vis-à-vis the head of house. Ownership of real property is vested in the head of the house, and he has final say in economic transactions. When brothers co-reside in the absence of their father, the oldest is considered senior and the head of the household. The wife of the oldest brother is likewise seen as senior to the wives of younger brothers.

---

[2] The statistics used in this and other chapters are defined and illustrated in M. J. Moroney (1965), Mueller and Schuessler (1961), and Downie and Heath (1970). The computer programs used include those prepared by the Population Study Center (PSC-VAR-III and PSC-ZERO-III) and by the Statistical Research Laboratory (Constat), of the University of Michigan.

The relative positions of father to son and mother-in-law to daughter-in-law are culturally defined to demand obedience and deference on the part of the latter to the former. These relationships, however, do not easily carry over to older-younger brother and older brother's wife-younger brother's wife relationships. While the oldest brother of a set of siblings is always deemed the senior and is paid a great deal of respect by his younger brothers throughout his life, the relative statuses of younger brothers vis-à-vis one another is not so clear. Situations of would-be fratrilocal residence could involve two married brothers, neither of whom would be the senior of the entire set of siblings. In such cases, even though the older of the two would be considered head of house, he would not bring the strong respect-defined status of eldest brother (ağabey or ece) to the position. Even where the eldest of brothers would be in a position to head a fraternal household, his wife would have considerable difficulty administering the women's sector of the home without conflict with the wives of younger brothers. Not only does she lack the right to complete deference which is attached to the position of "mother-in-law," but there are other reasons why she would find it hard to dominate such a domestic arrangement. The wife of an older brother might well be younger than the wife of a younger brother. The status of her natal family might be lower than that of younger brother's wife. Her bride price might be lower as well, and a high bride price is a fact about which women were prone to brag in talking with the investigator's wife. Any of these factors would make it hard to maintain the status differentials implicit in a household of co-resident married adults. The high potential for domestic conflict and fragmentation effectively precludes not only fratrilocal residence forms, but also residence of a married man within the tent of his uncles or other close kin.

FILIOLOCALITY

Not only is the ideal of patrilocality altered in local interpretation according to the circumstances outlined above, but the rule itself becomes inverted with the passage of time.[3] Even if there is

---

[3] Aram Yengoyan has very helpfully furnished me with a copy of his dissertation. His discussion of residence, in particular, was useful in providing insights into Yörük patterns of residence. He notes that the changing composition of a household and in changes in the life cycle of the individual can alter the residence type: for example, he finds "geriatric filiolocality" to be the rule in cases (in the Philip-

RESIDENCE AND NEW HOUSEHOLDS 99

no change in family structure occasioned by separation, changes in
the age and physical condition of the head of house and his wives
can affect the form of residence. The residence of widows, and
infirm widowers is properly with married sons, and thus is best
termed filiolocal. The son by then has become recognized as the
head of the household and his father or mother's residence is defined with reference to that fact.

There are a number of reasons why, although this is a particularly common form of residence for widows it is not common
for widowers. Foremost among these is that if a man remains
single upon the death of his wife it is a public announcement that
he has resigned his primary social roles and that he will not take
an active part in the economic affairs of his home. Almost without
exception, the few more-or-less physically sound males who have
not remarried are either senile or considered mentally unstable.
If a man who is physically healthy does not remarry within a fairly
short period after his wife's death, he is likely to become the butt
of increasingly blunt jokes about his sexual prowess and intellectual abilities. As long as a man remains married, he is socially
considered the head of house even though a married son may conduct most of the business affairs of the tent. There are more widows
than widowers for the actuarial reason that men marry later than
women, and marry women younger than themselves. There are no
filiolocally resident widowers among the nomadic Yörük, although
there are several such cases among sedentary families. There
are 14 widows residing with married sons who are not regarded as
heads of household. The women (if post-menopausal), unlike widowers, enjoy considerable respect and a freedom of movement
denied to them in their married state. They are, in fact, somewhat
feared for their gossip and sharp tongues. Senile widowers are
not treated with particular respect, and often their infirmities are
publicly played upon if no close kinsman in present.

WOMEN AND POST-MARRIAGE RESIDENCE

The position of Yörük women with regard to residence after
marriage is best seen in terms of how their statuses are defined
in relation to their husbands, or to the heads of the households in

pines) where an elderly couple is divided by death (1964:145). Raymond Kelly and
John Speth offered many suggestions and comments on the manner in which residence
is often inadequately detailed ethnographically, and this chapter is the richer for
these.

which they come to reside. Prior to marriage, of course, both
sexes invariably dwell in their natal tents. Much of the description
of post-marital residence from a female vantage point is subsumed
in the fore-going discussion. There are, however, differences
which have to do with polygyny and the optional junior levirate.

In the instance of polygyny, a woman's residence status is
partially defined by the co-wife. Thus, she can be either the first
of two or more co-resident wives (*koca karĭ* or *koca avrat*), or the
second wife (*ortak*). The first of the co-resident wives is regarded
as the mistress of the household. There is only one case where a
man who is not the head of the house has two wives, and this involved the acquisition by levirate of his brother's widow. Slightly
more than 8 percent of all married, neolocally resident women
(15 out of 173) are in polygynous unions (see Table 16). Poly-
gynously married women almost invariably reside neolocally for
the reason that it is very difficult for a man to acquire two wives
until he is in control of his own herd. His father will not supply
bride price for two women.

The optional levirate works to give a widow (*dul*), particularly
one with children, the possibility of marrying her deceased husband's younger brother by the same father.[4]

If she does not have children she may well go back to her
natal tent. This is further conditioned by the existence of a marriageable younger brother of the husband, and by the younger
brother's own opinion in the matter. Levirate is involved in seven
cases (32 percent) out of 22 recorded marriages known to be dis-
solved by the death of the husband whose widow is alive. Four (18
percent) widows have remarried outside the deceased's natal tent.
Eleven (50 percent) have continued as heads of their own households (as *dul kadĭn*) rearing their own children without husbands,
but camping with and protected by the deceased husband's close

---

[4] The junior levirate, as in most things that involve brothers, refers only to
brothers who share a common father, not those who may only have a mother in
common. Half brothers with different mothers are regarded as true brothers. An
interesting, if tragic, case occurred in the field when a recently married man was
murdered. He was still residing in his father's home, and had a half-brother by
his father's second wife (polygynous) of 16 years of age and a full brother of 12 years.
It was decided that the bride should remain in the family and that she should marry
the 16 year old boy. However, the deceased man's mother protested and insisted
that the bride go to her son, the 12 year old. It was not resolved while the ethnographer was in the field but it is suspected that the bride was given to the older,
more suitable boy.

patri-kin. The culturally esteemed practice, if there are no single brothers of her husband, is not to remarry but to raise the children in the husband's household, or to camp along near it. The children remain, in any event, in their father's household so for a woman not to choose the levirate or widowhood calls for her to leave her children after weaning.

Of the three choices available to her, only the decision to remain dul kadïn, head of household, affects her residence status. This status as head of the domestic unit will erode with time as her sons assume responsibility for more decisions. Further, the decision for continued widowhood or remarriage is conditioned by the manner in which her husband met his death, and whether or not she has children, especially males. If her husband died by violent means, she is more likely, some say, to remain dul in his memory (hatïrasï için), or to marry his younger brother should a suitable one be available. If there are no children she is more likely for the above reasons to remarry and her bride price, if given, would go again to her father.[5] A woman does not lose her natal lineality through marriage.

INHERITANCE AND THE FORMATION OF NEW DOMESTIC UNITS

The preceding discussion has shown the variability of postmarital residence among nomadic Yörük as measured with respect to the natal tent of the recently wed male. Quite apart from variability in practice, the rule itself is subject to diverse interpretations in the light of such factors as the state of the family herd, number of years of co-residence with the father, and whether or not there are other married sons at home. In presenting the analysis, frequent reference was made to neolocal residence and the separation of married sons and their wives from the groom's natal tent. Not only do more than 95 percent of married men whose fathers are dead reside neolocally, but also 30 percent of those with living fathers leave their natal tents.

All of the married men with living fathers, and those men with dead fathers but possessing living married brothers, are in some degree ignoring the strongly put cultural rule of patrilocal residence. Therefore a presentation of the processes by which new

---

[5] Bride price for divorced women and for widows is low, often not asked for at all.

households break off from established ones is a necessary prelude to an analysis of the factors which govern the residence of any household in the proximity of other selected households.

Any society, nomadic or sedentary, is faced with the common problem of households replicating themselves through time.[6] No matter whether the household is extended with the joint occupancy of a home by a large number of related people, or simply the domicile of man, wife, and single offspring, it must necessarily break up in a regular fashion. At just what demographic and generational point this occurs varies considerably. Also, as the term "cycle" implies, the household is always in the process of developing into something else and is not completely stabilized at any time. Not every household conforms to the same economic pressures in this respect.

Thus, not only might we expect that a shift in the means of production would alter such a pattern for the group, but we would expect variation within the group as well. Table 20 and Figure 9 indicate the range of variability of household size. The social makeup of domestic units among the sedentary Yörük does not differ significantly from that of the still nomadic lineages. However, the dynamics of household formation, the economic processes which necessarily underlie the domestic cycle, are radically changed with settlement. Moreover, it is apparent that there is a substantial difference in the mean number of people per household in the sedentary and nomadic population. Nomadic households average one person more in size, a difference that is statistically significant and is most likely related to the fact that large domestic units make economic sense in the pastoral economy. The effects of these changes for the political economy of the sedentary community are discussed in Chapter VII, as is the family economic basis for pastoral nomadism (Chapter VI).

The amount of capital held by any family is critical to the formation of new households; furthermore, in the society as a whole the ability of any form of property to generate more capital largely determines the pattern of development which brings new residence units into existence and retires those of the previous generation. Critical in this process is the extent to which household labor can be employed to increase capital holdings or income proportionate to consumption demands.

---

[6] The dynamics of household economics will be detailed in Chapter VI.

TABLE 20

HOUSEHOLD SIZE AMONG SEDENTARY AND NOMADIC YÖRÜK

(344 households)

Household Size	İslahiye	Nogaylar	Sayburun	Total Sedentary	Nomad	Row Total
2	1	1	2	4	6	10
3	5	2	4	11	6	16
4	8	1	5	14	12	26
5	11	1	10	22	10	32
6	10	6	3	19	21	39
7	13	6	3	22	18	43
8	12	8	10	30	21	52
9	8	3	6	17	23	38
10	9	3	1	13	17	30
11	1	3	0	4	13	17
12	2	4	0	6	8	14
13	1	0	2	3	3	6
14	0	0	1	1	2	3
15	1	2	0	3	5	8
16	0	2	1	3	1	4
17	0	0	0	0	1	1
18	0	1	0	1	3	4
19	0	0	0	0	0	0
20	0	0	0	0	1	1
Column Totals	82	43	48	173	171	344
Median size	7	8	6	7	8	7
Mean size	7.0	8.7	6.8	7.4	8.3	7.8

In the broadest sense it can be said that while sheep even in small aggregates can generate more sheep for their owner, land does not create more land unless held in sufficient quantity to enable its owner to purchase more from his profits. This is commonly done at the expense of someone else in the community who is losing land. Increases in animal holdings are not so directly related to differences in family fortunes at any given time, but are more dependent on the reproductive rates of the species herded. Increase in land is achieved only upon reaching a hypothetical take-off point, one that is likely to be above the mean size of land holdings in the community.

Among the nomadic Yörük, inheritance or the acquisition of a share of the family's herd is the most common means by which new households are formed and provided with the initial capital necessary for economic self-sufficiency. Yörük village practice, while in form similar to nomadic custom, does not enable new households

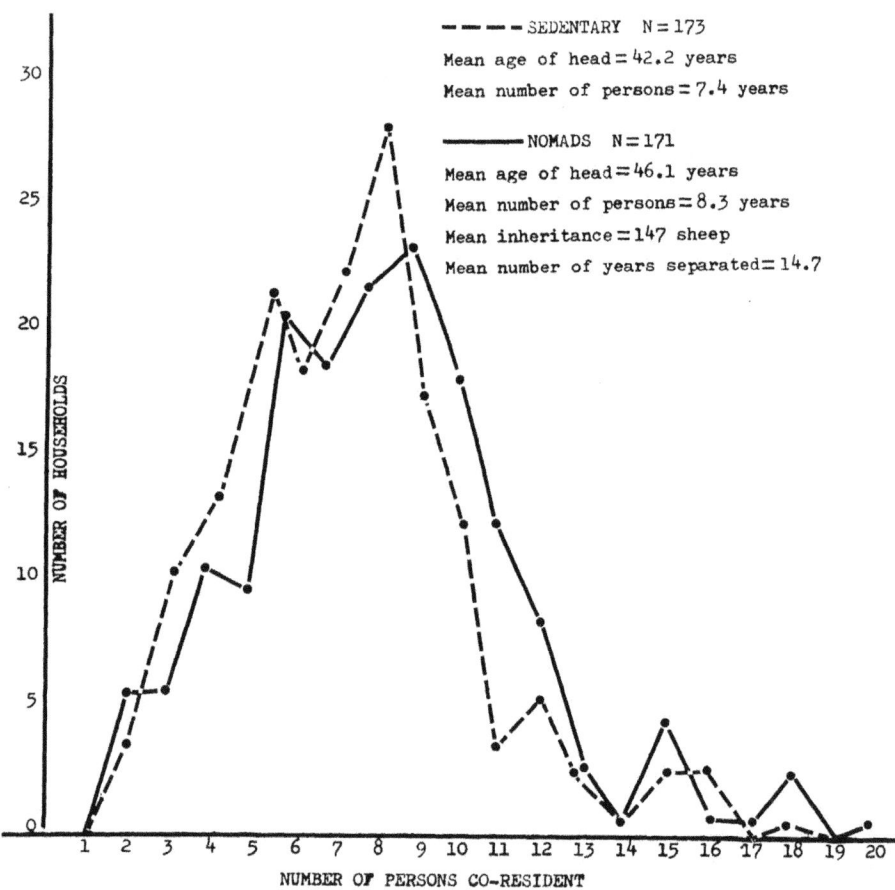

Fig. 9. Variability in household size among sedentary and nomadic Yörük (344 households).

RESIDENCE AND NEW HOUSEHOLDS   105

to assume full economic autonomy and, for the most part, does not establish units self-sufficient enough that they do not need to rely on selling labor to survive.

Inheritance rules among the nomadic Yörük differ both from village practice in the area and from Turkish law. Furthermore, although both nomadic and sedentary Yörük inheritance practices are rationalized by the participants as conforming to Sunni Islamic codes, they are, in fact, at considerable variance with the religious tradition they purport to follow. Contrary to both Turkish national codes and religious law (*shari'a*), daughters do not inherit at all and receive little dowry in many cases, although gold coins are given to the bride as her personal property both by her father and her father-in-law.

Widows do not inherit real property except in trust for minor children, which they must give up entirely should they remarry. Again, contrary to Islamic law, sons once separated from their natal tent do not inherit upon their father's death, but they must be satisfied with the patrimony received when they established their own households. With regard to household formation, the most pertinent rule is that, among the nomads, a son often receives a share of the family herds prior to the father's demise.

Stated concisely, no son owns property as long as he resides in his father's tent, or with an older brother if his father is dead. As a rule, sons separate from their natal tent only after marriage and according to birth order. Older sons marry first and consequently split away from their father before their younger brothers. Separation and the concomitant division of the family herds and transport animals can be occasioned by the father's suggestion that it is time for a married son to leave the household. This, however, is rare, as the more sons and their brides live in a tent, the more secure the labor supply and the easier the daily routine of animal care. There is a strong relation between the number of sons in a household and the ability of that tent to manage its livestock efficiently. Most commonly the decision to separate (*ayrīlmak*) is the son's, often precipitated by a quarrel between his wife and other members of the family. Sheer population growth within a household can cause considerable friction, as all of the members live together in a single unpartitioned tent (see Table 21 for age distribution among heads of household and the number of years separated).

The customary share of the family's property is calculated according to the number of male children plus the father residing in the tent. In a tent with a father and three sons, the son who separates first will receive one-fourth of the sheep, at least one camel, and a similar interest in any other capital.[7] The next son to separate will receive one-third of the then existing property, etc., down to the youngest son, whose duty it is to stay with the father in his tent until his death. The residual property, including the tent itself, falls to the youngest son in a system of quasi-ultimogeniture. Changes in the father's economic condition after a son has separated do not affect the son's share in his lifetime.

In general, the system works to favor the younger sons. Not only does the youngest son inherit the bulk of the property if he is the only son remaining with his father, but the natural increases in herd size after every division means that approximately the same number of animals is divided among fewer shares. This fact is readily acknowledged by the nomadic Yörük as a peculiarity of their inheritance practices.

Apart from the pressure of population growth within the household, there are social demands which encourage the separation of married sons from their fathers and younger brothers from the households of their elder brothers. Full participation in community discussions, the non-stop gatherings of adult males in each others' tents, is the prerogative of household heads only. While adolescent boys and all males may attend these gatherings and be offered tea, only the heads of independent tents are listened to with respect on subjects of general concern: to migrate or not, market conditions, pasture selection, and the solving of disputes. Even where married brothers have elected to stay together in one tent after their father's death, the eldest of them is held to be the head of household and the others his dependents.

However, for any son to separate there must be some assurance of success as an autonomous unit. Since separation and the division of the family herd is final as far as the son or brother involved is concerned, it is undertaken in most instances only when the new household feels that it can stand on its own. Among the Yörük who rely on animal husbandry, labor is a critical factor. Ideally a man separates after at least one of his own children is

---

[7] Inheritance is not as inflexible as suggested by the formal rules. The father has complete say in dividing up the herd in his lifetime, and the sons have to be content with his decisions in these matters. Consequently sons who part on extremely bad terms with their fathers may receive only a token number of sheep. Some sons receive more than their share. If possible, a camel is also provided.

TABLE 21

SCATTER PLOT OF YEARS SEPARATED FROM NATAL TENT AND AGE OF LIVING HEADS OF HOUSEHOLD

(154 cases, widows omitted)

mean age at separation = 29.1 years

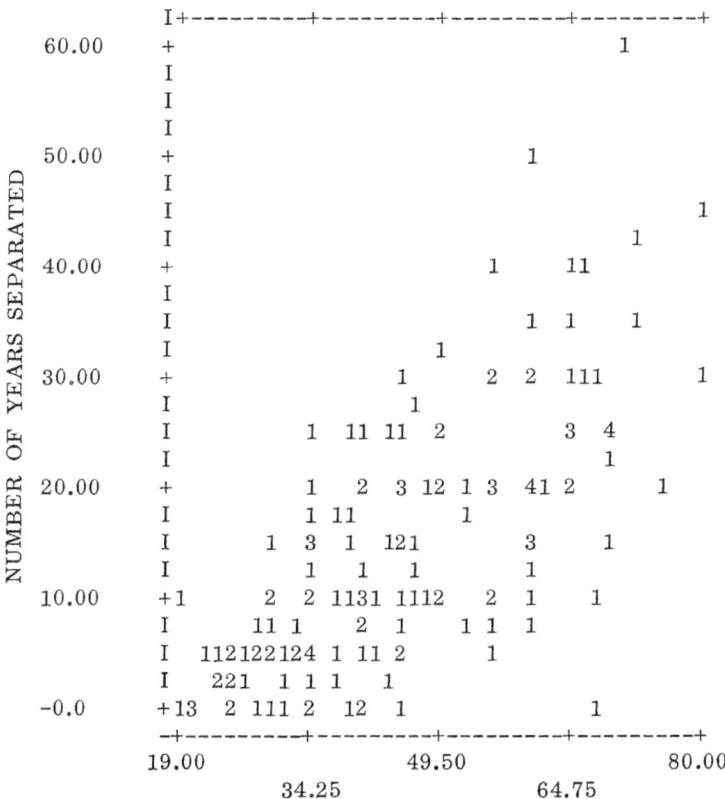

AGE OF HOUSEHOLD HEAD IN YEARS

old enough to help with the herding, but a household can be established before it is completely self-sufficient in this respect. In such cases the new tent can mix (karıştırma) its sheep with the animals of a relative or, occasionally, with those of the natal tent. The small herd owner shares in the care and maintenance of the combined flock proportionate to the number of his animals. Thus, he is able to gain time in which to build his flock and a supply of labor up to self-sufficiency. It should be noted that self-sufficiency for a newly separated nomadic tent is attained with both fewer animals and less manpower than for a more mature family unit. Not only does the family have fewer people to provide for, but it will not have any obligation to pay bride price for some time. Also, its social status will be relatively low and the constant requirements of hospitality will not be the financial drain that they are on the more important tents of older families.

Statistical variability in inheritance is summarized and partially analyzed in Tables 22 and 23 and Figure 10. Much of this information need not be repeated, although the highlights might usefully be underscored.

From Table 21 it is apparent that the presently youngest head of household is 19, having separated in the year of the study. The average age at separation from the natal tent is 29 years. The household demographic juncture at which this occurs is highly variable and cannot be accurately characterized in terms of "averages." The extremes have been already noted: few sons remain long in the natal tent after their younger brother has brought his own bride home and few leave before this happens or before their younger brother is of marriageable age. If a man is an only son it is unlikely that he will ever establish neolocal residence, except in a *de facto* way upon the death of his father. Within these limits, whether a man will remain in the natal tent and, if so, for how long depends on such highly particularistic factors as his desire to assert his own autonomy, his wife's relations with his mother, and his own relations with his father and brothers.

Although we have noted that most decisions to establish neolocal residence are born of intramural conflict among members of one hearth, it is significant that the five households who were denied anticipatory inheritance rights have all separated within the last three years. It is quite likely that hostility in some cases might still be resolved, and the customary division of the family herd carried out. To disinherit one's true son is extremely shameful and, they say, is an act justifiable only by the most serious unfilial behavior.

Adopted sons are not considered, in most instances, to have a claim to inheritance equal that of a "true" son. Adoption is rare, and is usually either done where a couple is without a male issue, or out of "charity" where a parentless child without relatives is

TABLE 22

HISTOGRAM OF INHERITANCE OF SHEEP AMONG NOMADS

(5 cases of no inheritance excluded)

NO. OF OBSERVATIONS = 145

```
                 I---------+---------+---------+---------+
   3.0000000     +
              77 I*************************************
  62.800000     +
              27 I************
 122.60000     +
              13 I******
 182.40000     +
               7 I***
 242.20000     +
              10 I*****
 302.00000     +                    total households = 171
               2 I*                   missing data  =  21
 361.80000     +                     no inheritance =   5
               1 I*
 421.60000     +
               0 I
 481.40000     +
               4 I**
 541.20000     +
               2 I*
 601.00000     +
               0 I
 660.80000     +
               0 I
 720.60000     +
               1 I*
 780.40000     +
               0 I
 840.20000     +
               1 I*
 900.00000     +
                 I---------+---------+---------+---------+
                 0        20        40        60        80
```

(number of sheep inherited by head of household)

15 intervals established

mean inheritance = 147 sheep

TABLE 23

PERCENTILE RANKING OF INHERITANCE IN SHEEP AMONG NOMADS

(150 cases, 21 cases of missing data)

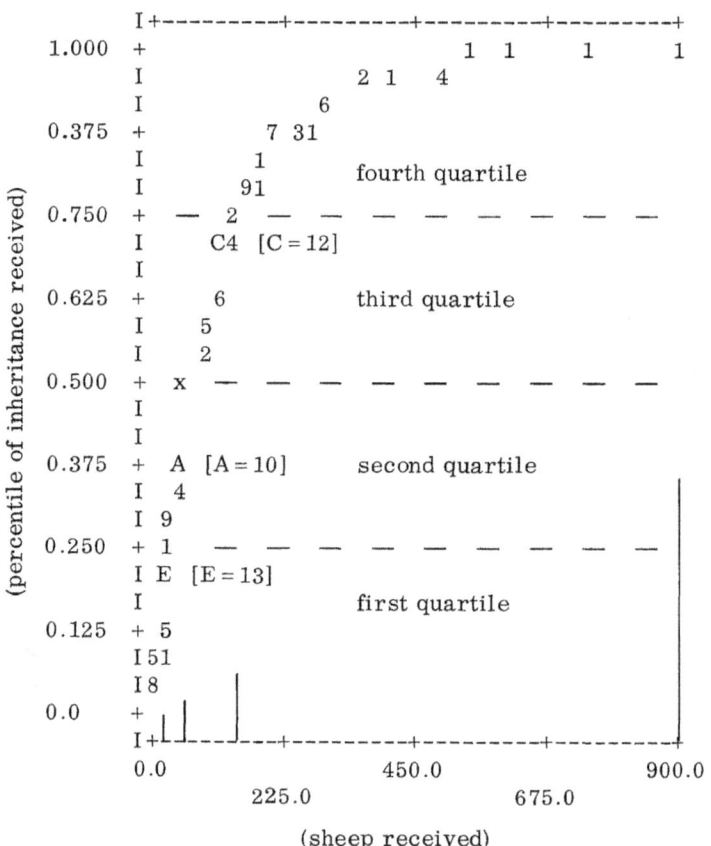

taken in by a family who can provide for an additional member, and use his labor. Girls are not adopted, and adoption in general is considered somewhat questionable as the non-consanguinal quality of the kin ties are never obscured, and always publicly commented on by others. The inheritance received by the only head of household known to be adopted was extremely small. In this case a man of Kurdish parents who were killed in the upheavals of the post-World War I period was taken in by a Yörük family. The man, now head of his own tent, has two married co-resident sons and is considered a "full" member of the tribe and of the descent group of his adoptive father, but his Kurdish origin is always recalled. He was not given a bride by his adoptive agnatic kin, and his sons both kidnapped their brides.

Sons who separated during the period of study (10) received on the average 200 sheep each, excluding those whose inheritance was

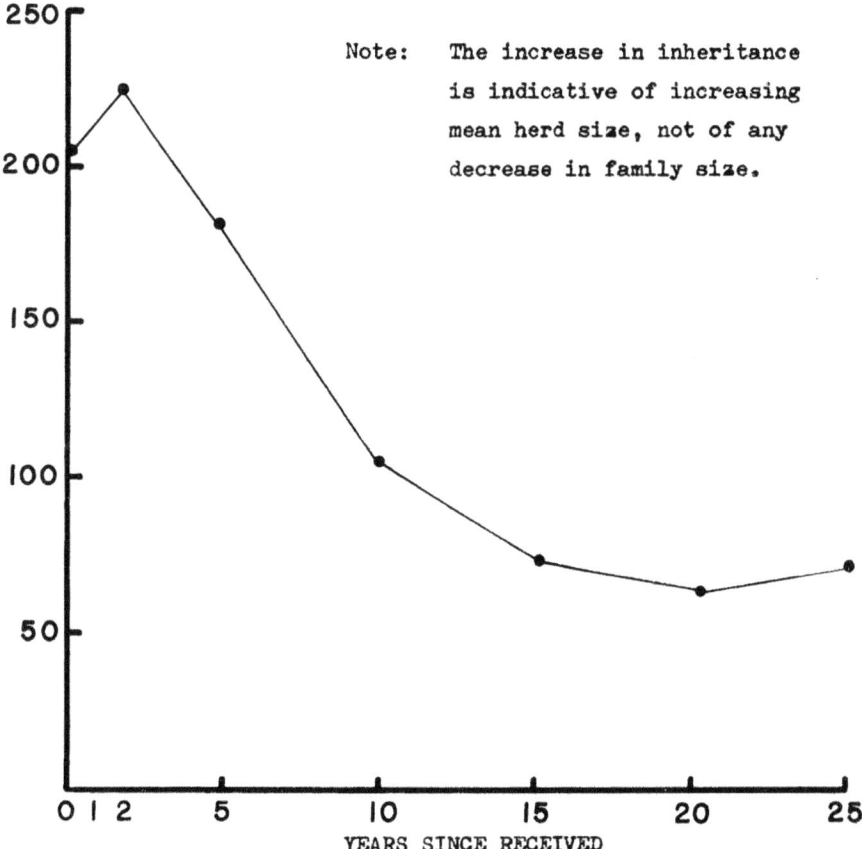

Fig. 10. Graph showing changes in mean inheritance of sheep over the past 25 years (now living household heads).

not yet settled on them. In general it is possible to say that despite great variability in inheritance received, there is a tendency that is statistically evident for inheritance to increase in more recent years. Figure 10 presents this in graphic form. What is particularly interesting is that this tendency for increased inheritances provides independent confirmation of increased mean herd size, which while clearly indicated by the large sizes of today's flocks (268 = mean) can only be intuited due to the lack of written documentation. There is absolutely no reason to suppose that family size is smaller today or the number of sons fewer; if anything the opposite is true.

A high degree of statistical confirmation for this hypothesis is evidenced by the Eta^2 test of the coefficient of determination, where $\eta^2 = 0.54$, or "explains" 54 percent of the variability in heritance (P = 0.05), with the independent variable being the number of years separated.

When the father dies, the remaining property in sheep or cash (including land and income-producing capital) can either be divided up among the sons not yet separated, or it can be maintained as the capitalization of a joint enterprise of these brothers. In either case, the eldest co-resident brother assumes the father's role as head of house and primary decision maker. If the remaining sons comprise one married son and his minor brothers, the property will not be split up until the single men marry and separate under conditions similar to their separation from their father, had he lived. There is no distinction between sons of the same father and different mothers in this respect. If there are more than one married son in a tent when their father dies, it is probable that the strains of maintaining a joint household will dissolve the household in a short time, and the herd will be divided equally among the sons. The tent and most household possessions go to the younger son. He cares for his mother. If there are more than one widow left by a man, they usually split up and are cared for by their true sons, not necessarily the youngest son in the household.

If there are no married sons residing in the tent upon the father's death, the property is held in trust for them by either their mother or their father's brother. The latter is seen as the natural provider in this instance, but often the widow assumes head of household status if she is capable and if the tent is self-sufficient in labor. Numerous cases were cited to the author of paternal uncles who abused their avuncular positions to deny their nephews their rightful share of the herds. Such accusations are partially due to the suspicious nature of Yörük when it comes to economic transactions and their readiness privately to accuse others of peculation. They are amplified by the fact that a man who administers a herd on behalf of his younger brothers, or his nephews, is as likely to suffer reverses as anyone else in the economy. Furthermore, he will have to engage in numerous market transactions, make payments for pasture and other overhead expenses, some of which are likely to be infelicitous. What is usually the case is that if a married brother or paternal uncle manages or holds control of property on behalf of minor sons of the deceased, he awards them a share upon marriage in his total holdings much as he would his own sons.

The net effect of the system of partible anticipatory inheritance and separation by the married man from his father's home is that sons are in positions to interact as near equals with their fathers, and as equals with their married brothers. Accordingly, the normative practice of immediate post-marital residence does not answer the question of how households are distributed vis-à-vis one another at any given time.

RESIDENCE DEFINED BY THE PROXIMITY OF TENTS

The newly established unit, like the parental tent itself, is faced with continual decisions concerning with whom it is to associate in camping and migrating. Anthropologists frequently do not distinguish between the rules of immediate post-marital residence and the outcome of the decisions of where to live which confront members of independent households. Although patrilocality is strong in ideology and practice regarding post-marriage co-residence, the overall residential (settlement) pattern is not so easily characterized. For example, in Yörük society a large variety of kinship-based dyadic ties exist between each member of a tent and hundreds of members of other tents. Many of these ties are not given prominence in stated cultural norms, but can and do determine some of the options open to any tent in camping with others where it is seen desirable that some kinship relationship exist so that neighbors are not "strangers" (*yabancĭ*). Most of the ties among households which are relevant to migratory and camp group composition arise from descent and kinship (including affinity). Only a hired shepherd who is also a head of an independent househould would regularly camp with non-kin, should his employer be unrelated.

THE PROBLEM OF DYADIC KIN TIES

The problem of dyadic kin ties and proximal residence, put simply, is that each of the 1,415 individuals in nomadic Yörük society is related to individuals outside his/her own tent by ties of shared agnatic descent, consanguinity, and affinity. Randolph and Coult (1968:83, 85 ff.), using a computer, determined that sets of spouses in the Bedowin Hawaashleh tribe (Negev) trace an average of 350 kin-type relationships, with some sets possessing over 700. The Yörük of southeastern Turkey are directly comparable in cousin marriage frequencies, rates of endogamy and genealogical depth to this Arab tribe. Therefore, a similar multiplicity of kin-type ties among members of the tribe can be assumed for them. This will be somewhat less for randomly selected pairs than for spouses, but nevertheless a high number of ties are predictable. Although a large number of such ties exist for each member of the household, not every member is in an equal position to influence camping patterns. Unmarried dependent children exert little impact on their social environment.

The stated preferences refer to the heads of households and strongly favor close consanguinal kinsmen as neighbors, particularly agnates (*yakĭn akraba*, emmi uşağĭ). Tents of a mahalle or kabile generally camp together, they say, and never to camp with kabile members calls into question one's status as member of the descent group in practice. Even though camp groups do not carry names there is enough of a patrilineal bias in their composition that clusters of tents encountered on the road or in yayla pastures are characterized by Yörük as being "of the 'so-and-so' lineage" (e.g., Osmangiller). The same group when approached will almost invariably turn out to be more complex than that, and usually will include tents whose only ties to other tents are through matrilateral (e.g., *dayĭ uşağĭ*) linkages or affinity. Such families are not *ipso facto* dependent or client members of the group, but rather the group itself is continually in a state of flux with tents joining and leaving it regularly.

The most emphatically articulated rule of residence after separation is that sons should be near living fathers and brothers. It is only problematically achieved in practice. Separated sons are often seen camping apart from their living fathers and brothers, and frequently move and camp away from their siblings.

These stated preferences have to do with the relationship of the head of a domestic unit to other heads of tents. There are social pressures emanating from dependent married members of the household which affect camping options. Some of these pressures deflect behavior from the norm of camping with close agnates and other close kin, while other factors arising from the kinship nexus of dependent married members of the household reinforce the tendency to be with close kin.

For example, the marriage of one tent's son and another's daughter affects the relations between the households and thus camping. Yörük feel that for an indefinite period of time they should not have too much to do with a tent to which they have given a daughter. This practice of quasi-avoidance can last over a year during which the new bride customarily does not see her parents. Meetings between the parents are very formal during the first years of marriage of their children, and the visits to each other's tents are infrequent. The closer the pre-existing ties of kinship, the shorter and less formal is avoidance between the households. With time the effects of affinity between a married son and his in-laws may encourage the tents to camp together. This is not too likely as by the time relations have become informal, the son and his wife probably will have separated from his natal tent.

The high rate of kidnapping is relevant to a consideration of camping decisions. When a marriage is formed by kidnapping the mutual avoidance of the two families is virtually complete for a considerable period. While it is true that with time relations become normalized and that men often use affinal connections created by their kidnapping, this does not happen soon enough to benefit the boy's father while the kidnapped girl is still in the boy's natal tent. For the two households to come into close contact would invite trouble, especially from the girl's brothers. The rate of kidnapping, discussed in Chapter III, may well have an unexpected effect on residence patterns.

Since kidnappings more often occur across lineage lines than do regular marriages, one would expect that in-law avoidance would tend to reinforce camping with close agnates. This is the case for those who kidnap non-kin. But a more important and negative effect on the rule of camping with close kinsmen stems from the relatively lower rate of kidnappings among close kin because such kidnappings invariably upset normative patterns. The conflict and ill-will generated by any kidnapping is considerable. When the girl is taken from a "strange" family, the behavior of the man's tent to his kinsmen is little affected as "the odds are" that they would not be in close interaction with them anyway. However where the girl is taken from an agnate or close consanguine, the receiving tent will find itself avoiding precisely those with whom its relations had hitherto been closest. When the tent whose son has kidnapped a close kinswoman finds its options to camp with lineage mates or consanguines reduced, it will seek to activate the ties it has with more distant kinsmen. Paradoxically, many of these will prove to have been formed by kidnappings in the previous generation.

Although never stated in preferences for camping, the ties created by the marriage of the head of house, like those established by the marriage of his sons, affect camping decisions. This is evidenced in two ways. One, the wife of the head of house has much to say in the daily decisions of migrating and household organization. Secondly, the head of house can use ties of affinity created by his marriage which link his tent to her consanguines.

The tent moves on the average about 30 times a year. Each move involves a choice of camping neighbors, although once camped on either winter or summer pastures it is difficult to move away without forfeiting grazing money already paid. The formal power to make any decision to move is left to the head of household, although it is rarely arrived at without discussion among members of the tent the night before. The major decisions as to which pastures to rent are debated for considerable time beforehand as they involve allocation of considerable amounts of capital in rental fees. There is little doubt that the head of house usually makes this important decision.

The wives of heads of households with whom the ethnographer traveled never failed to voice strong opinions about matters of migration while on the road. Also, the actual movement of the tents is undertaken in the pre-dawn morning, usually before 4:00 a.m. The work of loading the camels and getting underway is the responsibility of the women of the tent and they often find it an occasion for rivalry to see which home can be earliest on the road. Even when no visible consensus has been reached among the men the night before, the first muffled sounds of tents being folded and the complaints of camels led to their burdens seemed to prompt the women of still slumbering tents into action. Sometimes they moved even though the animals had not gone on ahead the evening before as is usual when a tent has decided to migrate. Soon the camp site would contain only a few stragglers and old women packing children and outdoor equipment on donkeys while the camels moved down the road. On one occasion the women of a rich man in the lineage (two wives and three daughters-in-law) were taken by surprise as the women of neighboring tents got started well before they awoke. Their embarrassment was great and their revenge, to the ethnographer, at least, appeared appropriate. The following morning they quietly awoke at 2:00 a.m. and when their sounds roused women of the other tents, the entire camp group was led stumbling through the night to the next camp site.

Daily decisions to migrate with a camp group are not as important as one would expect. Once a tent has decided to leave either summer or winter pastures with a group of tents, the daily decisions to stay with them or not are largely determined by the nature of the grazing along the roadside. In the spring, grazing is so poor that there are few junctures where a tent can stop for a few days, letting the rest go on. In fall, grazing is better and tents often choose to stay on a day or so longer than their camp mates, but usually rejoin the same group at a later point.

The long-term effects of affinal kin ties to a man's wife's family and relatives are more important in setting the general camping pattern and create alternatives to camping with one's brothers. The woman herself may wish to camp in winter or summer pastures with her agnates, perhaps her sisters, and the economic consequences of such bonds are greater than decisions to camp together with others on the road.

The fact of patrilineality in descent and the general "male bias" of the culture should not be taken to obscure the fact that women are also much concerned with their agnatic relatives, as well as maternal uncles and close cousins. Yörük women are visibly attached to their brothers and their fathers. They are raised in close association with their close kin from infancy to pre-pubescent adolescence. Childhood ties carry considerable affect. Also the ties created between men by their marrying sisters is considered one of great trust. If a man has to leave his wife alone outside of his father's tent he will entrust her to the keeping of his wife's sister's husband (*bacanak*).

These factors lead to an interesting anomaly in Yörük social organization. There is a strongly stated emphasis on patrilineality and lineage solidarity through the unity of brothers and the sons of brothers. There is customary avoidance of in-laws and the in-laws of one's children which strengthens the cultural emphasis on vertical patrilineal ties. However because these ties also involve the female in the networks of affect and mutual responsibility, every marriage that is not of very close agnatic kinsmen automatically puts the household in the potential position of having to choose between the husband's and the wife's agnates in joining temporary camp groups. What is noteworthy, too, is that one measure of the strength of the lineage is that women do not lose their lineage identity through marriage. Ironically these same ties can deflect the residence pattern from being rigidly that of patri-kin camping together. Given the variability of camp group size from two to 20 tents, a statistic here would not express accurately the rate of non-agnates camping with a group. In many cases, out of the numerous ties that existed in a camp group between a tent and other tents the closest ones were those of the wife to other head of household or to other married women. Even where the camp group was primarily composed of members of one lineage, the closest ties uniting tents, and quite possibly the reason for their being together, were those among women.

By informant accounts and by field observation it is possible to say that every tent has, on occasion, joined camp groups to which only affinal ties existed or to which these were the only close kin-type relationships. For example, out of the 11 tents of the Satılar lineage which the ethnographer was able to follow closely over a 12-month period, nine tents made long-term (e.g., of several months) decisions to be with tents more closely related affinally than by other criteria. Five of these decisions cut across lineage lines, although more distant consanguinal ties also existed, and three were with close affines who were also distant agnates. A ninth tent of the lineage, headed by a widow with a co-resident single-but-grown son stopped camping with her deceased husband's family because of a disagreement and joined a tent group containing her brother and her married daughter (see Table 24).[9]

It should not be concluded from this that nine out of 11 tents regularly camp with affines at the expense of close agnates. Rather, out of all of the many major decisions to camp for long periods with a concomitant payment of rental money, there were nine instances where affinal ties were utilized in a visible way. Of course in any camp group affinal ties will be likely among close agnates and other close kin, but it is not possible to determine which are foremost in motivating a tent to join a group. The camp groups are, in fact, highly agnatic regardless of whether the composition is determined by affinal links among agnatically re-

TABLE 24

CAMPING DECISIONS INVOLVING CLOSE AFFINES AMONG TENTS OF ONE LINEAGE DURING ONE YEAR

Satılar Household (out of 22 total)	Nature of Kin-Type Ties to the Tent Most Closely Related in the Group Joined	Locality	Time (months)	Reasons for Joining
1. Kara Çavuş G. (wife=no kin)	wife's mother's brother	spring & yayla	7	Conflict with agnates over a bride for his son
2. Hüsein Ö. (wife=FZD)	wife's father's brother, wife's mother's brother	yayla	4	Conflict with father over early separation
3. Kabak G. (wife=no kin)	first wife's brother	kışlak	6	No particular reason
4. Kabak G.	daughter's husband	yayla	4	To aid his daughter married to a poor man
5. İbrahim Ö. (wife=no kin)	sister's husband, wife's brother, sister (kid. mar.)	yayla	4	No particular reason
6. Ahmet G. (wife=FFBD)	wife's brother	kışlak, road	7	Conflict with brother
7. Mustafa A. (wife=FBD)	(MBS), brother's wife's father	kışlak	7	Conflict of his wife with his mother
8. Rüstem G. (wife=MBD)	wife's father's brother	kışlak	7	No particular reason
9. Ayşe G. (hus.=MBS)	left dead husband's brother to join her true brother	yayla & road	4	Conflict over animal debt with dead husband's brother

lated women or by shared descent among men. What is important for the Yörük adaptation to a highly variable political environment, and one in which access to resources is dependent on other ethnic groups, is that a wide number of camping options exist which can be used as needed.

Of social structural interest is the fact that there is no necessary congruence between patrilocality following marriage in the father's tent and the way in which neighbors are selected and options to travel together utilized. For example, two men each related as MBS to each other and each being of different descent groups might well camp together, and both may have at his side separated married sons. The sons would, of course, be patrilocally located while the nucleus of the little group would be quite different. Such combinations were often encountered in the field. What seems to give impetus to the final form of the camp groups as highly agnatic units is the economic basis of the groups as a means to rent pasture collectively.

The analysis has established that a broad range of options are available in residence, and has also shown that they are not restricted to those isomorphic with agnatic lineage membership. Nor does post-marital domicile which is patrilocal in rule and practice limit a significant reliance on affinal ties of kinship among independent households in choosing camp neighbors. The ideology of residence and the dispersed nature of marriage patterns through such processes and kidnappings outside the lineage allow an individual tent to choose from a variety of groups within which he can cite ties of kinship to some if not all tents.

V
CAMP GROUPS AND THE ACQUISITION OF PASTURE RIGHTS

CAMP groups are formed by households selectively exercising their options to camp with agnatic or other kinsmen (see Chapter IV). Such groups or clusters of tents vary in size from two to occasionally more than 20 households. It is rare that a family will camp alone for very long, even should it seem advantageous to do so for reasons strictly pertaining to grazing.

The factors which preclude isolated, dispersed camping can be mentioned without anticipating the analysis of camp groups and pasture acquisition. The need for sociability has already been referred to in Chapter I as a reason for members of the tribe not utilizing the small pastures available about half way along the route they take to reach yaylas in Kayseri Province. This facet of Yörük life cannot be discounted, since, quite apart from considerations of security and grazing, Yörük of both sexes greatly prize the restrained conviviality of kinsmen and close friends. They gather daily for tea or coffee and to exchange opinions, or simply to idle hours away with pleasant banter and good humor. The men meet daily in a tent of the camp group, each well-founded home having its turn, where the seemingly ceaseless exchange of small talk, opinion, and pithy commentary on the behavior of anyone not present constitute, in the words of local wits, the *meclis* or parliament. Even if security were not an issue, no family would readily sacrifice the pleasures of visiting and being visited, of giving hospitality and receiving it.

Apart from the high value Yörük place on social intercourse among their fellows, for most families, security is a problem which must be coped with. The problem is twofold: security from theft which involves non-Yörük almost exclusively, and protection against violence directed at persons of the household, usually by other Yörük. While few households at any time contain a member who is being actively sought as object for revenge in feuds, many contain men in the ambiguous position of being potential objects for violent assault by those with whom their relations are bad (*açĭk* or open), but among whom avoidance is assisted by the intervention of neighbors. Further, certain families not centrally featured in a blood feud (*kan davasĭ*), might find themselves suddenly furnishing a victim should they provide a vulnerable, though ethically borderline target. It has been noted that the outer limits of vengeance are indefinite.

More critical to the sheer survival of a family as an economic entity than its purse is the safety of its herd. Isolated households and herds protected only by the men mustered by one tent are vulnerable to the unwanted attention of sheep rustlers who, using trucks, can carry off entire flocks for sale in distant markets. Two families were utterly impoverished in this way while moving south from summer pastures. In both cases the tents had separated themselves from a larger group in order to remain longer on fallow cotton fields. More dramatic, to the ethnographer, was a similar attempt made on the herds of his host, then camping with five other tents. The intruders were driven off when spotted by a shepherd who noticed that only half of his flock had followed him over a small rise. His shouts brought the entire camp out, and achieved the recovery of the animals.

The area used by the Yörük is not lacking in administrative control; nor is it beyond the daily exercise of governmental jurisdiction by officials of the state. Many acts of personal violence, however, particularly those stemming from honor and vengeance, cannot be seriously reduced by jail sentences and the apprehension of the perpetrators. Paradoxically, the increased efficiency of the Turkish transportation system makes rustling a more profitable crime than ever before, and one less easily curtailed by local law enforcement.

The composition of Yörük nomadic camp groups cannot be directly related to the labor requirements of animal husbandry for extra-tent cooperation in herding and tending the flocks (cf. Swidler, 1972:70-75). Most tents are self-sufficient in this respect and the only households which are absolutely dependent upon outside aid are those whose herds are so small that they must rely on selling their own labor as hired shepherds, while mixing their meager flock with that of their employer. The only households in this category are a few recently separated young families, and one long established but recently impoverished tent.

While not critical, there is one substantial advantage to be had in camping with another tent in regard to labor-saving arrangements in herding. In the spring, shortly after the lambs are dropped in early to middle March, they are separated from their mothers during the most of the day in order to ensure a saleable milk production. At first they are kept in a special reed enclosure in a corner of the house tent, but when they are a few weeks old they are let to run loose throughout the day. They still must be kept apart from their mothers during most of the time or they will completely strip the ewes of milk. Usually two tents trade lambs during the day, each family mixing the lambs of his neighbor in his own herd, while giving his own lambs in turn to be kept elsewhere. Because ewes do not readily accept strange lambs to nurse, the milk production is effectively secured. Occasionally the lambs are deliberately let to obtain a full-ration of milk, and at unexpected times they may sight their mothers and rush uncontrollably to nurse, thus ruining a day's milk sale. Neighbors who exchange animals in this are called *katişĭk* for the period in which they do this.

Apart from this, neighbors are expected to lend assistance to one another when animals are lost, but generally they do not actually help search for them. Rather, a man will inquire about a neighbor's lost animals when he travels from tent to tent on his own business, and if he finds them, will see that they are returned. Animals found at large are always cared for by the finder, but never is an attempt made to conceal them from their owners. As each member of a household is able to recognize virtually every one of the several hundred animals they may own, it would be difficult (and extremely humiliating if caught) to claim feloniously the strays that are inevitably found along the route of migration. Mature animals are identified by ear notches (*in*) and by colored patches dyed on their backs (*damga*), as well as by details of physical appearance: facial coloration, ear type, spots, and deformities. Animals were continually seen being returned to owners by finders, and although families might not be on particularly close terms, no instance of even heated discussion of ownership claims occurred. It is taken as an article of faith among Yörük that every man knows his own animals, and knowingly to retain another's lost or stolen animals is considered extremely bad behavior. In fact, it is said with considerable emphasis that animals cannot be stolen or destroyed even by rival parties in a blood feud.

In summary, there are few if any truly collective supportive functions of a camp group in pooling labor apart from security and practical help during the two month period following lambing. The groups are not named, have no year-to-year continuity, no claims on particular areas of grazing and no legal or other collective responsibility for members. Each family provides its own labor without any significant pooling of group manpower, women milk their own herds only; men and women shear their own animals and search their own strays; and young men and boys primarily guard their own flocks. Small items of foodstuff, however, are lent upon request among neighbors and when an animal is killed (usually just before death would occur from natural causes) all of the men gather as a matter of course for a communal meal. The importance of the camp group for nomadic Yörük adaptations is not how it relates to the immediate tending of the livestock, but in how it serves to put persons in situations of direct social interaction, and as a vehicle for the acquisition of temporary pasture rights.

While the problems of security and the desire for regular social interaction largely account for why Yörük travel and camp in aggregate, it does not explain the composition of the groups. We have already outlined the multiplicity of kin-type ties which can be used to phrase the relationship of one tent to another. There are two factors which make it impossible to predict camp group composition from simple lineage identity: most importantly, lineages do not own or collectively control land; and secondly, a head of household does not gain or lose lineage identity by virtue of residence alone. An analysis of camp groups must look beyond the ideology of descent and the kinship system.[1] It is necessary to consider the camp group as a vehicle for the temporary acquisition and use of land rather than as the source of rights to lands. The highly agnatic composition of groups using pastures is not a function of descent lines having any special claim to portions of the landscape, but is a by-product of the economic and social transac-

[1] Barth (1961:25 ff.) provides perhaps the most detailed analysis of camp group composition in a nomadic pastoral society. Such groups among the Yörük differ significantly from those described by Barth for the Basseri of South Persia. Yörük groups are not named, and cannot be used as units for which marriage can be usefully described as endogamous or exogamous.

tions that are critical to the rental of grazing tracts. These are more intense among agnatic kinsmen.

THE CONTRACTUAL NATURE OF PASTURE RIGHTS

In terms of nomadic pastoralism, the Yörük may be an extreme case in that at present all pasture available to them falls within village borders. All access must be negotiated anew each season with non-Yörük title holders: in the yayla most often with village officials competent to dispose of village commons (mer'a), and in the region of winter quarters with large landowners.

Considering first the winter quarters (kĭşlak), all available pasture is contracted for upon cash payment for a specified season. The written contract is usually drawn up between the village headman (*muhtar*) or private landowners and a Yörük herd owner. The latter assumes full responsibility for the collection of rent and for possible damage fees from other sub-leasees. The contract specifies the total cash rent for the pasture, its borders, and the date by which it must be vacated (usually May first). Pasture fees are calculated per tract of land by the villages, while among the Yörük these are prorated per head of mature sheep, ranging in the case of the latter, from 9.00 to 20.00 T. L. ($1.00 = 12.00 T.L.) in kĭşlak, and making an average of nearly 13.00 T.L.

The usable terrain itself is unevenly distributed between non-arable hillside scrub lands and the more extensive fallow grain fields. Winter pastures everywhere are exhausted by late April. The tribe, however, begins to move to summer pasture earlier to avoid difficulties that occur if they remain in the winter pastures after crops begin to develop. Keeping their herd away from cultivated fields during this season is difficult and there is a greater risk of conflict with the peasants and landowners if they remain too long in the lowlands. The threat of conflict and damage claims may serve an ecological regulatory function in preventing overgrazing of pastures, in which the occupant has no proprietary interest and which he is inclined by paying rent to overexploit.

The fallow land (*firez*) and planted fields (*ekin*) are interspersed, and only the skill of the shepherd can prevent crop damage or even complete destruction. This becomes an increasingly troublesome problem as spring wears on, and the impetus warm weather gives fall-sown wheat makes herding in this season a matter of constant watchfulness. Rich landowners often employ special watchmen (*ekin bekçisi*) to ensure that damage, if not prevented, is at least charged against the errant herdsman.

Yörük state that it is *contra* the precepts of Islam, even *haram* or prohibited, to ask for or accept money in payment for grazing damage caused by animals. This belief, convenient for the herder, does not command any attention among the agricultural population. Even the Yörük nomads articulate it with the wistfulness of those speaking of an ideal world where man's nobler spirit prevails. In any event, the damage claims are usually argued and only paid up when the herd owner is confronted with the damage and with the possibility that the claims might be pressed with government assistance. The latter is an extremely credible threat since the government is primarily interested in agricultural production.

Damage claims and payments are not without their repercussions within the Yörük society. First, no man willingly admits to damage unless the evidence is overwhelming and, if on the road, few would hesitate to move on without paying, should that be feasible. Damage claims are collectible by law once damage is assessed by a government agricultural agent. If the herd is identified the owner is easily traced and charged. However, the herd is not always identified and serious debate among shepherds and owners sometimes takes place to set the blame.

Thus the effects of crop damage can split a camp group and lead to serious trouble among contending members. One herd owner, camping with maternal and affinal (non-agnatic) kinsmen caused repeated severe crop damage to the fields of a wealthy Kurdish landowner. In the final incident he attempted to cover his guilt by driving a few sheep of a neighbor into the damaged field. When everything was settled, and the truth brought into the open, the culprit was forced to abandon the camp group and the pastures he had rented, as well as to pay a substantial indemnity to the crop owner. Whereas well-established Yörük, both sedentary and nomadic, frequently act as go-betweens in arranging damage settlements with non-Yörük, no one acted in this capacity for the man who violated a basic premise of neighborly behavior.[2]

---

[2] Conflict occurred among sedentary Yörük of two sublineages in the village of Nogaylar over animal damage money (*zarar parasi*). Animals from a family damaged fields owned by families of the other Yörük group. The latter demanded payment, but the leader of the group which did the damage insisted that it was wrong to make or accept such payment. In the end they agreed to pay the money into a fund for religious use.

The contemporary impact of nomad animals on local agriculture is not so much in the direct involvement of the sheep in the crop cycle, but in how their owners interact with the non-Yörük populations. Manure, for example, is not introduced in a critical way into the agricultural system, but is collected (around the animal tents) and sold by Yörük to non-local farmers who truck it to another province for fruit trees. Crop damage or the threat of it would create an economic hardship on the villagers trying to make a living from poorer soils where returns would not sustain a margin of loss due to predation. However, the government's influence in this area of peasant-nomad relations is near complete and in many cases the damages collected by villagers are in excess of what was caused by herd incursion. The real force of nomadic Yörük presence is in the extra cash income which is injected into the local economy every winter when over 45,000 head of sheep and 400 to 500 head of camels are put on land rented at rates averaging over 10.00 T.L. per head of sheep, and more for camels, to total over 500,000 T.L. in cash. Not only that pasture is rented, but also there is a substantial demand for such local feed grains as barley, wheat straw, and cotton seed mixes which are purchased in local markets. Each tent averages about 4,000 T.L. in such animal production related outlays (see Table 25 for expenses related to summer pastures).

Turning now to the problem of highland grazing, summer pastures (yayla) are situated in Kayseri province. These lands are held by agricultural populations which, because of the severe winters, cannot fully exploit them for animal husbandry. Village herd size is regulated both by the amount of hay which can be stored for winter feeding, and by the ease with which pasture pays a profit to the village treasury by rental to the nomads. Whereas climate and the topography create the condition of excess pasture in summer, what is done with it is determined by economic return. The villagers could, in fact, exploit the common pastures to a greater extent by bringing in herds from elsewhere for summer fattening but, by leasing the land to the Yörük, they secure a good return with little effort or risk. The grazing is exclusively wild semi-Alpine grasses, with few fallow grain fields available, except, briefly, just prior to decamping in the fall. The pastures themselves are often situated at considerable distances from the villages to which they belong. Although large tracts of grazing area might result from contiguity of the individual pastures, the boundaries established by legal title delineate the units leased

TABLE 25
DISTRIBUTION OF TENTS ACCORDING TO NAMED YAYLAS, AND COST OF PASTURE RENTAL
(1969)

Number	Yayla	Number of tents	District	Total Cost (T.L.)
1.	Frenk Yaylasi	4	Pinarbaşi	12,000
2.	Salderesi	5	"	10,000
3.	Kefen	4	Sariz	10,000
4.	Kirkgeçit	10	Pinarbaşi	22,000
5.	Asagi Karagöz	4	"	10,000
6.	Yukari Karagöz	2	"	5,000
7.	Göl Yaylasi	5	Sariz	19,000
8.	Beş Ceşme	6	Sariz	7,000
9.	Kiz Kaç	2	"	4,400
10.	Destiye	5	"	7,500
11.	Üç Pinar	2	"	2,500
12.	Sari Çiçek	2	Pinarbaşi	6,000
13.	Binboga	6	Sariz	8,000
14.	Kurdağ (Beyçayir)	3	Pinarbaşi	7,000
15.	Çukur Yurt	3	"	7,000
16.	Kara Pinar	6	"	14,000
17.	Aşagi Beyçayir	6	"	9,500
18.	Kel Tepesi	3	"	5,000
19.	Immiza Yaylasi	4	Sariz	5,500
20.	Keçeli	10	Tomarza	20,000
21.	Otebaş'dan beri	6	"	--
22.	Büyük Gökbil	3	"	6,500
23.	Aslan Taş	20	"	23,300
24.	Çem Yaylasi	10	Pinarbaşi	7,500
25.	Solak Yaylasi	9	Pinarbaşi	1,000 (one month)
26.	Kepelek	6	"	5,000
27.	Mesçit	5	"	12,500
28.	Koç Pinar	10	"	7,000
29.	Kartal Pinar	5	"	8,200
30.	Bostanlik	3	Sariz	4,500
31.	Yedi Oluk	2	"	6,500
32.	Kumarant	9	Pinarbaşi	17,000
33.	Dumanli	6	"	16,500
Totals		186		306,900

Notes: Mean cost per mature head of sheep: 8.00 T.L.
Mean size of group using a named yayla: 5.3 tents
Mean cost per tent (excluding Nos. 21,25): 1765 T.L.

by the nomads, and mark the division of summer grazing territories among camp groups.

There are by field count 60 named yayla tracts that can be used by nomadic Yörük in Pĭnarbaşĭ, Sarĭz, and Tomarza districts (see Chapter I). Actual camps any given year are fewer than these for two reasons. Not all yayla pastures are necessary for the nomadic herds, as outer limits of the size of the animal population carried by the summer grazing lands is set by the nature of the worst season, winter pasture. The kĭşlak zone is the restrictive season because unlike the situation in yayla, there is no significant amount of excess grazing area that is not used. Some of the yayla pastures used by Yörük studied here are rented by nomadic Yörük of other tribes or sections who winter on the seaward side of the Amanos range in Adana province. The rest are leased by merchants from surrounding provincial centers to fatten livestock for fall slaughter.

The yayla pastures themselves are largely owned by villages of all ethnic types as common land (mer'a). The proceeds of pasture rental go to the village treasury (*sandĭk*) to be used for such pan-village expenses as school maintenance, the village road, and water works. The villages sometimes make minor investments from this fund to improve sources of yayla water, usually by cleaning out free-flowing springs, so that nomadic herds will be able to use the tracts. This, however, is not the rule and very little of pasture monies paid to villages and villagers are employed in a way that benefits the Yörük. The pasture areas themselves are usually well watered in spring from natural sources and a few pastures have usable wells. The Yörük do not do more than to maintain the springs in a clean condition, although they say that in the past they dug wells for their own use.

In one pasture visited, the Yörük occupants had arranged water troughs and toward the end of a dry summer were carrying water twice a day laboriously from a brackish well. This did little more than extend the grazing season a few days for them, still less than it would have been on better watered pastures, and it is not common practice in other camp sites. Well-watered sites seem to be somewhat more expensive to rent, although it is said that the scale of pasture fees roughly parallels the size of the tract and the quality of the grass. There is considerable variation in the amount *per* head of sheep paid in summer as well as in winter pastures.

About five years prior to the study, the government ordered that villages wishing to let mer'a lands to non-village residents do so only through public auction, supervised by the district governor in the district centers. This directive is primarily aimed at ensuring that the rental money paid reaches its proper destination in the public purse, and that village muhtars do not appropriate it to private ends. It was suspected that village officials were arranging private deals for pasture rental and declaring less income than actually received. It was also thought by villagers and the government that Yörük were able to bribe village officials for cheap rental contracts. These charges are not without substantial basis in fact.

Current practice is somewhat divergent from what the local representatives of the state have in mind in organizing the public auction. In most cases would-be leasees agree on a price with the village representative prior to the auction, at which time hitherto heavy bidding among Yörük stops when the sum is reached. On some occasions there is truly competitive bidding, but this is much frowned upon by the nomads for its bad effect on pasture prices. One case of competitive bidding occurred between unfriendly members of one lineage and heartily strengthened the ill-will that already existed between them. Such public displays of antagonisms are rare in Yörük society.

The contracts are written up in legal form and, unlike the practice in winter pastures, are checked by government officials to ensure that the sum agreed upon is not substantially less than that of the previous year. The officials have local interests at heart in regulating Yörük-peasant transactions. Payment is in cash due soon after the herds are on the pastures. Actual negotiation takes place before the arrival of the Yörük tents when each household sends a man on ahead to make the arrangements. The dates of the auction are announced well in advance.

MIGRATION

The movements of pastoralists are limited in an absolute sense by the physical tolerances of their livestock and the ecological setting. Yörük sheep are a variety of the broad tailed strain adapted to fairly cold conditions, but not resistant to hot weather or heavy snowfall. Winter pastures are unusable during the summer heat which begins in early May and lasts until late September. Summer pastures are snow-covered in most cases until late April, and snow remains in patches on some through July and middle August. In all cases Yörük are on the yaylas before the disappearance of snow fields, which are often important sources of water.

The threat of a late or unseasonable snowfall in the valleys leading up to the pastures is, paradoxically, more critical than in the summer pastures themselves (see Table 5). This is because herds on the road are being pushed through in forced marches, undernourished and highly susceptible to disease. Sudden snow, cold rain, or stream flooding is a major concern to the herdsmen. Not every herd owner, however, is able to cope with this through the same migration strategy. Those who leave early in April find choice grazing but risk higher animal losses. Those who move later in the season bring their herds over roadside fields almost totally devoid of grazing and must push through in forced treks of twice the normal daily length. Those who adopt the strategy of early departure from winter quarters lessen their risks considerably by leaving the winter wool on the animals. This is not a viable option for many middle or poorer nomads who need the immediate cash from wool sales to meet creditors in town.

Yörük herds are in poor condition by mid-point in the spring march and often find supplementary illegal grazing in roadside fields of winter wheat. On the other hand, villagers take advantage of the shepherd's difficulty in keeping flocks together in broken country by stealing stray animals. At the same time, occasionally village animals find their way into nomadic herds but they are usually returned. Although wealthier nomads have useful personal contacts in most of the villages traversed, it is only the presence of governmental authority which restricts violence to isolated incidents and enforces settlement of crop damage.

The trek down to winter quarters is impossible until the temperature has dropped in the valleys that must be traversed. This happens in middle September and allows serious discussion to begin among the nomads about their return south. Their journey, lasting a month and a half, is then a more comfortable migration for the animals as grazing is plentiful on the recently harvested fields. No attempt is made to move south until it is clear that crops are off the fields along the route, and cotton is picked in the area of winter residence (see Table 26).

Most of the grazing in the fall is free, as villagers recognize the benefit of sheep manure on the harvested fields, and as in most cases no single fallow stubble field offers enough grazing to make it worthwhile trying to rent it out. However, cotton fields are fre-

TABLE 26

SUMMARY TABLE OF VILLAGE AGRICULTURAL CYCLES
FOR AREAS TRAVERSED BY YÖRÜK*

	Seeding in fall	Harvest of fall-sown	Seeding in spring	Harvest of spring-sown
Kışlak	October 25	June 25	March 10	September 25
Göç Yolu	September 1 to November 1	July	March 30 to May 15	July 30 to September 15
Yayla	September 15 to November 1	July 7 to August 20	March 1 to June 15	July 10 to September 30

*Adapted from Table No. 5, Köy IşleriBak. Yayinlari No.'s 64, 65, 96

quently rented to Yörük where it is apparent to the owners that good grazing remains on the leaves of the plants. Sometimes there is sufficient cotton remaining on the plants after harvest to make it profitable sending the children out to pick it from fields rented for the sheep. This is never more than a small matter of a sack of cotton or two, and not a reliable means of paying for the fields rented.

Forage and camping sites are particularly limited during the spring migration owing to agricultural activity, but are plentiful during the fall move when fallow grain and picked cotton fields become available. The right of nomads to pass through village lands along their migration route is recognized by local authorities, although this is customary and not statutory.[3] Conflict over damages

---

[3] In the spring villagers collect a fee for Yörük herds crossing village lands (*yol parası*) which amounts to an average of 5.00 T.L. per herd per village. As the herds may cross a number of village lands during a night's migration it is a sub-

to crops and theft of animals is normal during the month-long spring migration, but not so common in fall.

LEADERSHIP, ECONOMIC DIFFERENTIATION, AND PASTURE ACQUISITION

The sources of political power and the foundations of leadership are apt to be diverse in any community. This is particularly true of the nomadic Yörük. Among sedentary Yörük, for the most part, men who acquire power do so through use of their superior wealth in land. These men are sometimes rewarded with political office (recognized by the state) to which they are elected by their tribal constituents in the village. The situation is different among the nomads. The state recognizes no office among the nomads, and the nomads maintain no named formal positions in the tribe to which men can aspire. The only linguistic term of personal distinction implying leadership is ağa, and it is very widely applied as a simple honorific to men to whom the speaker wishes to show respect regardless of their effective rank in society. Nomadic Yörük society is essentially egalitarian as it is structured today. Nevertheless certain men do come to be recognized as leaders and lineage spokesmen and achieve a degree of social status not afforded to the average household head. Some of the circular routes to this form of social success will be detailed in this section in as much as they relate to pasture rental and camp groups.

There is no over-arching political structure uniting the lineages apart from descent ideology. Certain men exercise limited control through economic sanctions and the manipulation of public opinion, but they hold no recognized office. These leaders emerge largely by their wealth and their ability to sway the opinions of others, both closely related personal attributes. There is no one-to-one correlation of leader to named lineage; some larger groups may have two or more leaders while entire small lineages may lack an effective one. There are approximately nine individuals from six kabiles who are widely, but not unanimously, recognized as lineage spokesmen, and who are normally referred to as ağa in that sense. As leadership is not expressed through formal office

stantial penalty. The district governor of Göksun attempted to stop this practice which is illegal. When the villagers protested that the money was needed to pay the costs of hiring watchmen for the planted fields, a compromise was reached according to which the Yörük would pay only authorized officials of the villages, and would receive a receipt.

access to such positions is unrestricted by qualifications other than wealth and effective social status. No chiefly families maintain hereditary control.

Yörük informants define the status of ağa (not the use of the honorific) as being achieved by men who possess three attributes in abundance: wealth, ability for considered public speech, and generosity. Family line is never mentioned but it is unlikely that a man whose father was a notorious offender of Yörük conceptions of proper behavior or whose parentage was in doubt could qualify as an effective ağa. Yörük conceptions of the prerequisites of superior status can be expanded upon. Not every individual in the society possessing these qualities is regarded by his peers as an ağa. What seems to distinguish ağas who hold real power and unambiguous social position is the way in which they coordinate their economic, social, and charismatic powers.

Wealth, in order to be used in acquiring or maintaining political influence among the Yörük, can not simply be the "static" ownership of a large herd. It has to be held in a way which involves others of the society, particularly in dependent relationships. Further, whatever material capital is held must somehow be "insured" against short-term loss which would put its owner in the politically damaging position of having to call in outstanding debts or obligations. The economic histories of most nomadic Yörük heads of households betray a great deal of fluctuation in economic standing, even though the individual is or has been fairly wealthy. Life histories of influential men show little of this. It is the high rate of fluctuation in wealth during the lifetime of the individual that is characteristic of most nomadic pastoral societies and that underlies the economic mobility so often commented upon for such adaptations (see Barth, 1961:115 ff. for an excellent discussion of this for the Basseri of South Persia). For a man to achieve high status in a society lacking formal political office or religious functionaries, a prerequisite would be a stable economic base. The potential for strong leadership roles is limited by the inherent instability of the mode of production when compared even to Yörük sedentary communities.

It is self-serving for a man with political aspirations to extend economic support to others. This can be seen as two sorts of aid or economic relationships. In one, the rich can provide outright charity which is not to be reciprocated by the grantee and which benefits the giver through enhancing his overall reputation in the community. Generally the recipients are religious men, itinerant non-Yörük teachers who are semi-literate in Koranic scripture but well versed in the lore surrounding those passages that point out the heavenly rewards for donors who support their mission. Every man gives such charity (*zekât*) as he determines he owes according to a formula which demands one sheep a year to be given for every 100 owned above 40.[4] Women whose fathers gave them sheep with their marriage gifts also pay, just as they should pay a tithe on the gold they own, but they rarely do.

Apart from the fact that this wealth flows out of the Yörük community, it differs in a definitional way from simple hospitality. Even though all give charity who consider themselves able to do so, the more a person gives the better he is regarded. Rich men can thus translate some of their wealth into prestige, even if they do no more than give the accepted zekât at the usual rate. It is the gift that counts, not the hardship behind it.

Of more direct significance is the selling of sheep to kinsmen. Such actions can, in many respects, be considered the functional analogue of a redistributive system. That is, families who need to replenish diminished herds can do so by drawing on the wealth accumulated by others, generally close kinsmen. Even credit granted at high rates of interest (the word *faiz* or "interest" is never used) is considered as supportive action. It is often in this way that a man in Yörük nomadic society acquires influence and further ensures his economic position by such investments against the losses which can reduce a well-to-do family in a very short period to near poverty. Although factors affecting the distribution of wealth and the domestic cycle are treated in Chapter VI, it is useful to examine here how families acquire and maintain large herds through capital investments.

As has already been noted, many aspects of wealth differentials and economic mobility can be related to the acquisition of the most critical resource in the society: pasture. Pastures are rented, and the fees paid for grazing tracts are increasing annually. The requirements for large cash outlays have had a significant impact on Yörük society. First, rising pasture fees have significantly increased the mean number of animals needed to supply a household. Thus, the pace of settlement has seemingly quickened as average family herd size has gone up. Second, certain members of the community, those known as ağa, have been able to transform a generalized economic hardship into personal gain and economic security. This is accomplished by their ability to supply cash

---

[4] For a discussion of zekât see Levy (1959:249 ff., 309).

credit to kinsmen when it is needed for pastures and other related expenses. The profits from the credit arrangements in turn release the grantor from some of the exigencies of total reliance on one source of support: animals. The manner in which this is done also affects the final composition of the camp group which, although it can be seen as variable when viewed from an individual's vantage point, is actually quite regular when seen socio-centrically. This is because even though a tent may be regularly changing its immediate neighbors, the groups themselves formed of members of one lineage seem to return to a limited number of the many pastures available.

Formerly competition for good grazing would likely occur, if at all, only between lineage divisions in the tribe, with poorer families of strong lineages benefiting to the same extent as their richer kinsmen. Today, despite an "egalitarian" ideology which obscures this, individual wealth is crucial in securing pasture.

Wealth, however, is directed to this end in a circular manner and it is not the case that those with more capital or credit possibilities can simply monopolize the choice grazing tracts. There are a number of factors which tend to equalize access to grazing, and to ameliorate the divisive effects of a cash rental system whose economic impetus would be to put the rich herder on the best pasture and the poor on the marginal sites. One, the cost of grazing within a leased territory is reckoned *per animal* not per household or herd; thus the price, though not necessarily the effective cost, of grazing is equitably distributed. Furthermore, within any pasture rented, all herds graze at will and no family from among the contracting parties is able to monopolize the better areas.

In opposition to such leveling institutions, what does decrease economic mobility is the dependence of animal owners on ready credit, supplied here by the wealthier tribesmen. This is somewhat analogous to situations elsewhere, such as in Iraq and among settled Kurdish tribes in Turkey, where tribal leaders have gained legal title to formerly open pastures (see Barth, 1953). Here, however, the leaders generally remain nomadic but use their influence to secure effectively cheaper use of, rather than title, to land.

Differential effective cost of pasture for categories of wealth among the Yörük is a function of their involvement in a cash economy. That they are so involved is not as unusual a circumstance as might be thought from the literature. Barth (1961) and Hütteroth (1959) detail cash transactions for the Basseri of South

Persia and Kurdish tribes of eastern Turkey respectively. Kolars describes Yörük economic exchange with a village in Antalya, with respect to its importance in the agricultural system (1963). Planhol discusses the geographical parameters of such interaction for southwestern region as a whole (1958). But otherwise the economic context of nomadic pastoralist groups in the Near East is little explored.

For purposes of this chapter, suffice it to say that the value placed by the Yörük on animals and animal products reflects the prevailing conditions in the best of several regional markets. Livestock value, of course, is adjusted by cost of credit in sales among Yörük which varies according to length of payment, economic standing of buyer, and demand for certain types of animals within the tribe.

This latter circumstance is due to the fact that while Yörük sheep are sold per weight directly in markets, Yörük themselves cannot purchase non-Yörük strains for breeding stock. The sheep herded by the Yörük nomads (*kiçik/geçik*) is one strain of the same general Anatolian fat-tailed breed (*Ak Karaman*) tended by villagers of the region. However, the Yörük state that village sheep do not do well when kept in the open, and cannot withstand the often cold nights of both kışlak and yayla. Conversely, the Yörük strain suffers high mortality rates when maintained throughout the year in the lowlands, thus making it unacceptable to sedentary pastoralists. It is possible to distinguish Yörük strains from at least two other common varieties of sheep in the region by appearance. Because these strains of sheep are not usually interbred, exchange of animals among Yörük takes place outside the market place, but is still reckoned in cash. Accordingly, the price of breeding animals after a bad year may be higher among Yörük than the market value of equivalent non-Yörük stock.

The influence of the market can be seen in other areas. Wool prices are set by national markets, as are those of white cheese (*beyaz peynir*), though the latter are influenced by monopolistic practices in the purchase of the raw product by entrepreneurial tribesmen.[5] Furthermore, a shepherd's labor, other than that of

---

[5] Wool prices during the study were steady at 12.00 to 12.50 T.L. per kilo of raw wool, having risen from 10.00 T.L. in the last three years. Wool is purchased by Yörük middlemen who collect it from the tents and resell it at a small profit to dealers for factories. These middlemen are often regular herd owners who make extra money in this way. The wool producer benefits in that he does not have to

sons, has a cash value directly mirroring the going rates for such work throughout the region.[6] No regular labor in herding is contributed to any other tent without cash payment or specified reciprocity. All barter exchanges of significance are calculated against market prices. Need on the part of the purchasers does not affect price except as it affects withholding power and ability to negotiate as an equal. Richer herdsmen are more likely to sell in a seller's market and buy in a buyer's market.

The amount of goods consumed which are produced by the households varies from season to season. In winter when there is no fresh milk, only stored cheese, butter and, at rare intervals, meat, are supplied by the domestic unit. Bread, the principal foodstuff, is made from wheat-barley flour purchased in the market, as are *bulgur*, rice, dried fruit, loose tobacco, tea, and sugar. The capital outlay for tents, camels, and equipment, including large tents for the flocks in winter,[7] is much the same for all wealth categories. This means the relative operating cost for small herds is higher than for large ones. Concomitantly, the economic withholding power of small herd owners is less, and their credit expenses higher. As pastures are obtained through cash credit for most herders, their involvement in the national market system is of prime importance.

The camp group closely mirrors the tribe's integration with the local agricultural and national economic systems. No Yörük family can afford to reside alone on pasture sufficient for more than its own families. Families camping together share their

---

risk damage to the wool in storing it until he can get it to a dealer, or pay the expenses of carrying it to market. The profits are not large for the middlemen. Lamb's wool is sold in small quantities at a higher price in late summer. Milk was being sold to Yörük dairy owners at 1.00 to 1.50 T.L. per litre. Prices late in the season are higher than initially because milk fat increases as the volume decreases.

[6] The wages of shepherds range from 300.00 to 450.00 T.L. per month, with clothes, food, and lodging included. This is rather higher than prevailing agricultural wages in the area. If non-Yörük are hired, the shepherds are usually Avşar. Even when working for a close patrilineal relative, a normal wage is expected.

[7] In the last 10 years Yörük wintering in the İslahiye region have begun to use large canvas tents for their animals (*mal cadiri*). The style is a direct copy of Kurdish house tents with numerous poles placed in rows of three each down the middle. The material is tent canvas purchased in town and made up to their specifications by local tailors. They cost about 600.00 T.L. each, and represent a fairly large capital outlay necessitated by the growing inability of the nomadic Yörük to sustain large kill-offs of animals while operating in a full market economy. Each such tent holds about 250 animals.

grazing expenses prorated *per capita* of livestock (see also Beşikçi, 1969:116-118). Annual cash expenditure for pasture rights alone averages somewhat more than 11 percent of the value of the breeding stock carried throughout the year. If grain or feed is purchased in winter, this figure may double. This, combined with shepherd's wages for families with insufficient manpower, maintenance of camels, losses due to disease and normal attrition, can considerably narrow the profit margin.

The total amount of grazing available and the nature of its access routes determines the total animal population which can be supported by the tribe. How this animal population is distributed among family units is a function, in part, of differential ability to negotiate favorable sources of grazing. Further, the number of people supported by this animal population is a function of the exchange value of animal products relative to products of sedentary society.

Both summer and winter pastures are commonly leased in advance of the arrival of the herds, and there is no benefit to be had in being first in line of migration in this respect as all tents are equally able to send a representative ahead to contract for grazing. Thus one might expect the spatial distribution of tents to change greatly from year to year as no ideology of territoriality can be pervasive over legal claims of pasture owners and their desire to rent at best rates for cash. As previously mentioned, a very definite pattern of camp groups based on kin ties does emerge as a result of primary least holders favoring patri-kin as co-resident debtors.

The distribution of tents during the two seasons of pastoral rental reflects the actual contracts arrived at by a small number of household heads who negotiate with owners of grazing land. The fact of co-residence implies, in many cases, some economic dependence or at least close cooperation between the primary lease holder and his neighbors. Clientship, as much as exists, is generally maintained along lines of kinship.

Milk is available for sale from late March to mid-July. However, sufficient milk cannot be sold prior to spring pasture to purchase grazing from such proceeds alone. And few animals are available for ready sale during either season of pasture rental. Wool, which could serve as partial payment for summer grazing, has to be sold by the majority of tribesmen in the area of winter quarters in order to meet debts to local shopkeepers for foodstuffs purchased during that season on credit. Ideally, cash earned by the marketing of these products might be carried over the following period of pasture rental. However, this is impossible for most families because they often have longstanding debts incurred as a result of their need to increase breeding stock by credit purchase of animals in order to replenish herds decimated by disease.

Thus, milk becomes the way credit is acquired for grassland as it offers the only potential for local middlemen to capitalize on simple marketing techniques, converting a product difficult to transport and store into marketable cheese. While each household makes a variety of cheese for its own consumption, the quality acceptable in the urban market is unobtainable except when processed on a fairly large scale. This manufacturing is commonly in the hands of lineage leaders who draw on patri-kin for milk supplies. The parallel development of high grazing fees together with the concentration of the dairy business in the hands of lineage leaders is not accidental. The semi-annual need for large amounts of credit has opened the way for those with sufficient capital, or large herds, to secure a steady supply of milk at submarket prices. Fall pasture money is advanced against promises of milk in the coming spring and summer. The price is fixed by collusion among a limited number of buyers at about 20 percent below market value, as represented by non-Yörük village dairies. Indebtedness influences the residence pattern further in that once the milk is sold in advance of delivery, the seller is obligated in most cases to live within a half-day's walk of the dairy tents, which the owner locates near his camp at a good source of water.

The need for credit, even when not phrased in terms of milk, exerts strong pressure on kinsmen to cluster around the lineage leader, who is able to negotiate for desirable tracts with the advantage of having a reputation for prompt payment and settlement of possible damage claims. Household heads, and in particular important men, in order to facilitate pasture rental cultivate friendships in villages. Largely as a result of this there is a strong tendency for lineages themselves to localize, with camp groups returning year after year to the same pastures. Camp groups in winter quarters are much smaller than in summer, ranging from two to five tents as opposed to the summer average of six households with a maximum concentration of 25. Nevertheless, in winter there is a similar bias for households to return each season to a limited number of the actual pastures available.

While there are other social and cultural pressures for the co-residence of patri-kin, the state of partial economic dependence clearly lessens the options open to many individual tribesmen. More critical to economic mobility is the fact that, although rich and poor alike are utilizing the same quality of grazing, the effective price paid for access is substantially more for those who have to sell milk futures to pay for it. Also, there is more pressure on owners of small herds to over-graze and thus to run down their animals. Richer men are able to leave diminishing pastures sooner, and can complete the often difficult route up the mountains before the main body of tribesmen. By this means they are able to use their cheaper access to pasture to secure their herds against loss of breeding stock, which is a constant threat to the average herdsman. This is not to suggest that economic influence is used to secure formal political office, as has been the case with many settled tribes, but rather it is used to maintain a preferential economic status through manipulation of the credit requirements of their kin.

VI
DOMESTIC PRODUCTION, CONSUMPTION, AND THE DETERMINANTS OF VARIATIONS IN WEALTH

MANY aspects of what is often ethnographically presented as "the economy" have already been outlined. A detailed analysis of the herd, the household, and the domestic cycle will underscore many of the earlier general remarks about pastoral land use with a more precise, quantified formulation.

The materials discussed in this chapter are topically arranged in two general divisions. In the first, the types of herds utilized, production curves for selected herds, and averaged patterns of consumption are presented in general terms. This will provide a useful background against which data taken from every household in the population can be more closely analyzed in the second portion of the chapter.

THE HERD AS THE UNIT OF PRODUCTION

Apart from ventures of temporarily shared risk, each household strives for economic autonomy. The basis for this autonomy is the herd. Two different types of flocks are kept for the maintenance of the domestic unit.

Toklu

The least common is the herd of male yearlings (*toklu*) raised entirely for their cash returns in urban markets. Such herds are not, of course, self-perpetuating and are put together by the cash or credit purchase of male lambs of six months of age in the fall. The toklu herd is never the only herd owned by a family; it is held in conjunction with a balanced flock with reproductive capacity (*koyun sürüsü*).[1] The lambs for a herd of male yearlings must be collected in numbers greater than can usually be supplied by a single herd of ewes, and are occasionally purchased from peasants as there is no restriction on strain or breed since they are not used to form a stable herd. Usually the animals are of the Yörük breed (*geçik*). Few families raise male lambs to maturity; therefore they wish to sell them in the fall of their first year. This is because toklu must be herded separately from female animals after reaching six to nine months of age. The toklu herd does not provide subsistence *itself* directly, but only via the market place. Whether sold or kept to maturity, male lambs are an important source of cash income to the family (see Figs. 12 and 13).

Credit (*veresiye*), very common in animal sales among Yörük, is usually essential to the formation of a toklu herd. The high cost of such long-term credit can be critical in determining the profitability of such types of livestock management. On the surface it appears to be a very lucrative type of investment. The herdsman buys lambs and less than a year later sells sheep at well over twice the price paid for them. During the research period, lambs sold roughly at 75.00 T.L. while the market value of good yearlings was between 150.00 T.L. and 200.00 T.L. Prices vary according to factors having to do with both the condition of the animals and national trends in meat prices. If the animals are sold with the wool unsheared, their prices are higher.

However, the profit is narrowed by the need to hire shepherds and by supplemental grain feeds required in the severest months of winter (January and February). Each herd must be accompanied by at least one responsible grown shepherd, and preferably two. Extra herding labor is needed in most cases because herds of ewes and male yearlings do not graze well together; such labor is usually

---

[1] In many ways the function of the toklu herd in the nomadic Yörük society is analogous to the *emanent* system among the Yomut Türkmen of Iran, whereby wealthy men buy animals in excess of their own herding capacities and give them to the care of other families (Irons, 1969:255-257). Both toklu raising and the practice of emanent among the Türkmen serve to circulate capital investments by the rich within the tribal community. The Yörük do not give animals to the custody of others except under special circumstances as they feel the rewards to the owners are too unsure. The absentee caretakers have few compunctions about radically increasing their own meat consumption.

not available from one household. Sheep require constant attention in order to fully utilize their pasturage. If left to themselves, sheep will not consume anywhere approaching the amount of forage they would under a good shepherd's supervision, or so state the Yörük. They must be led from one tract to another. The problem with toklu seems to be that they are hard to manage when herded in conjunction with ewes, and that it is difficult to keep both types of animals grazing at the same time. Shepherds say that ewes often will refuse to eat at all when in a herd with the male yearlings. The wool that will be produced before the animals are marketed is usually held sufficient to cover the cost of hiring a shepherd, but cutting the wool lowers the market value of the animal.

What makes such investments risky is the need to buy the lambs on credit, which pushes the initial cost of the animals up 30 to 50 percent. The cost of credit is never referred to as "interest" (faiz), but is calculated through a number of circumlocutions. The cost of credit or *de facto* interest is the difference between the cash market value of an animal purchased and the value agreed upon as the sum to be repaid. Mature sheep bought on three years' credit have an agreed-upon-value for final repayment easily double that of current market prices. Credit costs in the purchase of toklu are usually less than those exacted in the similar purchase of mature sheep, reflecting the difference in the length of time in which repayment is expected. Frequently sheep are purchased on an installment scheme whereby the payments are regularly spaced over three years. Obviously this would make little sense when buying toklu which are to be sold within the year. Toklu are usually bought on an agreement to pay the total price by one year or at the time of sale (*satış veresiye*). These agreements are written contracts (*senet*).

A less common form of credit used for toklu is known as "*Ana ölmezse, kâr yarî yarî*" (If the principal does not "die," split the profit in half). Here, the seller of the lambs agrees with the buyer on a price above which he will collect one half of the profits at final sale. Should the animals die, the buyer is responsible at the price agreed upon. It is a variety of joint venture where the man who puts up the capital assumes little of the risk and has a claim on half of the profits. This type of agreement, because of its expense, is used only where the seller perceived a high potential for default. Some men have explained this as a way of doing *tokluculuk* (running yearlings) by having another do the herding and assume all responsibilities for loss, which a hired shepherd would not, in return for half of the profits. The form of credit extended and the cost are largely set by the demands of the sellers of the lambs as there is a ready cash outlet for these animals by sale to dealers in several nearby centers: Pīnarbaşī, Maraş, and Gaziantep. The high rates of interest charged are realistic appraisals of the risks involved.

There are a number of bad, or at least well soured, debts in evidence among the Yörük, and conversation in tents often turns to such matters. Foreclosure is possible but hard to carry out if it means wiping out a family's livelihood or if it involves close kinsmen. In foreclosures or forced settlements, the creditor rarely receives full return on the debt. The usual procedure is to carry the debt interminably until it can be settled in installments. Debts (and credits), while not prized in speaking of them, are rightly thought by the Yörük to be fundamental to their adaptation to a highly fluid market economy where continual cash flow is needed to maintain even the small herder.

The families most likely to engage in tokluculuk are those with large amounts of ready cash available to invest and who can thus escape the high cost of credit or get cheaper credit with an advance payment (*peşin*). It is not a route to rapid wealth, although a number of men have tried it in hopes of making large profits in a short period. One family was greatly indebted during the field work period because of a credit purchase of a herd of toklu which was decimated during the particularly severe winter of 1967 (see Table 1). In that case the creditors were non-kin of another lineage. They have agreed to wait for repayment but expect regular installments on the debt, which amounts to more than the total capital in sheep and camels owned by the family.

In general, the raising of toklu is an economic strategy that is most profitably utilized by the already wealthy pastoralist family. This has to do with the differential ability of families in different categories of wealth to absorb the risks of cash indebtedness when the outcome of the investment, if successful, is a cash return which does not likely serve to build up a balanced herd. Most families, in order to afford this sort of speculation, are already herding as many sheep in a balanced flock as they can maintain with their domestic supply of labor. Tokluculuk seems to function in the Yörük economy as an alternative area in which wealth can be deployed to generate more income, while still remaining within the framework of pastoral nomadism. Land, as Barth notes (1961:111-115) is often the means by which rich herders secure their capital holdings when animals are held in numbers beyond the point where they provide a good return. However, in this region of Turkey, land is at a premium and is difficult to purchase on credit. Animals in the form of toklu provide an outlet for the moderately wealthy to use their "good names" and credit facilities without becoming entangled in the complexities (and expenses) of buying land in an area where other residents are of different ethnic groups.

Koyun Sürüsü

The type of herd that forms the mainstay of every nomadic household is, like the tent itself, based on the continuity of its members. This herd, although dependent on the care of the herdsman, perpetuates itself as a breeding population. It is comprised of rams (*koç*), about two per hundred ewes (*koyun*), immature yearling rams and ewes (*toklu, şişek*), and lambs (*kuzu*).

Yörük rams have a productive breeding span of about four years, beginning in their second year. Ewes bear young from their second winter through their fifth or sixth under ideal conditions. They are culled out and sold soon after passing their first winter without freshening. Ewes are referred to by the Yörük according to the number of seasons they have lambed, for example a *dörter* is one which has lambed four times. Older sheep are called *kart koyun* and are candidates for sale even if they have not proven barren (*kīsīr*), should the family need money. The median age of animals in the "typical" herd is about three years (see Fig. 11). The gestation period is about 150 days and spring lambs are ready for sale at the end of the yayla season before or during the downward trek to winter pastures. Rams are kept separate from the ewes during the later portion of the summer, and are allowed to cover the sheep during mid to late September. The lambs are dropped, in the main, within a 15-day period in March.

The numerous factors which affect variations in wealth among households and types of domestic units will be taken up shortly. Before going into such problems, it is necessary to present some general facts about production and consumption. Since the family owning a herd is making its livelihood in the context of a cash economy, the flock's productivity must be gauged by two measures: production for direct consumption and production for conversion into consumables by way of market exchange.

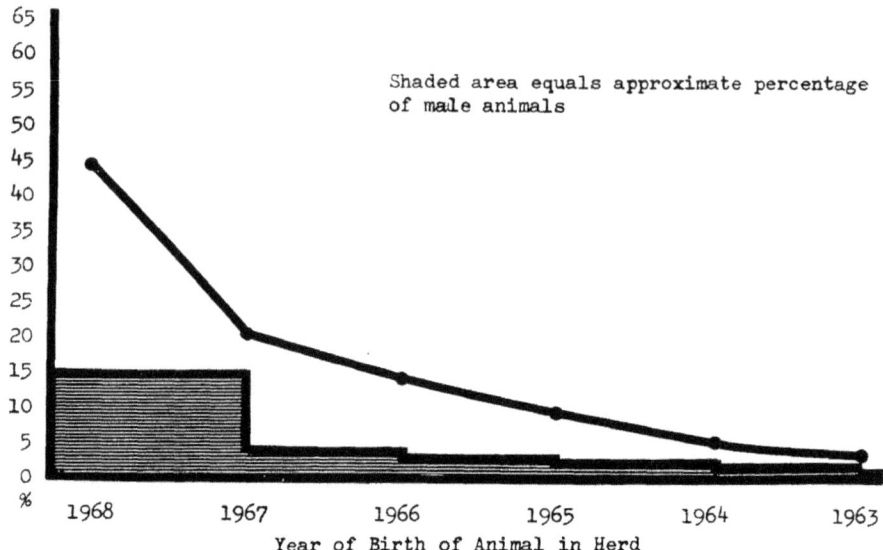

Fig. 11. Age distribution in median sized herd of sheep (245 animals). Shaded area equals approximate percentage of male animals.

Productivity of the Domestic Herd

The animals comprising the balanced household herd (not toklu) produce in three primary areas: more animals through reproduction, wool, and milk. All of these areas of production have been introduced in earlier sections, particularly in Chapter IV, but will be treated in more detail here.

The Natural Reproduction of the Herd. The most critical dimension of the domestic learning is the herd's maintenance and increase through natural reproduction. The rates of reproduction and the relationship between mortality, birthing, and herd size are shown graphically in Figures 12 and 13. Figure 12 represents 11 family flocks randomly selected with respect to herd size and history. Figure 13 presents the herds of most of the families of one patrilineage, exclusive of those in Figure 12.

Overall sales amount to a mean of 54.3 animals per herd of all age-sex groups as evidenced over a three-year period for the sample herds. Total average annual rates of reproduction are much higher (about 70 to 75 animals per 100 *mature* ones in a herd) with mortality and the incorporation of female offspring accounting for the difference between total production and sales. Several things are apparent from Figures 12 and 13, apart from the general averages. Since animal production represents the difference between bars B and C (animals born, animals died) it is clear that there is a tendency for this to be proportionately greater, that is to say, more productive, in large herds than in herds falling in the lower quartile of flock size (under 149 animals).

This could be important in determining socially differentiating features in the political economy if it were not for other factors which counteract such concentrating tendencies, for instance, the fluctuation in productivity of most herds, even within the limited span of three years. This variation is often related to annual differences in weather during kışlak, where most of the mortality occurs, for weather greatly influences both *bırakma* (spontaneous abortion) and resistance to diseases. Kışlak 1967-68 (K_2) was a very cold winter with heavy but uneven snowfall (see Tables 1 and 2). Kışlak 1968-69 (K_3) was a mild winter with little snow and mortality among sheep was correspondingly lower. Even though the wealthier herd owner can, perhaps, suffer periodically high rates of mortality among his animals with more equanimity than a poor man, fluctuations in mortality radically reduce the stability of every family's income base. Every herdsman is acutely aware of this and, apparently in response, each attempts to minimize any outward sign of distinction in wealth, just as he readily alleges such presumption in others.

In terms of the animals themselves, their sale rather than their meat is of first importance for the family. They are rightly considered capital (*sermaye*) and are never rashly allocated to the cooking pot. Animals are eaten only when they are on the verge of death. Then they are quickly dispatched by knife across the throat in accordance with Islamic law. If an animal dies of natural causes it is never eaten, sold, or otherwise given for human consumption. As many animals die in a manner that renders them ritually unusable as are butchered for the hearth.

Apart from meat consumption directly conditioned by herd mortality, animals are slaughtered on special occasions. At Kurban Bayramı (Feast of Abraham) one or more animals are sacrificed and eaten by members of the tent, their neighbors, and by non-Yörük poor who come for small portions. Animals are killed

150 THE YÖRÜK OF SOUTHEASTERN TURKEY

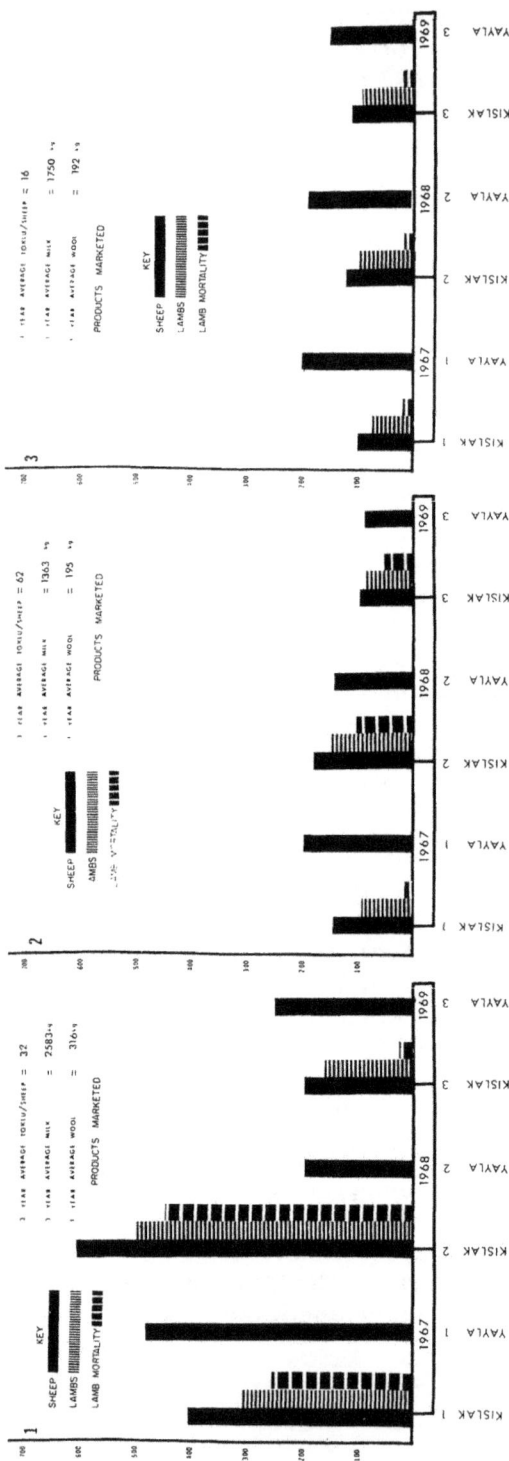

Fig. 12. (nos. 1-9). Fluctuations in herd size, lambing and mortality over a three-year period: 1967 through 1969 (annual cash sales per herd, in kg, in boxes).

PRODUCTION, CONSUMPTION, WEALTH 151

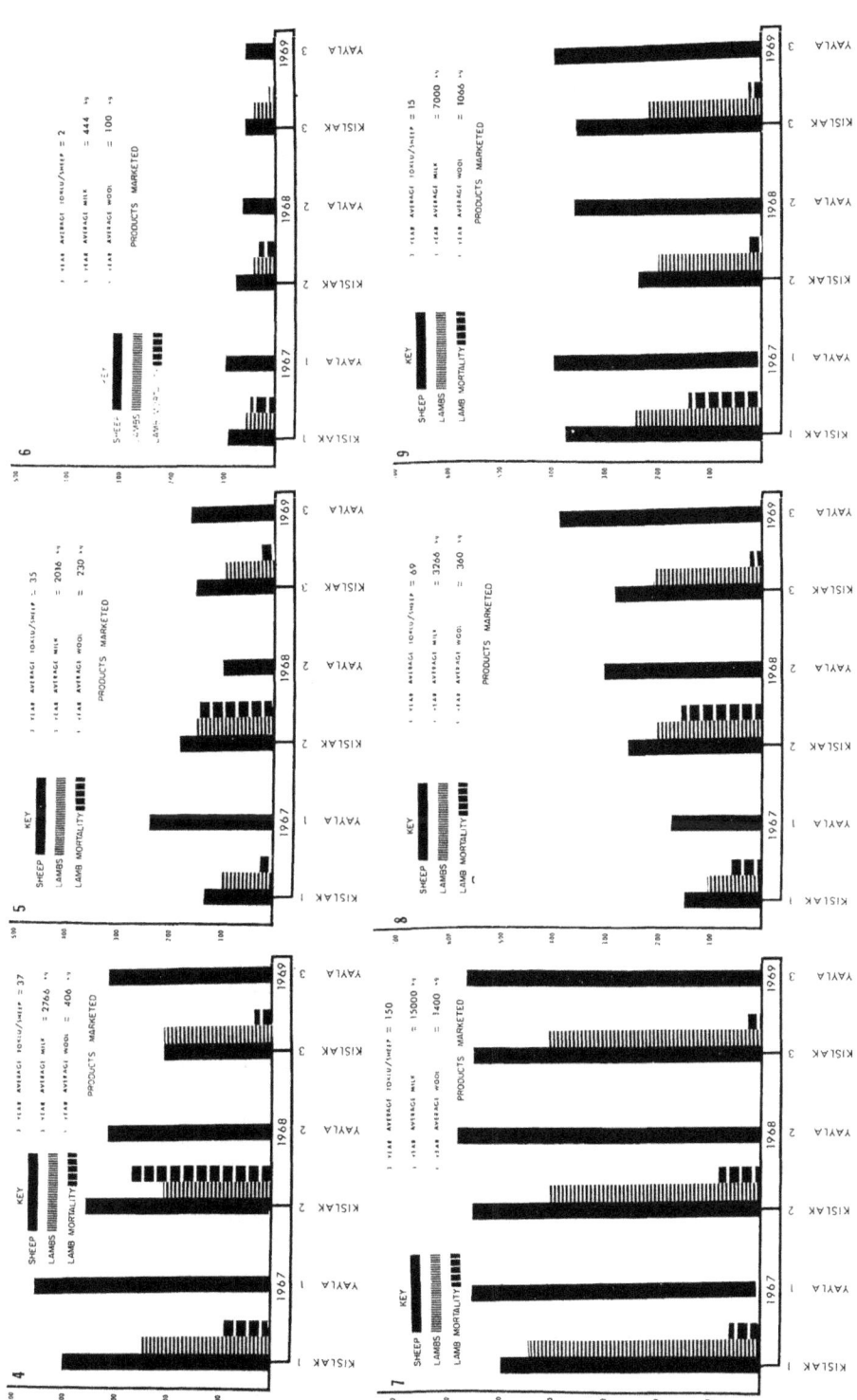

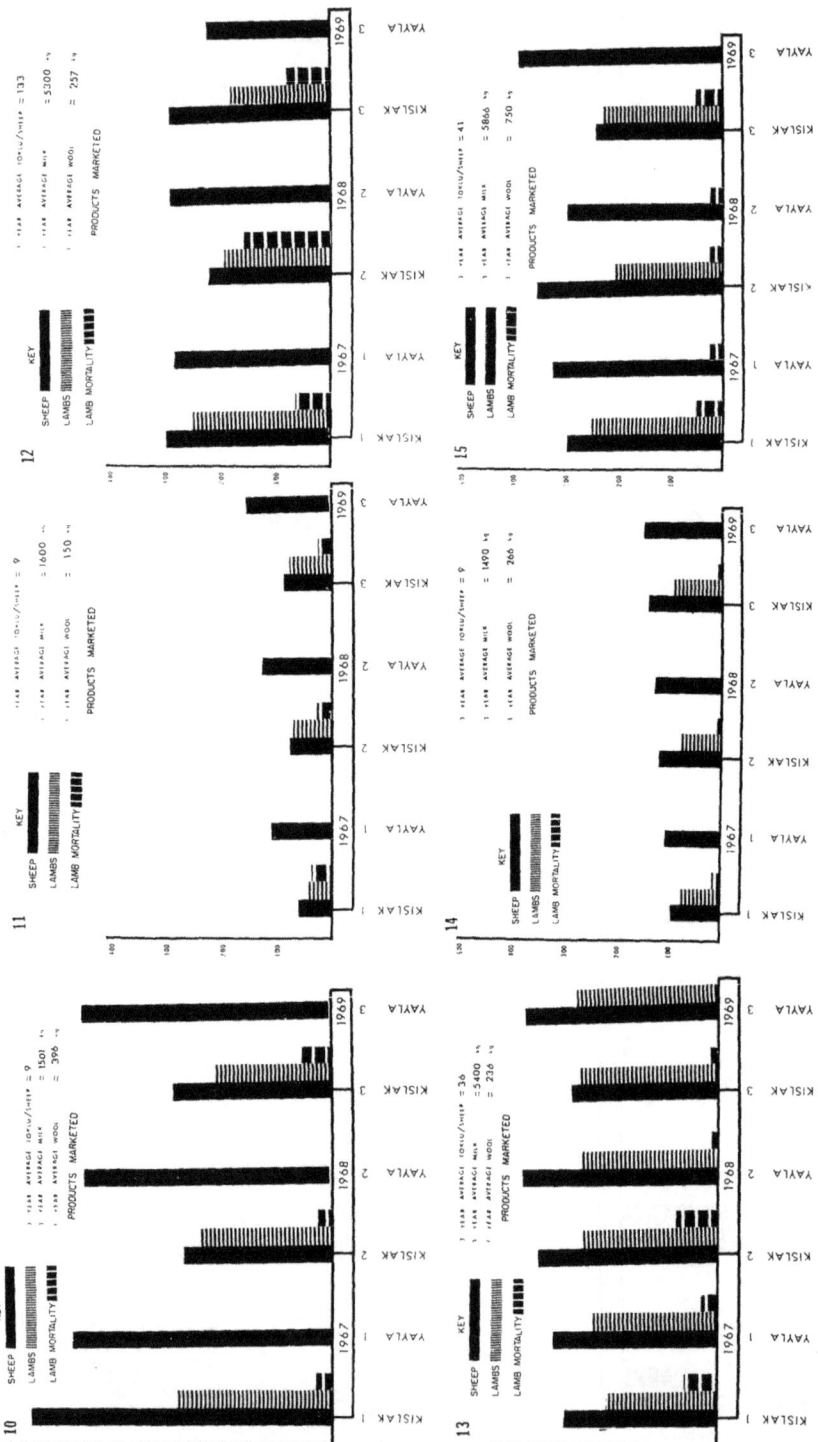

Fig. 13. (nos. 10–21). Fluctuations in herd size, lambing and mortality over a three-year period (cash sales, in kg, averaged for three years).

PRODUCTION, CONSUMPTION, WEALTH

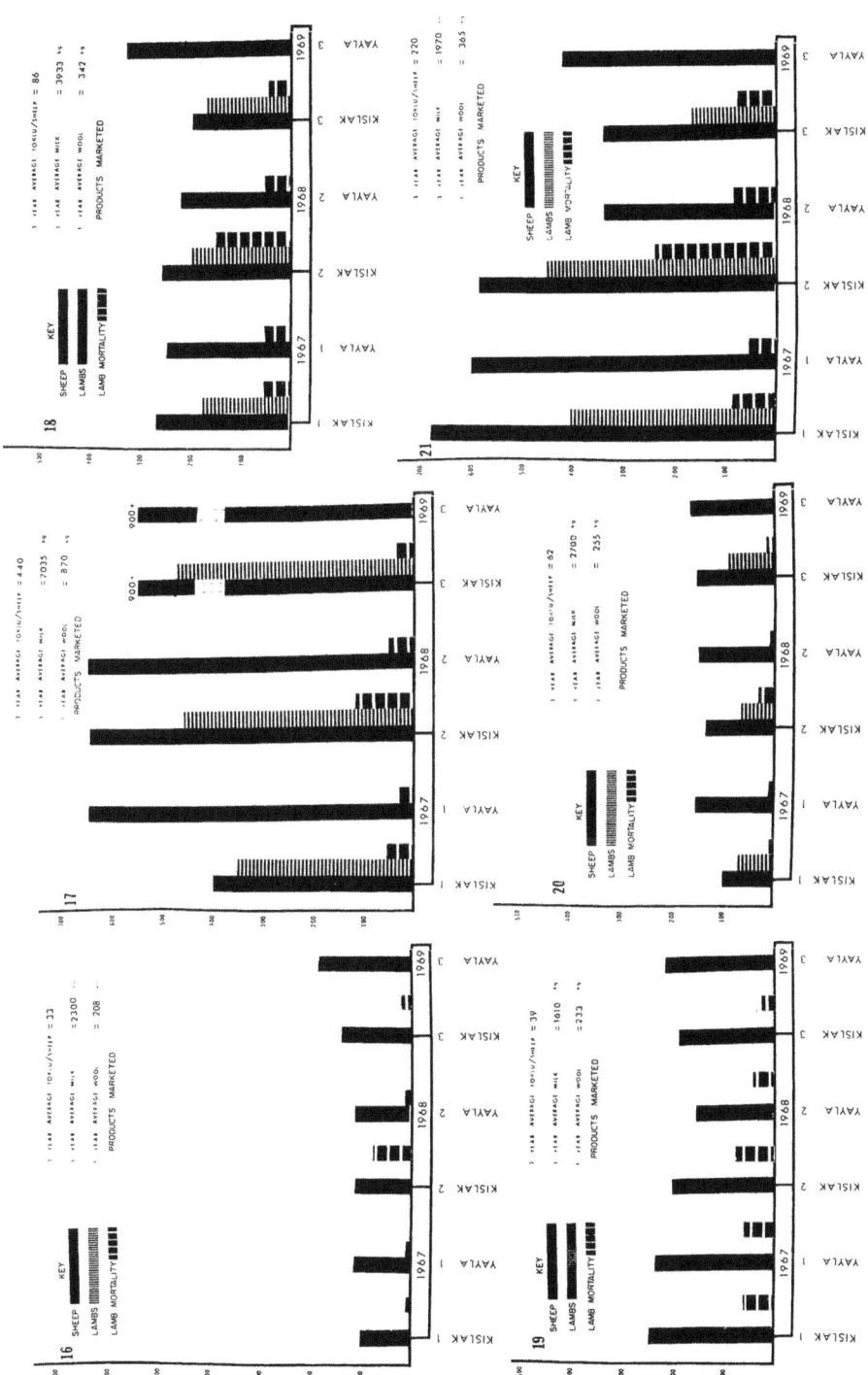

for important guests such as government officials, for the birth of a male child, at the erection of a new tent, to solemnize an important event such as an engagement, and to mark death memorial days (*matem*) and *mevlit* (recitation of the story of the birth of Muhammad). About five to 10 sheep a year are consumed in this way from the average herd of 268 animals; a wealthy man with greater demands on his hospitality might kill as many as 20 to 30.

Wool. Wool (*yün*) is frequently the largest single source of cash income, but paradoxically its social importance is less than that of either meat or milk. Wool can be incorporated into the household economy only in a limited way, and in goods for which the household's need is easily satisfied or put off. Secondly, although it is certainly of great economic importance as a means with which to pay for foodstuffs bought during the winter months in kĭşlak, it usually does not directly involve herdowners in special long-term relationships with specific purchasers, as does milk. The debts undertaken with urban storeowners for food staples, etc., are paid with wool not through any direct agreement to do so or through barter, but via other market routes. Unlike animals, which can be sold if need be at any time, wool is not a suitable means of responding to household economic emergencies, because it can be sheared only once a year in quantity.

It might be mentioned, parenthetically, that camels—which represent considerable capital (two to eight per family)—are also a means by which a family can react to a sudden demand for cash. The camels are a cross between Arab dromedaries and two-humped Bactrian breeds and cost about 1,500 T.L. to 2,000 T.L. per mature animal. They are used only to carry household goods on migration, and are not milked or ridden.

Household use of wool is for felt rugs (*keçe*), for flat-woven rugs (*kilim*), camel bags (*çul*), and such small items as belts and camel pack-saddles (*havut*). Clothing is made almost entirely of manufactured printed materials, ready-made items, or *pazar* (bazaar) tailored suits. Men wear European-style sport and suit coats over pants of a cut traditional for southeast Turkey, but one which is not traditional for the Yörük. Women wear traditional dress but of pazar purchased materials sewn at home on portable sewing machines, which are found in most tents and are the most substantial items taken by brides to their new homes. The tent itself is no longer made from the family's own herd as goats' hair is employed exclusively. Goats' hair (*kĭl*) is purchased from members of the Tekeli tribe either by the kilogram (1 kg. costs 10.00 T.L.)—about 50 to 60 kilograms are needed for a tent—or as a finished product made to order. Tents cost between 600 and 1,000 T.L. and are expected to last six to eight years.

Wool averages about 1.5 kilograms per mature animal and the mean sale of wool for the sample families over three years are 422 kilograms per annum. Since the mean price was 10.50 T.L. per kilo, the sale of wool represents a sizeable income, and one which does not fluctuate as much as do milk or meat. Some small amounts of lamb's wool are sheared and sold at a higher price in late summer.

Milk. Only in recent years has milk become a valuable cash-producing commodity. Older Yörük males sometimes claim to recall when milk was simply dumped by the roadside because it could not either be sold or used by the household in the quantities in which it was produced. This seems unlikely in the regular course of events and probably should be taken more as a verbal illustration of the dramatic changes which have put the Yörük in a completely cash market oriented economy where foodstuffs become crucial trade commodities. Formerly, only wool and animals were produced for sale, and then in amounts directly related to the need for foodstuffs and items outside the domestic mode of production. Now, as described in Chapter IV, the need to rent pastures has put virtually insatiable demands on the household's ability to produce for cash, as pasture prices are inherently inflationary.

Milk, apart from its recently developed relevance to pasture acquisition, is a major food staple. When it is available, a family consumes it with each meal, and it is drunk warm with *pekmez* (grape sirup) as a special treat. A sour milk drink (*ayran*) is much used. Yogurt is prepared daily and eaten with unleavened bread (*yufka ekmeği*) as a major meal of the day. A "cottage-cheese" (*çökerlek*) is eaten with hot bread and chives. Butter (*tereyağ*) is prepared by rocking separated cream in a skin or tin, both for winter and for daily cooking needs. *Beyaz peynir* (the white cheese ubiquitous in the Balkans and Near East) is eaten regularly and stored for winter use. Both cheese and butter are primarily made during the tail end of the milk season when the butter fat content of the milk is highest, and the total volume so diminished that the dairy tents are packed up for the year. Most tents have portable mechanical milk separators of Swiss patent which operate by a hand crank on the centrifuge principle. These separate the milk into highly concentrated cream and a largely fatless skimmed milk which is used for a dry cheese (*nor*). The butter fat rich cream is churned into butter or made into other products including a variety of enriched yogurt. Butter is stored in goat skins for winter use.

During the entire range of production, the household is consuming milk at a daily rate which, for a family of eight, declines from a peak of 10 liters to little more than a few cups by middle September. The dairy tents are closed by late July or early August. A herd (about 100 mature animals) monitored for production during the study produced 53.8 liters of milk on a daily average during the period it was in kĭşlak or moving across the İslahiye plain. During the period of migration to upland pastures production for both sale and use was drastically curtailed. While some days saw a nearly "normal" production, many days were milkless as the lambs needed all that was available. Daily production in this period averaged 100 grams per animal in milk usable in the household, compared with over 500 grams in kĭşlak. Once on the pastures, production immediately picks up and for a few weeks is at its peak, about 600 grams per animal milked per day. This soon begins to drop off rather steeply as pastures dry up.

CONSUMPTION OF MARKET PURCHASED COMMODITIES

Table 27 presents the mean annual domestic consumption of purchased goods and services for the households as averaged from the detailed statements of 12 tents. Mean family and herd size for the 12 is close to the overall median for the total population (seven to eight people, 245 sheep), so the figures might be taken, cautiously, as representative of general patterns. The data themselves were collected painstakingly through long discussion with heads of household, and assistance was rendered the informants by the ethnographer in preparing certain estimates. While some items may have been overestimated by informants in order to display an "ideal" pattern of consumption and a proper concern for the diets of dependents, it is likely that the overall mean is slightly low due to the omission of numerous minor categories of expenditure. Animal-related or income-producing expenditures were excluded from the table.

Not only is the reported mean annual expenditure of 9,136.45 T.L. strikingly large, but also the variety of items consumed is unexpectedly great. This is seen in Table 27 even though some items were either omitted or collected under broader rubrics. One item reported by a few families was margarine which although quite rationally purchased for use when butter ran out, seemed to the observer incongruous for a nomadic pastoral household.

In looking at each larger category, it is apparent that of the cereal and vegetable items consumed, flour or wheat for flour is the most important. The Yörük do not grind wheat when it is purchased in grain form, but take it to mills (@ .10 T.L./kg.). There is little saving to be had in doing it this way, but purity is assured. Also, some families mix barley flour (*arpa*) in wheat flour they have had ground. Of the 23 cereal and vegetable products listed, all but five are universally used. Rice is a luxury item for poorer tents, while lettuce and carrots are a matter of varying tastes. Baked loaf bread is bought only for a diversion, but it is not highly regarded.

Fruits, dried and fresh, are purchased in large amounts and featured often in everyday meals as either the basis for soup-like main dishes or as a compote. Pekmez sirup is a major source of sugar for all members of the household and is eaten as a main course with bread during winter months. Since sweet tea is consumed less by women and since granulated sugar is not used in any cooked dish, pekmez may be the primary source of sugar for much of the population. Tobacco is an important consumer good as, almost without exception, every married male is an inveterate smoker of cigarettes. No alcohol or opiates are used.

Table 27 also indicates the relative importance of village and market sources for the goods purchased, and the predominance of urban suppliers. All of the household non-food items and most of the foodstuffs come from the pazar. Goods bought from villagers usually do not involve direct dealings with the primary producer, but are transactions carried out through village peddlers who purvey their neighbors' produce to Yörük of numerous camp groups. Not infrequently, the same peddlers will buy meat butchered by Yörük when animals appear ill. The fact that the Yörük are known never to eat or sell meat not ritually killed makes it possible for them to do so. Otherwise it would be impossible to sell any meat not seen live on the hoof. In the main, items acquired from villagers are paid for in cash, and in every instance of barter the equivalencies are calculated by market measures.

Since herd products have already been described, it remains only to note several miscellaneous sources of consumables. Hunt-

TABLE 27

ANNUAL ESTIMATED CASH PURCHASES FOR DOMESTIC CONSUMPTION*

(12 households considered)

Item	English Name	Source of Item village	Source of Item town	Range of Variation min.	Range of Variation max.	Mean Amount per family	Unit Cost in T.L.	Total Cost in T.L.
1. firīn ekmeği	bakery bread		x	0 ea.	100 ea.	25 ea.	.75	18.75
2. buğday	wheat (grain)		x	0 kg.	2500 kg.	737 kg.	1.00	737.00
3. buğday unu	wheat flour		x	50	3000	1368	1.10	1504.80
4. bulgur	cracked wheat	x	xx	50	650	231	1.50	381.50
5. pirinç	rice (white)		xxx	0	150	52	3.00	156.00
6. makarna	macaroni		x	3	100	23	2.50	57.50
7. nohut	chick peas	x	xx	5	100	48	1.25	60.00
8. kuru fasulye	dried lentils	x	xx	30	200	94	1.75	164.50
9. mercimek	split peas	x	xx	3	75	28	2.50	70.00
10. kuru soğan	dried onions	x	xx	20	300	113	1.00	113.00
11. patates	potatoes	x	xx	35	500	200	.80	160.00
12. domates	tomatoes	x	xx	10	500	148	1.00	148.00
13. patlican	eggplant	x	xx	20	300	80	.75	60.00
14. biber	red peppers	x		2	100	35	1.50	52.50
15. kabak	squash	x		10	200	52	.40	20.80
16. taze soğan	fresh onions		x	10	200	56	.50	28.00
17. taze fasulye	fresh lentils	x	xx	10	200	56	1.25	70.00
18. hiyar	cucumbers		x	10	300	84	1.00	84.00
19. lahana	cabbages	x		2	100	33	1.25	41.25
20. havuç	carrots		x	0	50	14	.75	10.50
21. marul	lettuce		x	0	100	24	.50	12.50
22. kuru biber	ground pepper		x	1	50	13	5.00	65.00
23. turp	radish		x	10	100	43	.50	21.50
(sub-total for cereal and vegetable foods .... 3037.10)								
24. elma	apples		x	3	500	126	.75	94.50
25. armut	pears		x	0	100	32	1.00	32.00
26. kaysī	apricot		x	0	100	58	2.50	145.00
27. taze üzüm	fresh grapes	xx	x	50	250	189	1.00	189.00
28. incir	figs	x	x	0	50	20	1.25	25.00
29. dut	mulberries	x	x	10	200	45	1.25	56.20
30. portakal	oranges		x	15	200	95	1.00	95.00

PRODUCTION, CONSUMPTION, WEALTH 159

#	Turkish	English							
31.	karpuz/kavun	melons	xx		25	500	184	.50	92.00
32.	kuru üzüm	raisins	x	xx	15	300	173	1.75	216.00
33.	kuru incir	dried figs	x		0	100	36	2.00	72.00
34.	kuru erik	dried plums	x		0	50	13	1.25	16.15
35.	pekmez	thick grape sirup	x	x	30 lt.	400 lt.	170 lt.	2.25	382.50
36.	karma	thin grape sirup	x	x	0	200	60	1.35	81.00
37.	helva	halva (sweets)	x		0 kg.	50 kg.	24 kg.	6.00	144.00
	(sub-total for fruits and sweets)								1640.40
38.	siyah zeytin	black olives	x		0	50	10	5.00	50.00
39.	tavuk	chickens	x		0 ea.	10 ea.	1 ea.	10.00	10.00
40.	yumurta	chicken eggs	x		50	300	133	.25	33.30
	(sub-total for olives, chickens and eggs)								93.30
41.	kesme şeker	sugar in cubes	x		10 kg.	250 kg.	71 kg.	3.75	226.25
42.	toz şeker	sugar in bulk	x		25	100	63	3.50	220.00
43.	kahve (çiğ)	coffee (beans)	x		1	10	3	40.00	120.00
44.	çay (Turkish)	tea (Turkish)	x		30 pack.	200 pack.	68 pack.	4.00	272.00
45.	çay (kaçak)	tea (smuggled)	x	x	0 kg.	7 kg.	2 kg.	40.00	80.00
46.	tütün (gov't.)	tobacco (gov't.)	x		0 pack.	1000 pack.	464 pack.	.85	394.40
47.	tütün (illeg.)	tobacco (illeg.)	xx		0 kg.	8 kg.	2 kg.	13.00	26.00
	(sub-total for sugar, tea and tobacco)								1338.65
48.	gaz yağı	kerosene (lamps)	x		18 lt.	100 lt.	48 lt.	.50	24.00
49.	kibrit	matches	x		4 boxes	100 boxes	30 boxes	1.00	30.00
50.	giyimler ve kumaş	clothes and cloth	x		500.00 T.L.	3500.00 T.L.	1906. T.L.	--	1906.00
51.	kıl çadır	tent (dep./8 yrs.)	x		80.00	80.00	80.	--	80.00
52.	çay bardak	tea glasses	x		10 ea.	100 ea.	40 ea.	.50	20.00
53.	yemek tabağı	dishes (yearly)	x		1	5	2	5.00	10.00
54.	lamba şişi	lamp glass (shade)	x		0	10	4	2.50	10.00
55.	tencere kalayi	tinning pots and dishes	x		--	--	32.00 T.L.	--	32.00
56.	sağlık	medical (humans only)	x		75.00 T.L.	500.00 T.L.	261.00 T.L.	--	261.00
57.	çayhane	teahouse/restaurants	x		100.00	520.00	100.00	--	100.00
58.	seyahat	transportation	x		75.00	500.00	354.00	--	354.00
59.	tüfek masraf.	guns, ammunition etc.	x		00.00	500.00	200.00	--	200.00
	(sub-total for misc. items)								3027.00
	Total mean annual expenditure for foodstuffs (T.L.)								6109.45
	Total mean annual expenditure for dry-goods and services (T.L.)								3027.00
	Total mean annual expenditure for all household purchases (T.L.)								9136.45

*Minimum family size = 3 persons; Maximum family size = 20 persons; Mean size = 7 persons

ing is regularly engaged in as a sport. Primarily rabbits and game birds are shot, but it is doubtful if they are worth the money spent on weapons or ammunition. Children often collect fish when streams are low in the fall, but this is of little dietary significance. In the yayla pastures fragrant sweet tasting weeds are gathered for "mountain tea" (*dağ cayi*). These are dried and also used during the winter, but never to the extent that regular tea is used. Wild chives and other grasses are collected in the summer for use with yogurt. In the winter the fortunate tent will be able to collect good quantities of mushrooms, which although of little real importance, are a welcome addition to a menu made duller by the absence of fresh milk.

Animal manure, particularly camel dung, is often used as fuel for the cooking fires, but wood is preferred where available. Sheep dung is collected around the animal tents in the spring and is sold for a small amount to farmers outside the area who truck it away. Local farmers will not purchase it.

LIMITED PARTNERSHIPS

Implicit in the above discussion is the fact that the fundamental unit of common consumption and production is the single household. Each tent possesses its own means of support and there is little joint holding of income producing capital by members of more than one co-resident household.

An exception to this is when occasionally men from different households will buy sheep to market immediately. This is invariably a short-term partnership (*ortaklık*) to take advantage of momentary market fluctuations, and is not the primary occupation of the parties involved.

For example, in the fall men sometimes agree to buy their neighbors' six-month old lambs or yearlings for marketing. Older sheep and sheep which have proven infertile in the previous lambing are also collected in this way. Such animals are culled out of the herd each fall or when the need for cash arises. The usual procedure is for the owner and his sons to bring animals to market or to sell them on the pastures to urban traders who come there to buy them for later sale in city markets. However, not infrequently Yörük men will collect such animals and serve as middlemen for their neighbors and kinsmen. They collect the animals on "summer credit" (*yaz veresiye*) or "sale credit" (*satış veresiye*), meaning that they pay the seller before the end of summer or immediately upon the resale of the animals. The effective cost of such credit, unlike long-term credit, is not great and sometimes is not figured at all if payment is to be made within a very short period. The price of the animals is based on local market prices, and the middlemen secure their profits by either holding the animals for a slight upturn in the market or by shipping them in hired trucks to more distant markets where they have heard that prices are better. The men who engage in such activities, similar to those who collect wool, do not seem to make a large profit on balance and have to sustain a considerable risk. The sheep may die en route to the market, fall off the truck, or be damaged by careless driving. Also, if they are not sold immediately upon reaching their urban destination, it is likely that their condition and weight will decline, adversely affecting their value.

Rich herdsmen do not usually bother with such enterprises and regard them as overly speculative. The men who set up such limited partnerships are often close agnates and almost always near kin. The agreements are informal and temporary. They split the proceeds according to the amount of initial capital risked by each partner in hiring the trucks or making first payments on the animals. Losses are shared according to the same formula. Market information is obtained from individuals coming through the camps and local markets from various towns, and is often checked out by using the telephones available in town to call contacts around the region—local merchants, dealers, and relatives with whom the individual has had past dealings.

The men who engage in such speculation among the nomads are usually middle income herdowners attempting to turn their otherwise idle time in the fall to profit. It would seem that the long-term effects of such endeavors are more in providing a marketing service for others, rather than forming an easy avenue of economic advance for the entrepreneurially minded.

DISTRIBUTION OF WEALTH IN NOMADIC SOCIETY

There is no significant productive capital in nomadic society apart from the animals herded. Only six nomadic families studied owned shares in fields or urban property from which they derived a predictable income, and for none were such holdings the primary resource. Variation in herd size therefore is an accurate measure of a family's economic standing.

162   THE YÖRÜK OF SOUTHEASTERN TURKEY

The following discussion outlines variations in wealth according to descent groups and types of household, with reference to some of the factors which contribute to a family's ability to manage its animals. These concerns are directly relevant to an appreciation of both nomadic pastoral forms of land use and the political economy. Although many of the problems taken up in the subsequent sections have been discussed in the growing literature on nomadic pastoralism, few attempts have been made to quantify many of the obvious variables. Likewise, there is no published analysis which uses statistical tests to measure possible relationships between labor, patterns of domestic consumption, and wealth in animals. It is the objective here to provide such quantification and preliminary testing for co-variation among variables likely to affect the distribution of wealth.

Wealth and the Lineage

The mean number of animals owned by the 168 families for whom this information is available is 268.35 according to an economic survey conducted by the author in the fall of 1969. This figure includes lambs of both sexes born the previous spring. Median herd size is 245 animals with a mean standard deviation of 164.5. From Figure 14 it is apparent that despite the closeness of the mean to the median, the range in animals within the first standard deviation is considerable.

These animals are unequally distributed among descent groups just as they are held in unequal amounts by the households which comprise the lineages (see Fig. 17).[2] In spite of the obvious range of herd sizes evidenced within each descent group (Fig. 15 and Table 28), it is necessary to examine the degree to which such membership is associated with the differences in wealth among families. For lineage membership closely to determine individual wealth in most societies, different descent groups would have to enjoy varying control of crucial resources. This is patently not the case among the Yörük where not only do lineages lack collective rights, but also cannot bring force to bear in gaining access to grazing. Nevertheless, as developed earlier, there is a strong

---

[2] An example of wealth being drastically concentrated in the hands of one lineage was found in one of the two villages studied here. In Nogaylar, however, the reasons for this distribution have more to do with the fact that the earlier settlers were given free land and were of one large lineage. Latecomers, of all lineages, have had a difficult time acquiring property.

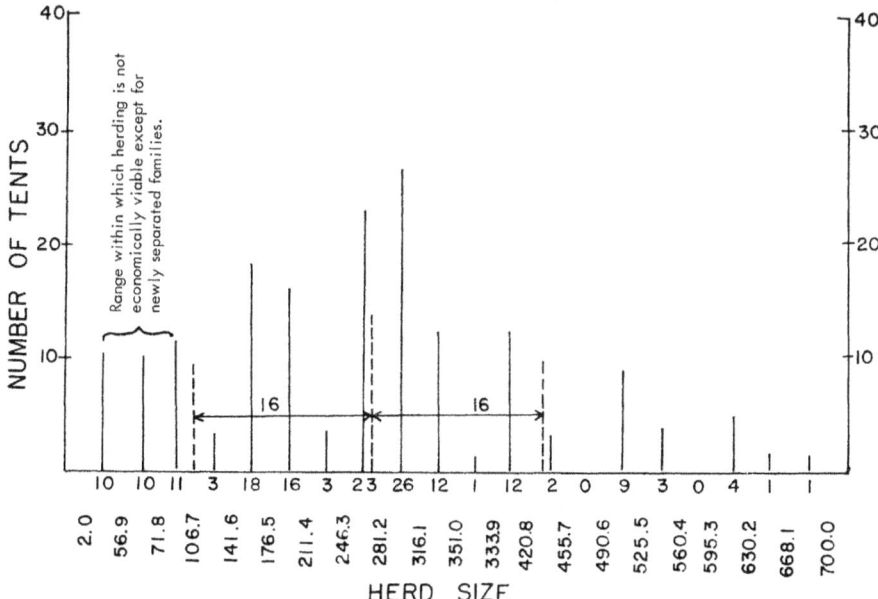

Fig. 14. Wealth in sheep among nomadic Yörük households, yayla, 1969 (168 tents considered, 20 intervals established, std. dev. = 164.50, mean, 268.35, median = 245). Number of tents in graph refers to number of tents in each category of sheep holding.

ideology which calls for supportive behavior among agnates, particularly in dealings across close descent lines.

In a similar vein, it might reasonably be argued that segmentation, although precipitated largely by such non-economic factors as conflict over marriage arrangements, pasture borders, and personal misunderstandings has an ultimate economic effect. Segmentation at a low level of genealogical inclusiveness, as is often the case, would have an equalizing effect in that it would prevent larger groupings from using their pooled strength in arranging preferential market and credit transactions to the detriment of the larger Yörük population. Since credit very clearly follows lines of agnation, a large lineage could come to represent an instrument for insuring its members by means of readier loans against the hazards which attend nomadic animal husbandry.

PATRILINEAL DESCENT GROUP	NO. OF TENTS	SHEEP MEAN	STD. DEV.
Göğebakanlar	44	315.5	194.2
Arabalar (Arab Aliler)	28	232.9	135.1
Çavuşlar	14	283.8	74.9
Satılar (Sadıkoğulları)	11	241.7	211.7
Kelebekler	11	333.6	99.5
Daz Kirliler	10	293.5	176.2
Haytalar	3	160.0	36.1
Cüce/Sermayeler	3	316.7	76.4
İzmirli	3	435.3	208.2
kölemenler	2	250.0	212.1
Tırtarlar	2	200.0	70.7
Kabaklar (İzmirli)	2	225.0	106.1
Hacı Çİller (İzmirli)	2	400.0	141.4
Sarı Keçililer	26	192.8	171.6
Osmanlı	8	255.6	153.3
Tekeli	2	250.0	0.0
(Other)	1	110.0	0.0
TOTAL TENTS 172		OVERALL MEAN 268.35	STANDARD DEVIATION 164.50

Fig. 15. Nomad herd size per lineage (survey taken in late summer 1969; includes previous spring's lambs).

TABLE 28
DISTRIBUTION OF HOUSEHOLDS BY QUARTILE OF WEALTH AND FAMILY TYPE FOR EACH DESCENT GROUP

Descent Group	WEALTH CATEGORY: SHEEP				FAMILY TYPE				Total
	1st Quartile	2nd Quartile	3rd Quartile	4th Quartile	Nuclear	Extend.	Poly.	Poly. Ext.	
Göğebakanlar	7	5	15	17	29	13	1	1	44
Satılar	3	3	3	2	8	1	1	1	11
Arabalar	9	4	8	7	23	5			28
Kölemen	1			1		2			2
Kelebekli		1	6	4	3	7		1	11
Çavuşlu		4	7	3	6	5		2	14
Hayta	1	2			3				3
Izmirli		1		2	2	1			3
Hacıçiller*			1	1	1	1			2
Kabaklar*		1	1		1	1			2
Cücü/Sermaye			2	1	1	2			3
Tırtar		1	1		2				2
Sarıkeçili	9	11	3	3	16	9		1	26
Tekelli	1		1			1			1
Osmanlı	1	3	1	3	3	5			8
Daz Kirli	3		3	4	6	2	1	1	10
Other Yörük	1				1				1
TOTAL	35	36	52	48	105	55	4	7	171

*Izmirli sections

This is the case, arguing from non-statistical evidence, and likely would be more so if the benefits of lineage solidarity were immediate enough to be appreciable to all of the participants. This latter is not so because an adult man in breaking with a collateral line does not lose all of his agnates, but only some of them. Furthermore, of those he loses, many no doubt were peripheral to his daily life. The net effect is, however, to narrow not only his but his descendants' practical network of kin *within* a named descent group.

When one considers only lineages selected because they are known to have members important in the mercantile life of İslahiye, another dimension of the problem of variation in wealth among households in different lineages suggests itself. The lineage best represented in İslahiye, and one which has more than one ağa of influence, is the Göğebakanlar kabile. Table 28, shows that 32 out of 44 nomadic Göğebakanlar households, 73.7 percent as opposed to the 50 percent expected where wealth was equally distributed within the lineage, are in the upper two quartiles of wealth in animals (see Fig. 16 for percentile rankings of wealth). The Kelebekli, Çavuşlu, and İzmirli descent groups show a similarly lopsided concentration of households in the upper half of the rankings by wealth (99 percent, 71.4 percent, and 71.4 percent respectively). All of these lineages have a substantial sedentary representation of rich men who are in local commerce.

The effects of such ties on wealth distributions in the nomadic community are played out in two diametrically opposed directions. On one hand, the lineages with wealthy men, and with more ample avenues of credit open to their members, can render more supportive assistance to families who must borrow to increase their productive capital. Secondly, at the extreme lower end of the economic scale, poorer families among the nomads will consider settlement a more viable alternative than would comparable tents of a lineage which did not have settled members. The latter would be expected to attempt to maintain themselves in the pastoral economy where the similarly positioned nomad of a partially sedentarized lineage would prefer to settle with the expectation of aid from kinsmen.

PRODUCTION, CONSUMPTION, WEALTH

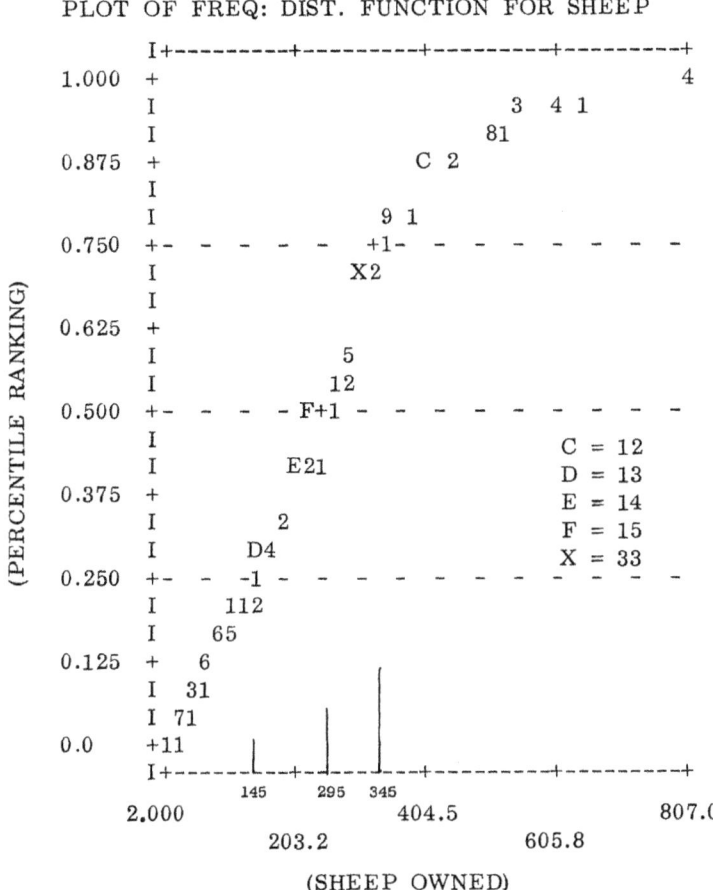

Fig. 16. Plot of rankings in wealth by percentile for nomad herds.

1st quartile = 35
2nd quartile = 35
3rd quartile = 52
4th quartile = 46
       total = 168 household herds

THE DOMESTIC MODE OF PRODUCTION

The pastoralist Yörük with some justification might be regarded as producing primarily for domestic consumption and the maintenance of the household. Although they are in a cash economy and dealings are phrased in terms of money, cash received for goods is deployed in ways which, for most, have goals other than simply the accumulation of more cash.

While there is considerable variation in the amount different families spend on consumer goods, and not all families are able to purchase certain desired food and apparel items in the same amounts measured *per capita*, there is remarkable uniformity in the nutritional standards among tents of all classes of wealth. All live in roughly the same quality tent, with few distinctions in external appearance that represent anything more than different family size. The usual areas to which increased wealth is directed are apt to be related to prestige. For example, rich men acquire second wives at high bride prices, devote much wealth to hospitality and charity, and interact with kinsmen in a preferential way. While such men may well be manipulating agnates for personal gain, the goal is not strictly monetary profit. If it were, many could expeditiously sever many kin ties which serve to recycle much of their profits back into the nomadic community through often risky credits and uncollected debts.

There are many theoretical issues raised by the problem of defining the goals of production which need not be gone into here. Much of this is simply by way of saying that domestic production is related, at least in part, to the need to provision the household unit within certain culturally defined limits. Given this, it is necessary to examine variations in the production of wealth in the light of differences arising from the variability of households in the society.

The Domestic Cycle and Wealth

Anthropologists tend to regard the "native" household as a social entity of great permanence. Yörük households, however, are formed by the unwished but predictable departure of married sons. The average length of time that a Yörük tent has been in existence is only 14.7 years.

The new household is launched on its independent course with a complement of personnel and animals detached from a parental unit. Its subsequent development in terms of wealth is contingent on a wide number of factors. Lineality, discussed above, is among these. More important, however, are those variables which directly condition a family's ability to utilize both the fact of supportive kin ties and the productive capacities of sheep.

These variables are either functions of the composition of the tent *or* are defined by the circumstances of its origin. In the former category are such factors as the number of people co-resident, their ages and sexes, and their abilities to assist in the provisioning of the unit. Other things which condition wealth stem from the causes for the tent's initial separation, most notably inheritance (see Chapter IV for background discussion) and the length of time since separation.

The extent to which variations in wealth are attributable to the make-up of the household can be taken as a measure of the different potential for production offered by different compositions. This, if founded on sound evidence, would be an empirical basis for an assertion that the Yörük nomadic pastoral economy is inherently responsive. The degree to which wealth variations reflect differences in inheritance, however, would indicate potential, although not necessary, restrictions on economic mobility, the basis of social inequality in most societies.

In sedentary agricultural societies of the Near East, operating as they do in a context of land scarcity, the amount of land tilled is likely to be determined more by the social position of the domestic unit and the wealth of the parental household than by the amount of labor available. In such situations, increased demands for consumption often outweigh any gain in productivity achieved through the increase in household size. Moreover, increased household consumption demands among peasants often are met with a tightening of individual belts, rather than by varying either production or worker productivity. It will be shown that in the nomadic society herd size or wealth is adjusted to the amount of labor available and the consumption demands of the tent.

Households have already been ranked according to their wealth in animals in Figure 16. From this ranking they have been further grouped in quartiles whose three internal cutoff points in terms of sheep owned are 149, 249, and 349. In Table 28 this construction is used to show lineage variations in wealth. The following discussion attempts to explain the factors placing families in a given bracket of wealth. Quartile measures are useful here because they summarize the finer distinctions shown in the histogram in Figure 14. As the quartiles contain virtually the same number of families, they can be used in the construction of contingency tables. They correspond with distinct modes in the distribution of animals among tents.

Types of households among the nomads have been listed in Table 28 by their occurrence among descent groupings. This typology will now be explained and utilized in analyzing variations in wealth. There are two reasons for this typology. Each type of the four constructed is a statement of varying specificity about the composition of the tent and its development. The types are not primarily based on any Yörük model of their own society, although the polygynous families can be regarded as the stated ideal of many household heads. Whether or not men professing to want second wives actually would take them if they could, is hard to say.

The first type of household is the *nuclear family*, defined here as the co-residence of one married couple and single dependents, including formerly married but now single individuals. This type of composition is useful to distinguish because it represents, for the most part, an expanding unit with no married dependent sons awaiting the opportunity to separate. It is the most common form of household (105 cases) and predictably the youngest. The second type, the *simple extended family*, is defined by its potential for fissioning, and contains two or more married couples and their single dependents. Married brothers living together are included under this rubric as are the more common arrangements of father, mother, and married son(s). This is less frequent in occurrence (55 cases) than the nuclear type and has a high potential for dissolution through the separation of the dependent married couple(s). The third type is the *simple polygynous family* which is defined as a nuclear family in which the head has two or more wives (four cases). This type is structurally much like the nuclear family but is usefully distinguished from the former because the families which constitute this type are mature ones, rather than the typical nuclear one which has its growth ahead of it. The fourth type is the *polygynous extended family*, structurally similar to the simple extended type in that the potential for fission is great. There are seven cases of the polygynous extended family. While it is not central to the typology's purpose, the four types do roughly correspond to what many Yörük informants would describe as the ideal progression of the household from its inception as a small nuclear unit to one in which the head has acquired both a second wife and

PRODUCTION, CONSUMPTION, WEALTH   171

married co-resident sons. The typology is only one of many possible.

Variations in demographic size within each type and the range of overlap are shown in Figure 17, and need not be taken up in the discussion. It should be noted, however, that despite the seemingly wide range of family sizes within each type, a chi square test confirms that there is significant association between household type and the number of people in a tent (Table 29). This should be kept in mind in considering the association between family type and wealth (to be taken up shortly).

Variations in Inheritance and the
Development of the Household

Each household is set up with an inheritance of animals. The amount of inheritance is, in main, a product of the wealth of the parental unit and the number of males in the tent at the time of

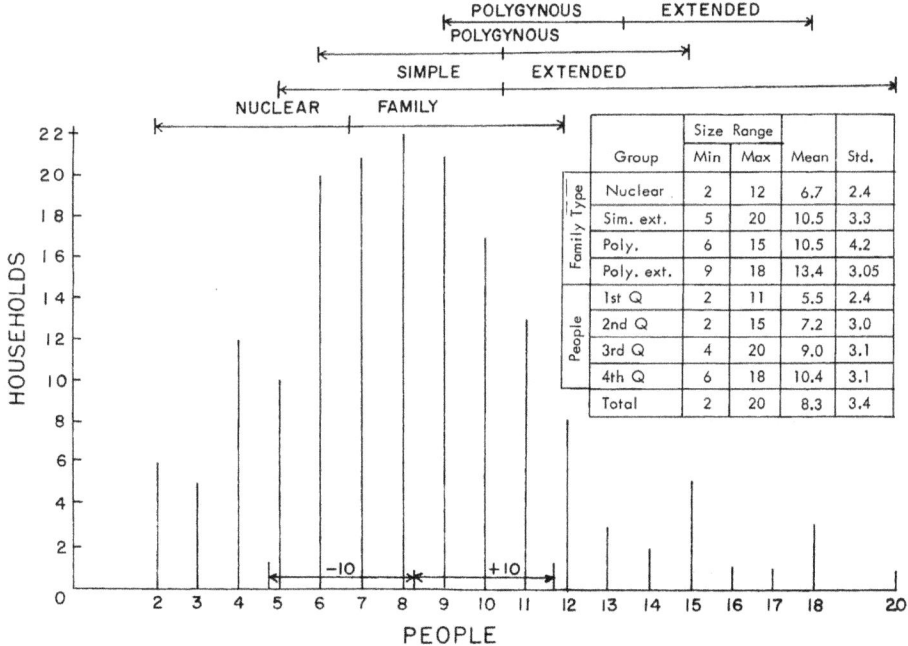

Fig. 17. Variations in family size and household types.

TABLE 29

CHI SQUARE TEST FOR ASSOCIATION BETWEEN FAMILY TYPE AND
NUMBER OF PEOPLE CO-RESIDENT IN TENT

(171 households)

Family Type	People By Quartiles				Total
	2-6	7-8	9-10	11-20	
Nuclear	46	33	21	5	105
Extended	5	10	14	26	55
Polygynous	1	1	0	2	4
Polygynous Extended	0	0	1	6	7
Total	52	44	36	39	171

Note: $x^2 = 65.2$
$p = .001$
$d.f. = 9$

separation. The son who separates has little control over these factors, although he may put off separation if the herd is particularly diminished by disease. In a structural sense inheritance, when considered as a variable affecting a domestic unit's present wealth, is an economic fact external to the dynamics of the household which has received it. While it may well condition the subsequent development of the family, as will be demonstrated, it is an economic fact that is not responsive to changes in demand or consumption. It is given only once.

Another matter over which the family has no influence is the time which has elapsed since the household's separation. As years pass, the household is involuntarily placed in changing patterns of social obligations and responsibilities which carry their own advantages and penalties in the household's attempts to secure its livelihood.

Primary analytic attention will be given to inheritance because of the obvious sociological implications for Yörük society if it is shown to condition wealth or family type.

Tables 30 and 31 illustrate the distribution of inheritance and the mean number of years each family has been in existence for both quartiles of wealth and type of household. In looking at Table 30, it is clear that there is some relationship between wealth groupings and the average number of sheep inherited by families ranked

TABLE 30

CIRCUMSTANTIAL VARIABLES AFFECTING WEALTH ACCORDING TO QUARTILE OF WEALTH

	mean values per variable		
Variable Sheep	Years Separated	Inheritance in Sheep	Number
1st Quartile, 0-149	6.8	43	35
2nd Quartile, 150-249	11.8	76	36
3rd Quartile, 250-349	17.6	114	52
4th Quartile, 350-800	18.2	201	48
Total	14.7	147	171

	standard deviations per variable		
Variable Sheep	Years Separated	Inheritance in Sheep	Number
1st Quartile, 0-149	6.8	42	35
2nd Quartile, 150-249	8.6	103	36
3rd Quartile, 250-349	11.8	124	52
4th Quartile, 350-800	12.4	203	48
Total	11.6	114	171

TABLE 31

PERCENTAGE OF VARIATION IN WEALTH: CURVILINEAR COEFFICIENT OF DETERMINATION ACCORDING TO AMOUNT OF INHERITANCE

Statistic	N	Significance	Coefficient of Determination
ETA^2	148	$p = <.01$	$\eta^2 = .64$

Note: Independent variable equals sheep inherited.

in this manner. The 48 families in the fourth quartile have, on the average, inherited more than four times the number of sheep than have families in the first. As the standard deviations for these means are also great, it is evident that the relationship is not narrowly rectilinear. The relationship of wealth to inheritance is not attributable to changes in family size through the years. If anything families are getting larger and, as was shown earlier, inheritances are also on the increase. Therefore, the correlation of inheritance with wealth or variations in wealth cannot be held a product of there having been more sheep and fewer people in the past generation. Rather, it indicates an increase in mean number of sheep owned per family. It is further related to the increased costs of pastoral production, in that it now takes more animals to maintain an individual in the nomadic economy.

Table 31 shows the distribution of values for this variable. The ETA^2 coefficient of determination ($\eta^2 = .64$) is very high; 64 percent of variation in present wealth of households is "explained" by differences in the amount of inheritance received (see Downie and Heath, 1970:90, 115-119). Since ETA^2 is curvilinear (and unsigned), it is a measure of both positive and negative determination. The extent to which large herds are predicted by large inheritances is partially shown in the coefficient of linear determination, r^2, which likewise is significant ($r^2 = .21$; $p = <.000$).

While this finding is of importance in suggesting that economic status is more dependent on parental wealth than is often supposed, it must be used cautiously. First, in looking at this and at other statistics as well, it should be kept in mind that the nomadic population is itself a sample biased toward the "middle" in that the poor are selected out more regularly than are the rich. Moreover, the ETA^2 coefficient, by its nature, excludes those cases in the independent variable column which are coded as having zero inheritance. It should go without saying that neither ETA^2 nor r^2 is cumulative, and the values for these coefficients when based on different independent variables run with the same dependent variables (e.g., herd size) are not mutually exclusive in the percentage of variation they explain. For example, both age of the head of household (Table 32) and the number of years the household has been in existence (Table 33) predict present wealth to a considerable extent. However, a social understanding of wealth variation is not achieved by merely weighing the differences among the coefficients for these factors. It is interesting that inheritance predicts

TABLE 32
PERCENTAGE OF VARIATION IN WEALTH: CURVILINEAR COEFFICIENT OF DETERMINATION ACCORDING TO AGE OF HEAD OF HOUSEHOLD

Statistic	N	Significance	Coefficient of Determination
ETA^2	168	$p = .05$	$\eta^2 = .64$

TABLE 33
PERCENTAGE OF VARIATION IN WEALTH: CURVILINEAR COEFFICIENT OF DETERMINATION ACCORDING TO YEARS SEPARATED

Statistic	N	Significance	Coefficient of Determination
ETA^2	142	$p = .05$	$\eta^2 = .53$

Note: Years equals the independent variable.

wealth, and it is also significant that age and years of establishment do the same. The latter is one measure (although a crude one) of the degree to which economic statuses are responsive to individual effort.

It is no revelation that inheritance influences wealth in societies where the means of production are rooted in a class-stratified economic system. The Yörük, however, have no pervasive class system, and possess a strong egalitarian ideology according to which each man's flocks prosper by the effort given them and, more to the point, numerous natural factors affect the herd's physical condition. Therefore, it is important to note that inheritance has a significant influence on wealth for the population at large. Had only the recently separated households been considered, the determination of wealth differentials by inheritance would be both higher and less useful for an evaluation of the possible social effects of the high coefficient.

While inheritance does significantly predict a family's later accumulation of wealth in sheep (Table 31), it does not work to stratify the society along economic lines. This is because a major factor in the distribution of inheritance is the number of males in the tent. Since this same variable is important in the production of wealth originally, those families with many animals are also those who will divide the capital among numerous heirs. Even though the herd is partially replenished after each division of anticipatory inheritance, it is still the case that rich men often cannot pass on anything approaching their total holdings intact. While men who receive large inheritances do succeed better economically than those who receive little, each generation will find its large inheritors coming from different families in a fairly random pattern.

The degree to which inheritance conditions the subsequent evolution of the household's form is more difficult to express statistically as the radically different number of cases for each family type together with the small number of categories in the independent variable column precludes the use of ETA^2. However, there are considerable differences between the mean values of inheritances ranging from nuclear, extended through the simple polygynous type of household which suggests that inheritance may be a conditioning agent (Table 34). Most likely the relationship is not a determining one, but rather reflects the influence of inheritance on wealth that already has been demonstrated.

There is a close association between family type and wealth (Table 35). Since there is less variation around the means for wealth by family type, it is possible to compute an ETA^2 coefficient of determination. Table 36 shows that a high percentage of wealth variation is explained by family type.

In looking at distribution of household types by quartile of wealth we find that of the 35 families in the lowest bracket, 34 are residing in what has been defined as the nuclear type, with one family of the extended variety. In the second quartile of wealth, 29 households are nuclear, nine are extended and one is polygynous. In the third quartile of wealth, this changes radically with 28 of 52 households being nuclear, 22 extended, and two polygynous. The highest category of wealth, families in the fourth quartile, displays a similar proliferation of extended and polygynous types of domestic arrangements. Twenty-four families are in extended households, eight in polygynous ones and 16 in nuclear types. This has been summarized in Table 35 together with the chi square test for association between wealth and type of composition.

TABLE 34
CIRCUMSTANTIAL VARIABLES AFFECTING WEALTH ARRANGED BY FAMILY TYPE

	mean values per variable		
Variable Family Type	Years Separated	Inheritance in Sheep	Number
Nuclear	11.2	89	105
Extended	20.3	149	55
Polygynous	14.2	260	4
Polygynous extended	27.8	163	7
Overall mean	14.7	147	171

	standard deviation per variable		
Variable Family Type	Years Separated	Inheritance in Sheep	Number
Nuclear	10.3	110	105
Extended	10.6	182	55
Polygynous	9.6	330	4
Polygynous extended	18.1	105	7
Overall mean	11.6	114	171

Wealth and the Composition of the Household

In an economy where a major impetus to production is provided by domestic consumption requirements, one can measure the extent to which income-yielding wealth varies with the demands of the unit of consumption.[3] The responsiveness of a family's productive capital to the internal dynamics of the domestic mode of production is central to the generally unstratified nature of Yörük nomadic society.

---

[3] Much of the subsequent analysis derives from approaches to pre-industrial economic systems suggested by E. R. Wolf (1966:14-16 ff.) and M. Sahlins (1971). The concept of an economic system in which the intensity of the domestic mode of production can be measured against domestic demands for consumption is first advanced by A. V. Chayanov (see Wolf, 1966:14-15).

TABLE 35

CHI SQUARE TEST FOR ASSOCIATION OF WEALTH
AND TYPE OF FAMILY

	Sheep by Quartiles				
Family Type	0-145	146-249	250-349	350-800	Total
Nuclear	34	26	28	17	105
Extended	1	9	22	23	55
Polygynous	0	0	2	2	4
Polygynous extended	0	1	0	6	7
Total	35	36	52	48	171

Note: $x^2 = 44.7$
$p = .001$
$d.f. = 9$

TABLE 36

COEFFICIENT OF DETERMINATION OF VARIATION IN
WEALTH BY TYPE OF FAMILY

Statistic	N	Significance	Coefficient of determination
ETA^2	168	$p = .01$	$\eta^2 = .45$

family type is the independent variable

Table 37 shows that families vary considerably in their composition when differentiated by the quartile of wealth to which they belong. Table 38 outlines the same variability according to the typology of household forms introduced earlier. From Table 37 it is apparent that some relationship exists between specific attributes of the household, e.g., the number of adult males and wealth in sheep. In fact, all of the variables listed show increases in mean values for each sequentially higher category of wealth. The number of people in a tent, in particular, rises sharply with each quartile of wealth.

The chi square test for association (Table 39) confirms a close fit between the size of a family and its wealth. According to the measure of curvilinear relationships, 57 percent of the variation

TABLE 37

COMPOSITION OF HOUSEHOLDS BY QUARTILE OF WEALTH IN SHEEP

Number of Sheep	People per Tent	Married Sons	Adult Males	Adult Females	Adolescent Males	Adolescent Females	Children	Number
A. Mean Values Per Variable							
1st Quartile 0–149	5.5	.03	1.21	1.09	.62	.56	1.94	35
2nd Quartile 150–249	7.2	.33	1.89	1.72	.83	.69	2.03	36
3rd Quartile 250–349	9.0	.62	2.58	2.21	.94	.92	2.33	52
4th Quartile 350–800	10.4	.81	2.98	2.46	1.10	1.10	2.69	48
Total	8.3	.50	2.28	1.95	.91	.85	2.29	171
B. Standard Deviation							
1st Quartile 0–149	2.4	.17	.73	.29	.95	.89	1.20	35
2nd Quartile 150–249	3.0	.53	1.04	.85	1.00	.89	1.30	36
3rd Quartile 250–349	3.1	.87	1.43	1.00	1.02	.99	1.69	52
4th Quartile 350–800	3.1	.84	1.33	1.20	.80	.83	1.74	48
Total	3.4	.75	1.36	1.06	.95	.92	1.55	171

TABLE 38

COMPOSITION OF HOUSEHOLDS BY QUARTILE BY TYPE OF FAMILY

Number of Sheep	People per Tent	Married Sons	Adult Males	Adult Females	Adolescent Males	Adolescent Females	Children	Number
			A. Mean Values Per Variable					
1st Quartile 0–149	6.7	.03	1.66	1.41	.90	.78	1.97	105
2nd Quartile 150–249	10.5	1.31	3.40	2.69	.85	.87	2.66	55
3rd Quartile 250–349	10.5	0	1.50	2.25	1.00	2.00	3.50	44
4th Quartile 350–800	13.4	1.43	3.14	4.14	1.43	1.00	3.43	7
Total	8.3	.50	2.28	1.95	.91	.85	2.29	171
			B. Standard Deviation					
1st Quartile 0–149	2.4	.17	1.03	.65	.97	.94	1.28	105
2nd Quartile 150–249	3.3	.60	1.16	.86	.89	.86	1.72	55
3rd Quartile 250–349	4.2	0	1.00	.50	1.41	.82	3.11	4
4th Quartile 350–800	3.05	1.34	1.46	1.34	.98	.82	1.62	7
Total	3.4	.75	1.36	1.06	.95	.92	1.55	171

TABLE 39

CHI SQUARE TEST OF ASSOCIATION OF WEALTH IN SHEEP
AND NUMBER OF PEOPLE IN TENT

(171 households)

Number of People	Sheep by Quartiles				Total
	0-145	146-249	250-349	350-800	
2-6	22	19	8	2	51
7-8	7	5	17	14	43
9-10	5	6	16	10	37
11-20	1	5	12	19	37
Total	35	35	53	45	168

Note: $x^2 = 54.8$
$p = .001$
$d.f. = 9$

in wealth is explained by the size of the household. This measure provides some documentation for the flexibility built into the nomadic pastoral economy: despite overall inequality in wealth, as demand increases in the form of more population to be supported, the domestic unit is able to respond with increased animal production utilizing the additional labor. Thus, wealth that is unequal in its distribution among families is continually under adjustment when measured by the number of individuals within the units.

This can be refined somewhat in order to distinguish the functions played in determining wealth by each of the dimensions along which household composition is measured here. The ETA^2 coefficients were computed for all of these variables and, without burdening the reader with more tables, it is sufficient to note that the number of adult males and adult females both predict wealth variations at very significant levels: $\eta^2 = .53$ and .51 respectively with $p = .01$. The number of married sons does not evidence any close relationship to wealth among families which have such sons, but is important in predicting wealth differences between those who do and those who do not have co-resident married sons (see Table 35). The number of adolescent males, females and children (ages 8-16, 0-7 respectively) does not correlate at a significant level with variations in wealth when taken alone.

This latter fact is not surprising for even though individuals in those categories contribute to the family's increased demand for consumption, they themselves are not producers. Therefore, it was thought advantageous in evaluating the consumption demands and the labor available for households of different categories to consider two new variables which would express the differing make-up of households in these areas: one showing the ratio of consumers to workers and the other indicating the ratio of workers to sheep.[4] Each household is scored for each of these analytic attributes; the general distinctions are based on the different capacities for contributing to the household economy according to age and sex. The main disparity is that between the high consumption of infants and adolescents (coded .5 and 1.0 respectively) and the lower work capacities of the same (coded 0.0 and .8 respectively). Adults were given codes of 1.0 for both their consumption and working abilities. These codes are admittedly arbitrary, but the larger distinction between juveniles and full adults is justified by the divisions of labor within the household. Although children are put to work as soon as they can effectively perform minor tasks, they do not contribute to major areas of production to any appreciable extent until adolescence. At that time, however, their consumption requirements seem to rise drastically. Their requirements for clothes and items of personal adornment, the expenses of minor gold coins for daughters, together with the nutritional demands of body growth make them seemingly more than full consumers.

In general, although somewhat arbitrary and tentative, the index of consumers to workers (or the dependency ratio) in a tent is a meaningful measure of differences in a vital area of the domestic economy. In its lower range, as it approaches 1.0, it expresses "minimum dependency" in that each consumer is also a worker. Or, conversely, the social demands of consumption are minimal per worker. The second index, that of sheep to worker, is a measure of output per worker in the household. Its analytic import is that as the ratio increases, it suggests increasing productivity as more sheep are maintained by each worker in the family.

[4] The uses made here of the indices of productivity and consumer to worker ratios are not in every instance the same as suggested by Sahlins. In main, they differ in that no attempt is made here to show how actual coefficients of consumer/worker to sheep/worker are deflected from an "ideal" linear regression whereby all productivity is in response to increased consumer demand. The concepts introduced by Sahlins are felt here to be extremely useful analytic tools, and he is not responsible for any flaws in their application to and interpretation of Yörük data.

TABLE 40

SCATTER PLOT OF WEALTH IN SHEEP AND NUMBER OF PEOPLE IN TENT

(168 observations)

```
          I+---------+---------+---------+---------+
    607.0 +          1         1         1         1
          I
          I
          I
    572.8 +
          I                              1
          I          1 1 1         1
          I
    538.7 +              1         1
          I            2 1    1    2  2        1    1
(sheep)   I
          I              1 1
    404.5 +          1 2 3   1 1 1 2 1       1
          I                            1
          I    1     1 1 1   1 3 2         1 1    1
          I       1    5 4   3 2 1 1 2       1     1 1
    270.3 +          2 3 1   2 1
          I    2     1 3 2   2 3 3 1
          I 1      1 5 1 3   2 1 1         1
          I 1        1 1     1 1                1
    135.3 +1 1 3   1 3   1   1       2
          I 2 1        1 1 1
          I   2 2   3 1 1 3       1
          I 3   2   1 1 1     2 1
    1.000 +        1 1
         -+---------+---------+---------+---------+
        0.000                11.00              20.00
                5.500                 15.50
                            (people)
```

| | | | COEFFICIENT OF |
STATISTIC	N	SIGNIFICANCE	DETERMINATION
r	168	p = 0.00	$r^2 = .49$
ETA²	168	p = <.01	$\eta^2 = .57$

(ETA² independent variable is people)

The ratio of consumers to workers decreases sharply in extended family arrangements as compared with nuclear families. This suggests that the nuclear form of household may be less efficient in operation in the sense that each worker has to "carry" more dependents. Further, there is a decline in the mean values for this index as one moves upward through the four quartiles of wealth. In the fourth quartile, the ratio of consumers to workers in households is, on the average, 1.26 whereas it is significantly higher in the first quartile, 1.44. The ratio of sheep to workers, or the index of productivity, displays a similar but more marked progression associating wealth with efficiency: 73.0 sheep are maintained per worker in the fourth quartile and only 27.8 per worker in the first quartile.

In terms of wealth in general, a significant percentage of variation in wealth is predicted by the consumer/worker index. The ETA^2 coefficient of determination for this relationship is $\eta^2 = .34$, with an attained level of significance of p = .05. This is preliminary statistical confirmation of the proposition that demand within the domestic unit conditions total production.

The Relationship of Labor to the Demands of Consumption

Apart from providing certain general measures against which types of family organization can be evaluated, the above two indices are analytically useful in another way. We have already noted that there is evidence that total productivity is adjusted, in part, to household consumption demands as measured by the dependency ratio of consumers to workers. Both indices employed together should provide an insight into how families react to increased demands in situations in which, theoretically, their production can be adjusted.

There is some empirical justification for concluding that a major response is increased labor output for workers in the family. Table 41 shows that 37 percent of the explained variation in worker productivity is determined by the consumer/worker ratio within the family. In other words, there is evidence that at the total group level, consumption patterns affect the intensity of labor or the efficiency of the worker. It should be kept in mind, of course, that full adjustment of production to simple domestic demands is not to be expected, since, as we have noted before, much production is deflected into the community at large through credit, etc.. In any

TABLE 41

SHEEP/WORKER INDEX OF PRODUCTIVITY VS. CONSUMER/WORKER INDEX

(Total Group)

Statistic	N	Significance	Coefficient of Determination
ETA^2	168	$p = .01$	$\eta^2 = .368$

Note: cn/wk = independent variable

TABLE 42

SHEEP/WORKER INDEX OF PRODUCTIVITY VS. CONSUMER/WORKER INDEX

(First Quartile of Wealth in Sheep)

Statistic	N	Significance	Coefficient of Determination
r	35	$p = .014$	$r = .42$
ETA^2	35	$p = >.05$	$\eta^2 = .66$

Note: cn/wk = independent variable

event, the relationship is strong enough to demand further explication.

In the preceding discussions, analytic recourse was made to the quartile divisions of wealth in Yörük society according to which families are ranked. These partitions in continuous gradations of wealth, have proved useful because families in one quartile often differ significantly in many other characteristics from those in other quartiles. For example, the quartiles can be used to compare the degree to which families of differing wealth alter their labor efficiency in response to the ratio of workers to consumers in the household. Examining the relationships of sheep/worker ratio versus consumer/worker index (Tables 41-45), it is clear that there is a significant percentage of variation in the sheep/worker index determined in each quartile by the ratio of consumers to workers. Although there appears to be considerable variation among the coefficients of determination for the four individual

TABLE 43

SHEEP/WORKER INDEX OF PRODUCTIVITY VS. CONSUMER/WORKER INDEX

(Second Quartile of Wealth in Sheep)

Statistic	N	Significance	Coefficient of Determination
ETA^2	36	$p = .05$	$\eta^2 = .38$

Note: cn/wk = independent variable

TABLE 44

SHEEP/WORKER INDEX OF PRODUCTIVITY VS. CONSUMER/WORKER INDEX

(Third Quartile of Wealth in Sheep)

Statistic	N	Significance	Coefficient of Determination
r	52	$p = .000$	$r = .66$
ETA^2	52	$p = .01$	$\eta^2 = .89$

Note: cn/wk = independent variable

TABLE 45

SHEEP/WORKER INDEX OF PRODUCTIVITY VS. CONSUMER/WORKER INDEX

(Fourth Quartile of Wealth in Sheep)

Statistic	N	Significance	Coefficient of Determination
ETA^2	45	$p = .01$	$\eta^2 = .59$

Note: cn/wk = independent variable

quartiles, a conservative approach to the statistic best serves the purposes of analysis. While the first, second, and fourth quartile (Tables 42, 43, and 45) do show differing ETA^2 values too much weight should not be placed on these differences as the distribution of the data is so loose that small variations are amplified by the coefficient.

There is one outstanding divergence from the general pattern among the wealth categories: the percentage of variation in productivity determined by the ratio of consumers to workers in the third quartile (Table 44), the wealth bracket which ranges from 250 to 359 animals owned. Families in this category apparently alter their output per domestic worker to an extraordinary extent: some 89 percent of the variation in worker output, as measured by the index, is determined by the ratio of consumers to workers within the tent. Since the data are largely linearly distributed, the r statistic is also useful. The coefficient of linear determination indicates that to a very high degree (44 percent), the families in the third quartile are able to increase productivity per worker in reaction to increased demand (Table 44). Thus this category of wealth is shown to differ markedly from the other three. Again, it would be misleading to attach too much significance to the difference between the coefficients for the different quartiles of wealth, but the high η^2 value for the third quartile suggests that families of that bracket are more closely attuned to domestic need in their production than are the other groups. In a *tentative* way, this range of herd size, when compared to the other three, might be taken as "optimum" for a domestic mode of production since not only is worker productivity high, but the variability of productivity is more clearly related to the demands of domestic consumption. Rather than put forth such a contention as a demonstrated finding, it is realistic to reaffirm that the importance of these measures is in the future analysis they suggest.

The overall implications of these findings regarding productivity, consumption, and demand within the family could be of some theoretical importance. By demonstrating how families of different wealth categories respond to demand arising within the household, it is possible to explain how the domestic mode of production is able to support a surplus of consumers in anticipation of later contributions to the labor force.

It was demonstrated earlier that the number of people in a tent is a good predictor of its wealth. However, in order to accept

the propositions that production is a response to population and that
the distribution of animals, while uneven among families, is moving
toward equalization in terms of individuals, it is necessary to explain how a family can invest in consumers and at the same time
increase production. A partial answer is supplied by the above
brief analysis of productivity as determined by household requirements. Workers in the tent can increase their efficiency under
such internal pressures. It is reasonable to expect that the ability
to adjust productivity to consumption, and to increase productive
wealth in sheep through increasing inputs of domestic labor will be
important factors in the demographic structuring of the Yörük population.

The discussion in this chapter has ranged over a broad spectrum of subjects and ideas; from general statements of production
levels and market requirements to the abstract concepts of worker
productivity and consumption needs. Certain aspects of production
and determinants of household wealth have been more precisely
formulated than has previously been attempted in the literature on
pastoral nomadism. Some of the tests have simply confirmed the
suggestions of earlier researchers regarding pastoralists: that
nomadic pastoralism is a highly flexible and responsive form of
production. Other portions of the analysis have devolved around
the use of analytic techniques developed by others and applied to
new data in the Yörük economy. Most notable among these is the
attempt to measure and compare productivity and the distribution
of wealth.

Two aspects of the analysis may have broader application in
research concerning other populations and other modes of production. First, a fundamental analytic distinction is drawn, distinguishing determinants of wealth rooted in the circumstantial place
of the household in society from those factors influencing wealth
through the internal dynamics of the family. Thus, it is possible
to evaluate the contributions of such fixed factors as lineality and
inheritance to the distribution of wealth, apart from such dynamic
domestic parameters of production as the family labor supply and
consumption demands.

Second, an attempt has been made to provide the reader with
as much of the analyzed data as is consistent with clarity of presentation. A fundamental problem in analyzing domestic output in
pre-industrial societies is measurement and quantification. Wealth
in sheep among the nomad Yörük is a more accurate expression of

their relative economic standing and total production than any more abstract indicator devised by the anthropologist and employable in the field. Students of peasant and primitive populations are forced to make a number of often tenuous assumptions regarding wealth and production because income-producing resources or capital are controlled through many intricate, often concealed, byways of the system. For this reason, the statements made in the preceding pages about the interrelationships of such variables as population, family type, and inheritance take on a special significance, not because of any subtlety of analysis, but because of the intrinsic precision of the units measured.

VII
NOMADIC SETTLEMENT AND CHANGES IN SOCIAL LIFE

SEDENTARY members of the Saçïkara and other Yörük tribes are vital elements in the social and economic life of the nomadic pastoralists. Settled Yörük are important in two major ways. First, sedentary Yörük—not only of the village described in this chapter, but of all the communities in the region—form the most important linkages a nomadic family will have to the national market system. The purchase of food staples, supplementary grains for their animals, and a wide variety of transactions with the non-Yörük world are conducted through sedentary Yörük kinsmen and friends. Those nomadic Yörük with agnates in either of the two villages in İslahiye where there is an appreciable Yörük population may be fortunate enough to gain the use of free or cheap winter grazing on mer'a lands controlled by these people.

Secondly, the sedentary Yörük community by its very existence widens the range of viable options open to the herdsman as he maps his domestic strategy. In an area such as the one traversed by the Yörük pastoralists where ethnicity is a major social marker, the realistic chances of success after settling are much enhanced if the settler can join kinsmen rather than strangers.

This chapter describes the settlement of formerly pastoral nomadic families of Yörük in a village in the İslahiye district of Gaziantep Province, focusing in particular on some of the factors that select families out of nomadic pastoral society and lead them to settle; the joint settlement of related families as distinguished from the isolated settling of individual households; the reasons why some are successful in the new economy and others are not; and certain changes in social life which have taken place as adaptive responses to changes in production and resource utilization.

The focus here is on how members of a nomadic pastoral economy adopt a different system of production, rather than on how the population shifts from one "culture type" to another. The analysis will assume that nomadic pastoralism is an economic strategy carried out by rational individuals attempting to achieve acceptable economic returns, not merely striving to conform to a self-image of themselves as "nomads." Consequently, any decision to leave pastoralism for another occupation is a rational one, given the information and technology available to the participants. The extent of any community's market involvement is an empirical matter which will likely vary from group to group, but in Turkey it is of significance in every contemporary case.[1] Among the Saçıkara, as we have noted, many of the daily transactions are phrased in an idiom of equivalent exchange such as with town-based peddlers and peasants who visit the high summer yayla camps to trade for wool, meat, butter, and small amounts of cheese. The underlying value, however, is determined by prices in the local markets, not fixed by custom or in any way unresponsive to supply and demand.

This point, obvious from the previous chapter, is somewhat belabored here because the assumption of this analysis of settlement is that the Yörük are making economic decisions in abandoning nomadism, as are those who do not settle. While similar individual strategies could be described for groups not so deeply immersed in a market economy, clearly market demands are part of the Yörük economic adaptation. Fluctuation in the price of wool and meat on the national scene have serious repercussions locally. The transition to a sedentary life, therefore, while involving a change of resource base and concomitant social adjustment, does not necessitate a shift from subsistance or precapitalist economy to a cash economy. That transition has long since been made by most contemporary societies in the Near East, and the present tribal structure is as much an adjustment to that fact as it is to the material prerequisites of herding.

---

[1] See Beşikçi (1969), Hütteroth (1959), and Kolars (1963) for accounts of such market involvement by nomads in Turkey.

The decision to settle, like all economic decisions, can be made only by family (tent) heads and not by a leader on behalf of the other members. Each household as an independent economic unit succeeds or fails as it chooses between differing economic strategies. Apart from alternative approaches to nomadic animal husbandry, including choice between concentration on milk production, wool and lambs, or the raising of male yearling sheep (tokluculuk) for the market, there is the ever-present question of taking up a sedentary specialization. There are now as many settled Yörük as there are those who are still nomadic.

Nogaylar village itself consisted at the time of Yörük entry of a small number of "Çerkes" or Nogay Turk families, the remnants of a larger population drastically reduced by malaria and emigration in the previous generation. As a result, four of the original Nogay families had come into control of the lands originally granted by the Ottoman government to approximately 100 families of immigrants from the Caucasuses in around 1856. Although the contemporary village contains only a small proportion of the population which can claim any Nogay ancestry, the name of the village derives from their presumed place of origin and that half of the village inhabited by non-Yörük is usually referred to as "Çerkes," which is how the Nogay are known in the area.

The legal process of settlement was fairly simple on the surface, although it involved the abrupt transition from nomadic tent life to the fixed residence of the settled farmer.[2] The Yörük, as required by law, immediately built dwellings in the villages, copying the Çerkes model of reed and mud (saz), two-roomed, one-story thatched houses. This would prove to be one of the few cultural borrowings from the Çerkes, soon to become intimate neighbors and close enemies of the newly arrived Yörük.

Settlement in the physical sense began in the fall of 1949 when two closely related lineages arrived at the north edge of the village, where they camped in the area bordering the village commons (mer'a) and away from the better watered lowlands. This was in accordance with the directions given by the Toprak Komisyonu

---

[2] The land granted must be used by the grantee, who must reside in the village in which the land is registered. The land cannot be sold for 20 years, and a nominal payment is required by the State which is of no financial burden. Land is assigned to individuals, not to families or tribes. Thus all adults of the group which settled together 20 years ago in Nogaylar have title to some land.

(Land Commission) which said that houses had to be laid out in regular rows along the village road which led to neighboring communities to the north. The 29 non-Yörük Turkish landless peasants who also received land under the same grant settled in the lower half of the village around the houses of the Çerkes. Most of these settlers, while they had been employed by the Çerkes' ağa, had not lived in the village proper on a regular basis. These basic social distinctions are maintained to this day.

DISTRIBUTION OF WEALTH AND SETTLEMENT

Considering here just the Yörük, it is appropriate to review some of the causes for the settlement of formerly nomadic households. On the one hand, it is useful to distinguish settlement due to poverty or other reasons where concerted group action is not attempted. This process is quite different from group decisions to settle. In Nogaylar, both approaches to settlement occurred. Seven households followed the initial arrival of 30 households. Another nearby village, Sayburun, and the district center, İslahiye, likewise display a dichotomy in the motivations and subsequent development of Yörük households who settled alone as opposed to group action by related families.

Distribution of wealth is obviously a factor in determining who will settle and under what circumstances. Animal holdings in the nomadic society represent wealth, as few households among the nomads both herd and farm. Total animal population for all nomadic sections is regulated by the amount of grazing available throughout the year. How these animals are distributed among households depends, we have already shown, on such variables as labor supply, size of inheritance, pasture fees, bride price outlays and return, and the family's ability to acquire and use cash credit. Herding skill and sophistication in the use of veterinary medicines are also important. Presumably, disease, inclement weather, theft, and other natural disasters strike irrespective of wealth, but their effects are felt differently by different wealth categories. This clearly dictates different options and strategies for families of varying economic circumstances.

The following is a summary of the widely cited model that Barth presents to account for the tents belonging to the Basseri nomads of South Persia which settle (Barth, 1961:101-111). The point which Barth makes, and which should be kept in mind here, is that there is a range of herd sizes within which animal husbandry is a profitable deployment of capital. Families falling at either end of the distribution range are candidates for settlement, particularly those at the lower extreme. Below a certain level, to be empirically determined for the population concerned, herding cannot provide sufficient income to maintain the household, and alternative sources must be sought. The converse of this is the upper limits of herd size, calculated per family, beyond which animals give a diminishing yield with respect to the capital and risk involved. Families whose animal holdings approach this level are led to consider other deployments of capital, often, among the Basseri as among the Yörük, land or urban shops.

Accordingly, families at opposite ends of the spectrum of wealth that settle do so under vastly differing conditions, with varying prospects for post-settlement standards of living. Families occupying the various points in the distribution of wealth among the nomads may be doing so in a very temporary manner; that is, they may be constantly in a state of flux regarding herd size, with little indication of stable classes. Once settled, however, the new resource base frequently is such that divisions of wealth are frozen. Such mobility as does appear is more likely to be downward than upward. We will return to this point later.

If herd size drops below the lower limits of subsistence, the alternatives are either to settle by selling the remaining animals or to go into debt in order to increase herd size.[3] The latter is usually preferable unless there is free land available or unless there are prospects for a good job. Credit is feasible if one is not already deeply in debt and if the family has the labor force, particularly sons, to manage animals purchased with credit. A reputation for good management and honesty, of course, helps in getting livestock on credit. However, the credit is so expensive that a series of disasters cannot but lead to bankruptcy and settlement as village or urban poor. Many of the families which have settled singly in the past 15 years have done so under these circumstances.

[3] The price of land relative to that of the animals herded is an important factor. There is reason to believe that land prices in the İslahiye are rising at a much more rapid rate than are animal prices. For example, a Yörük man sold his herd 10 years ago and bought 100 dönüm of land in a Kurdish village. Two years later he decided to return to nomadic pastoralism and traded the 100 dönüm of agricultural land for 100 good quality two-year old ewes (şişek). Today it would be impossible to purchase the same land for less than 1,000 to 1,200 T.L. per dönüm, whereas a sheep of the best quality will hardly bring 300-375 T.L.

While most credit sales of animals seem to be within the named maximal lineage (kabile), the rates of interest are high. Complete "foreclosure" is not common; however the animals sold on credit are often taken back if the buyer cannot pay. In these cases the herds have almost always been decimated by losses, and the high rate of interest reflects the high risk of giving livestock on credit to even the most reliable person. One function of this extension of modern capitalistic credit arrangements is to provide a form of partnership between two families who, in the traditional economy, would seemingly succeed or fail largely according to their own individual fortunes. The now widespread practice of credit sales of animals is a means of diversifying risk through a broader social network than would otherwise be feasible in a society without collective ownership or formal rules of obligatory mutual assistance in economic matters. However, when animals are not paid for and if the creditor feels that he cannot sustain the possibility of greater loss, he will take them back. Usually he will not take other animals where this would completely impoverish the family; he will leave the balance as an outstanding debt. Nevertheless, when animals are reclaimed, it is usually the beginning of a short migration that ends in settlement. Not only do natural disasters effectively reduce herd size, but market conditons and the rise in prices of needed supplies, combined with a current lag in price rise of animal products, also work to raise the lower level of self-sufficiency to a point where less fluctuation is needed to bring family herd size below the break-even point. The nomads' primary response to this is the introduction of grain feeding in winter, together with the use of large canvas animal tents for added shelter. While this enables the herder to bring more animals safely through the winter in İslahiye, it also disproportionately increases the overhead expenses for smaller herds.

Settlement as a means of reinvesting wealth, the obverse of the above, is occasionally, but less frequently, seen. Rich pastoralists, usually men regarded as lineage leaders, do attempt to diversify their wealth by purchasing shops or productive agricultural land. Most of the well-to-do ağas among the Yörük nomads have done this. The buying of such property may take years. Again Barth's (1961) analysis of the Basseri is relevant. This model of settlement, while largely accounting for many individual decisions to abandon nomadism, does not describe the group settlement of whole communities. In the case of Nogaylar, the better portion of a major descent segment settled together, with all herd sizes represented, not just the rich or the very poor.

GROUP SETTLEMENT

Sociologically and historically, group settlement is by far the most interesting form of sedentarization in Turkey and the Near East. The settlement of Nogaylar Köy is in many ways analogous to the settlement of large portions of the Hatay and southwestern Turkey (see Aswad, 1968 and 1972; Eberhard, 1953a and b; Planhol, 1958). Also, it is to be expected that the rate of sedentarization in eastern Turkey will increase yearly as pressure on land builds up due to population increases.

In a group decision to settle, the economic motivation underlying each family's choice must be different, although acting in concert with others. In the case of Nogaylar it is apparent that lineage leaders, not marginal herders, were instrumental in organizing the joint settlement. Quite apart from the special ability of such men, the ağas, to deal with the government apparatus more effectively, the job of establishing the preconditions for group settlement fell to them because the acquisition of land benefited them more than it did the middle range of nomads who had large enough flocks for a comfortable subsistence, but not so many that other means of capital deployment were necessary. Poorer nomads who had a pressing need for another economic start generally lacked the social stature within the tribe to influence others and had to rely on others for useful contacts with government officials. The tribal leaders, much like rural landlords, maintain contacts at as many levels of government as possible.

One immediate cause for increased desire for land by a broader range of families was the increase in pasture fees demanded of the nomads by peasant grazing land owners. This was accompanied by sporadic governmental curtailment (beginning in 1945 or so) of access to rich grazing in a 10 kilometer strip along the Syrian border. The rise in pasture fees seems dynamically related to the increase in Yörük population, or at least to the number of tents in the area during World War II, as the culmination of a general eastward shift of tribal sections into less densely settled areas. Households made the shift from Çukurova to İslahiye during and after World War II with the economic development of the former district.

The Kurdish tribes of İslahiye were settled before significant Yörük entry. If the Yörük might be thought to fill an ecological niche left vacant by forced settlement of Kurdish and Türkmen nomadic pastoralists, population growth both among the Yörük and local populations rapidly dictated still more shifts, either in location or from pastoralism to other types of production. Also, while pasture rates were increasing, another source of income was declining—that of leasing camels for agricultural transportation during the fall months when cotton had to be brought to market. By 1949, road transportation by truck had increased to a point where the commercial use of camels was eliminated; along with it went the additional income Yörük owners had previously received.

These changes raised the lower limits of self-sufficiency through a total reliance on animal husbandry. Likewise, more astute members of the tribe, particularly the richer ones, realized from developments along the southern coast (see Kolars [1963:10-50] for a discussion of these) that pressure on grazing was going to increase in the future and that land offered greater security.

While many of the nomadic Yörük recognized the value of land in the 1940's, as they do now, it was difficult for individuals to act on this knowledge. Also, it should be noted that until the rather dramatic increase in rural population growth was felt after World War II, nomadic animal husbandry was not an inferior way of making a living when animal and agricultural profits were compared on a household basis. There is little doubt that most of those families still nomadic in the area of study, although not necessarily those elsewhere, enjoy both a higher income and better standard of living than many small farmers, and they are many times better off than the landless daylaborer.

Most of the arable land in the fertile regions of winter pastures is located in Kurdish, Türkmen or Çerkes villages. Interethnic antipathy makes it very difficult to be a minority in a community culturally and politically dominated by another ethnic or religious group. Following World War II, a number of well-to-do nomadic Yörük attempted to settle as individual households in Kurdish villages through purchase of large fields (over 100 dönüm [1 dönüm = 1 dekar = 1,000 m^2]) of good land. To my knowledge, most have failed largely due to lack of cooperation on the part of the dominant villagers rather to a deficiency in technical skill. Such skills can be learned easily or hired, but it is difficult for a man respected in his own circle to accept an inferior position in another. Ethnicity in this area of rural Turkey is extremely important in channeling patterns of intermarriage, economic cooperation, political allegiance, and mutual aid in conflict.

Although close personal friendships develop among individuals across ethnic boundaries, in time of stress priority is always given to one's own community, no matter how narrowly defined. There is a strong Yörük prejudice against giving brides to outsiders, which in turn makes it difficult for them to secure women from non-Yörük (which they accept) and to create alliances in this manner. In many cases, linguistic barriers make it difficult for the Turkish-speaking Yörük to participate fully in the Kurdish community. This is, from all acounts, different from the situation along the southern coast of Turkey where there is presently no important ethnic or cultural barrier to settlement by isolated or scattered Yörük families. Indeed, much of the coast is populated by Yörük, some settled for several generations, whereas in İslahiye such settlement dates only from the last two decades.

Ethnicity encourages Yörük with large herds who wish the security of land, as well as the social gratification of wealth which they cannot find as a minority in a non-Turkish or non-Yörük community, either to purchase property in towns where Yörük live or trade or to settle in concert with members of their lineage in villages. Settlement in towns, as opposed to village settlement, is significant in the İslahiye region. Almost all settlement has taken place within the last 20 to 25 years, during which time 90 to 95 households have settled in villages, 82 in İslahiye and 25 in Fevzipaşa (note that Maraş and Türkoğlu are not included, but have Yörük populations, as does Kïrkhan in the Hatay).

Urban or semi-urban settlement is feasible on an individual family basis, and just about every Saçïkara lineage is represented in İslahiye. In such cases there is no special problem of social adjustment that is not economic in nature; most who settle now are driven to do so by poverty. Village settlement, due to ethnic definitions of loyalty and cooperation mentioned above, involves mass settlement and the co-residence of relatives to be successful. Of course, once Yörük are established, individual Yörük families can make their way into the community on the coattails of the early settlers. The available land, however, is usually taken by that time.

Group village settlement can be accomplished only if there is cheap or free land in quantity, permitting co-residence of sufficient households to relieve the settlers of dependence on the alien community in certain critical areas: supply of marriage partners, control of violence, full exercise of property rights, and the full use of village commons (mer'a). Although subsequent political development almost always has strengthened the political power of the richer settlers or lineage leaders, often formalizing with office what had been before an informal term of respect (ağa), this cannot be held out as the conscious aim of the efforts of these men to recruit co-settlers. In the case of Nogaylar, the objective was to secure a simple majority in a community where the initial response of the inhabitants was quite hostile. The recognized leader of the İzmirli kabile arranged for lineage members to register with the Toprak Komisyonu (Land Commission) and saw to it that the applications were followed up and that all were able to obtain land in the same place. Before being offered land in Nogaylar, he was offered land in Sayburun Village, along with Yörük of the same tribe but from other lineages. This he refused on the reasoning that the land offered was to be divided among too many households and that settlement under those conditions would be pointless. Later, land was found in Nogaylar Village which, while being farmed by the Nogay occupants, was legally treasury (hazine), or state land. The Toprak Komisyonu agreed to distribute this to the Yörük, and the amount given to family heads in the first division amounted to almost twice what they would have received at Sayburun: about 80 dönüm as opposed to 40 dönüm. This was done, however, over the strenuous opposition of the Nogay families who had until then made good use of the fields and felt the coming of the Yörük was an intrusion. In fact, some of the lands are still under litigation.

What was, perhaps, most disturbing to them was that along with losing free use of the hazine land, their own formerly landless Turkish agricultural workers also received land with the assistance of the Yoruk on the same basis of 80 or more dönüm per household. Not only was the ağa damaged economically, but his political power was diminished in a similar fashion. Economically, it seems that he has recovered with non-village business interests, but in the first election following the arrival of the Yörük, he lost control of the village to the successful candidacy of the Yörük leader for muhtar (headman). This will be elaborated on later, but is mentioned here to show the necessity for coordinated effort on the part of the Yörük in order to gain a foothold in the village against entrenched opposition.

Unanimity of purpose among the Yörük was achieved due to the fact that settling members who had no great interest in the fields they were to receive could simply establish legal residence, build an insubstantial house, and continue to migrate with their animals. Once registered in the village, they could use village commons (mer'a) for winter pasture without paying the fee which would normally be exacted from non-residents. Thus, settlement for some simply made nomadism more profitable through cheaper grazing, with little change in either actual residence or in life style. Now, 20 years after settlement, tents are still to be found in winter on the mer'a belonging to households which, although registered to vote in the village, move with the main body of nomads to yayla pastures in the spring, some 200 kilometers away. Apart from the obvious implications for Yörük village organization and economy, this "semi-sedentarism" is a point of conflict with non-Yörük villagers who would otherwise benefit from the leasing of this land for cash paid into the village treasury for public expenses. It is somewhat ironic that the families most likely to remain pastoral nomadic in a profitable way will probably be those families which first became registered members of villages and thereby secure access to free or inexpensive grazing on village commons.

SOCIAL CHANGE AFTER SETTLEMENT

While this will not treat all aspects of social change which developed since settlement, certain areas stand out as particularly relevant. The discussion will center around three general problems: fixed residence and the mahalle (village faction or ward), the development cycle of the household, and the evolution of new forms of political organization. These are not isolated issues, but problems closely related to one another and critical to an understanding of the most significant changes which have arisen in response to the new environment and the new means of production.

Fixed Residence

By settling, Yörük families sacrificed flexibility in residence group composition, a composition which was in continual adjustment to social and economic realities. Instead, they adopted one frozen according to house plots in a pattern set up by the government.[4] Secondly, the Yörük kabile took on a territorial connota-

---

[4] The physical layout of the village is attractive, with little sense of the regimentation often seen in the government-built communities where houses are provided. The field pattern is like that described for Mesudiye village in Konya by Hütteroth (1968:74 ff.).

tion; full membership in activities of the lineage presupposed co-residence and ownership of land in a specific locality.

In the traditional nomadic scheme, families camp together in ever-shifting patterns. No camp group endures intact throughout a complete annual cycle, as strictly environmental considerations limit the winter camp group to five to eight tents, whereas in summer, tent communities of up to 20 are possible due to better grazing and the more restricted nature of agriculture in the highlands. Groups of households moving between winter kişlak and summer yayla pastures rarely exceed 10 tents, for similar reasons. It is difficult to secure roadside camp sites and grazing for larger numbers of people and animals. Within the limits set by the size of the combined herds and the contractual arrangements made for pasture rights, the configuration of the group represents a social consensus which is in continual flux.

In 1949 the settlers in Nogaylar Köy set up their residences in a pattern which was to remain virtually fixed; to change only in a way conditioned by the initial layout. The resultant distribution of households reflects the then existing system of social interaction. The pattern expresses the overall division of the settlers into two branches of one patrilineage and, also, the tendency for economic and social relations to parallel the intensity of patrilateral kinship ties. Very often brothers in the village settled side by side or close to one another. The lineage, as noted before, is split between the descendants of two brothers of the previous generation, currently not represented by any living member. These sections occupy different ends of the village area settled by Yörük; the leaders of the now rival sides live in well constructed two-story homes as far apart from one another as is possible without leaving the village proper.

The nomadic mobility mentioned before has two important sociological effects on group integration: political and economic power of any individual is limited in that those who would be his clients or dependents can physically remove themselves from his reach. Secondly, disagreement, quick to arise among families, can be often resolved before real conflict occurs. Yörük society has evolved no elaborate mechanisms to adjudicate disputes or to mediate hostilities, but it does have clear provisions for the support of kin in conflicts and obligations of blood vengeance. Peacemaking is difficult at best and, in cases of murder, impossible until revenge is taken. The physical separation of the parties immediately concerned in a conflict, prior to physical violence, is an effective means of controlling relations among individuals who feel themselves estranged.

In the nomadic society households which dislike each other rarely need see each other and can keep considerable distance between their tents while still following the same migratory schedule. The option of moving away probably obviates the need for more socialized means of resolving conflicts, as well as possibly allowing violence to remain a useful social tool.

In Nogaylar, given the commitment to stationary residence necessary for full rights to land, movement becomes impractical as a means of relieving social conflict. There is no way households can ignore the presence of members of households with which their own close relatives have had disagreements. Both of the Yörük villages studied were rent by inter-Yörük conflict which had involved the use of violence. Although it is clear that most violence over minutiae of daily life is the surfacing of deeper, perhaps more significant, conflict, such as feuds of a previous generation, overt violence in nomadic society can be prevented more easily when time and distance can play their mediating roles.

Related to the same problem is the question of political power built on reliable support of certain individuals by others. Because of fixed residence, few can avoid taking stands on most issues of village concern, the resolutions of which often benefit some more than others. Households, related or not, cannot ignore the wishes and opinions of the large landowners of the village. In Nogaylar this has its expression in the two related factions, a split that took place before settlement but which became intensified with time. Areas where political influence is important include distribution of water for irrigation, the canals which carry it, field boundaries, and the use of public domain (mer'a). It should not be assumed that there is no scope for the use of political influence among the nomads. However, for the settled Yörük such situations are potentially more divisive insomuch as factions, once formed, can change only slowly.

Residence, then, has altered the previous system of control of violence by movement without substitution of an adequate mechanism for control and reconciliation. Fights among Yörük, related or not, seem to be long remembered and antipathies are often strengthened with the passage of time, not forgotten. Secondly, once households are committed to a territory which cannot be left without forfeiting certain property rights, they are inevitably drawn into whatever system of factions may have evolved. Simply because they are there, their support is sought by the different sides in any question that involves more than one family. As a result, there is no family that is not considered a supporter of one of the two sub-lineages, irrespective of kinship. The families of Nogaylar who are not of the dominant maximal lineage which has two sub-lineages in the village are nevertheless allied with one of the two local branches.

Among the nomads, as we have mentioned, although there is frequently ill will between families, even within lineages, there is no rigid division of the tribe, or any part of it, into excluding factions. There is nothing that approaches the two mahalle or moiety division that bifurcates settled Yörük society in the two villages studied. As a result, Nogaylar, a highly nucleated settlement with its houses all tightly packed into an oval shaped figure, is split down the center, separating the Çerkes mahalle from the Yörük. At the same time, the Yörük themselves are divided into two factions rationalized by a genealogical junction, and which have a strong territorial representation as well. The neighboring village of Sayburun is likewise split, although there the Yörük settlers are not living next to their Kurdish village neighbors. In that case the Yörük relations with their non-Yörük neighbors are considered good, and both Yörük factions have close dealings with Kurdish families from the main village, which is itself divided into two political mahalles. The village headman in the case of Sayburun is Kurdish, while the second or assistant headman is from the largest of the two Yörük factions. In Nogaylar, relations with the Çerkes are so poor that inter-ethnic hostility serves to force the Yörük into a semblance of unity.

Inheritance and the Formation of Households

Although inheritance is important in accounting for variations in wealth among tents, it also provides the majority of the new households with sufficient means to maintain themselves as autonomous entities. In the 20 years since settlement, neither the number of households nor the composition of land-using units has remained static. The land granted to adult settlers formed the primary resource of the household, much as had the family herd in pre-settlement days. Likewise, analogous to the management of animals among the nomadic Yörük, control of land use and disposition of land rested with the head of the household. Subsequent to the sedentarization of the first households in 1949, seven more have settled without benefit of government assistance and, with a single exception, have not accumulated the requisite land base for full reliance on the production of their own property. The village Yörük are now distributed among 43 households (Fig. 18). The latecomers have not, as yet, redivided any of their individually meager holdings, nor have any new residential units developed from these.

Accordingly, the following discussion of the dynamics of household formation refers to the former group of settlers. Of the 30 original households, five have undergone internal division; the formation of new residence units through the separation of formerly co-resident individuals. Seven new households have emerged in this way from five primary units. Table 46 summarizes the internal make-up of Yörük households in the village. Whereas the income from land is shared within the household on the basis of need, albeit culturally defined so as to vary by sex and status, households, irrespective of the degree of kinship to one another, are competing

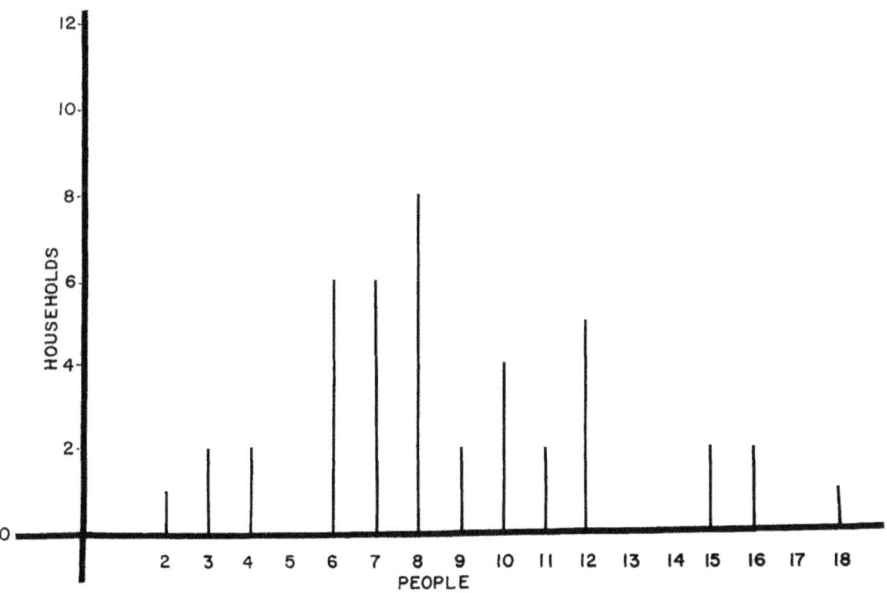

Fig. 18. Distribution of population over household units.

TABLE 46
COMPOSITION OF YÖRÜK HOUSEHOLDS IN NOGAYLAR KÖYÜ

Age of Oldest Male	Widow (oldest son away) and Single Sons	Married Man plus Unmarried Brother (no married son)	Two or more Married Brothers (no married son)	Nuclear Family	Patrilocal Extended Family	Polygynous Extended Family
60+					8	1
50–59				3	1	1
40–49				9	2	
30–39		1	1	12		
20–29	1		1	1		
Total of each type	1 case 2.33%	1 case 2.33%	2 cases 4.66%	25 cases 60.5%	11 cases 25.58%	2 cases 4.66%
No. of Individuals in each type	5	3	30	182 (mean=7)	133 (mean=12)	25

in different ways for rights to the limited resources available. In this sense, the members of the seven new households no longer interact in the same way with members of the domestic units from which they separated, even through the formal bonds of kinship and agnation remain unchanged. The property that formerly provisioned one domestic unit became the support of two or even three households. At the same time, as shown in Table 47, the number of potential male heirs (37) directly in line to claim rights in the land once belonging to only five households ultimately threatens the resource base of all established residence units. This is not to be thought of as merely a peculiarity of the rules of partible inheritance, but as the result of limited resources which are to be privately allocated.

The response of the Yörük to the dilemma of allocating restricted resources among a large number of real or potential claimants, who by virtue of their relationship to heads of households will have to depend for their future welfare on access to specific plots of land, is a shaky structure of half measures. Although insufficient time has elapsed since settlement to see the full consequences of the demand for land by those who wish to establish autonomous domestic units, certain alternative approaches can be discussed with reference to the seven new households formed from the original settlers.

Sons, adult and married at the time of initial land distribution in 1949, retain the rights to fields which they received at that time; however they usually divide the proceeds of those fields with their natal family rather than divide actual fields which were formerly worked in the father's name. The shares in these cases represent the amount of land to which the separately residing son holds title. In the cases where the father who originally settled is dead, but where separately residing sons remain, by far the majority (eight houses), the title to land is, apparently, unaltered while the actual proceeds and expenses associated with the land are shared according to the principles of partible male inheritance.[5] The land might well be the subject of later litigation, as this pattern of use does not correspond with Turkish law regarding property left intestate, which would equal shares to married and single heirs of either sex (Table 47).

[5] In some cases, the separated brothers have agreed on a title transfer of one field, but work others together on a share basis. In other cases, no formal transfer has been made of any specific field, but the proceeds of certain ones are regularly assigned to one household.

TABLE 47
JOINT LAND USE BY INDEPENDENT YÖRÜK HOUSEHOLDS IN NOGAYLAR KÖYÜ
(Five sets of co-users totaling 12 households)*

Status of Original Titleholder	Status of Co-user	Number of Land Sharing Sets	Number of Households	Number of First Generation (Direct) Male Heirs Having Possible Claim to Land	Years Since Land Use Established	Mean Number of Dönüm per Household
Older brother	Younger brother	1	2	7	4	62.5
Older brother	Two younger brothers	2	6	18	1.2 / 4.4	65.3
Father	Son	1	2	4	8	50.0
Father	Two sons	1	2	8	9.3	33.3

*Note the potential for extreme fragmentation of land by male heirs with legal claims, not yet separated

Thus there exists a system whereby individual domestic units rely on stipulated rights of access and disposal of specified properties, which is, as we have noted, strongly supported by a cultural tradition of private ownership of the primary income-producing resource. Alongside of this exists an *ad hoc* system of joint land usage among brothers sharing in a common estate, although such a practice is extremely rare among nomadic pastoralist sections of the same tribe and is strongly mitigated against by a cultural emphasis on household autonomy. This latter aspect of land tenure is complicated by the fact that titles (*tapu*) and the law of inheritance, the only legally enforceable claims to land, do not correspond with actual patterns of land use or with the demands of partible inheritance by males, whether at the time of the father's death or when separating from a natal unit in the father's lifetime.

The strains thus put on relations between separated brothers, or even between fathers and their separately residing married sons, are considerable. Indeed, one might speculate that if it were not for the rivalry between the two factions, to be treated in more depth somewhat later, the sheer force of conflicting economic interests would render such a tenuous system unmanageable.

Like the nomadic Yörük, those settled in Nogaylar and two other communities studied by the author do not distribute land or other important property to daughters. Dowry (*cehiz*) has only in the last few years been given to daughters in what is a frank imitation of non-Yörük practice. In includes certain items of household furnishings, but rarely equals either the bride price (başlĭk) or the share of the family fields the girl might legally claim. Cehiz in village usage should, and often does, equal bride price. Among settled Yörük now, the widow of the head of household goes to live with one of her sons who receives an additional share of the estate to care for her, called "mother's share," or *ana hakkĭ*. It is not clear yet whether the younger or older brothers are favored, as insufficient time has passed for a true pattern to become apparent. This stems not from a sudden awareness of a hitherto unnoticed moral obligation, although it is supported by Koranic law, but rather from the fact that when land was distributed the state registered some of the fields in the names of adult females as part of a formula which included family size in making the award of land.

According to title records, over 25 percent of Yörük-owned land is registered under women's names. Until now, it is claimed, no woman has attempted to dispose of this land except in conformance to her husband's wishes. No woman in the Yörük quarter of the village has inherited land and no attempt has been made by a husband to acquire the legal share of his wife's father's land which she might claim. The possibilities for conflict are considerable and can be expected to increase as pressure on land parallels population growth.

The pattern of actual field use does not correspond with the distribution of legal titles to land. Brothers farm land to which their sisters have a legal claim. Brothers have split without dividing their patrimony, with some setting up independent households; others with an equal share to land continued to co-reside with older brothers. Land titles have remained largely unchanged since they were issued, and land is registered in the names of deceased of both sexes. All this leaves the problem of distribution to yet another generation—one that is to be more and more desperate to secure economic self-sufficiency as this goal becomes harder to achieve.

Those who settled after the initial distribution have acquired little land and have little likelihood of doing so. The landless find that their labor is of little help in the acquisition of land. It is also difficult for a family with only a small patrimony to increase its holdings. What a man receives from his father or brothers is likely to be the maximum that he will ever own if, indeed, he manages to hold on to that. Land everywhere in the district is in short supply; those without land are many and prices are restrictive. To buy land to increase one's patrimony necessitates considerable credit, and it seems the use of land to buy more land is the prerogative only of large land owners. Yörük with substantial herds which they can sell also can purchase land, but, as we have mentioned, it is difficult to do so except in communities where Yörük are already settled.

An economic alternative which further separates the landed from the landless is, paradoxically, the option of combined herding and farming. Three families in the two villages studied have split following the father's death, with one brother managing the fields and the other taking the herds to the summer pastures and living there in tents during that period. The brothers alternate in their roles and apparently divide all profits evenly between them. Membership in the village gives them rights to free winter pasture on the village mer'a. The poor or small land owners do not avail themselves of what might seem to be an ideal solution to the problem of fully maximizing the use of their labor to increase cash income and capital. They, too, have a right to village common land and usually have the necessary labor power and skills for animal management. What deters them is both their work as hired hands in the late summer cash crop harvests of their neighbors and their utter lack of capital or credit with which to acquire animals. Most, in fact, came to the village having failed at herding as nomads. To set up a herding operation, one needs enough capital to buy the livestock, pay cash for pasture rights in the yayla, and support shepherds through an initial period in which there is little direct animal production. Accordingly, animals provide an important means of subsistence as the primary resource becomes strained, but only for those who have substantial holdings to begin with.

The natural progress of the domestic cycle in the sedentary community leads to the differentiation of two classes of households: the landed self-sufficient and the landless dependent. With time it seems safe to predict that more of the now self-sufficient will fail to expand property holdings in keeping with the number of heirs to share in the division of the contemporary estate. The distinctions of wealth which were temporary among the nomads become rigid among the sedentary households. Even though there are many apparent similarities in the formal structure of the domestic units of the two specializations, these are not the only criteria for comparison. For example, the fact that labor is of little use in accumulating capital among the villagers means that large families with little land will not easily improve their position, as they might in a pastoral nomadic economy. Anticipatory partible inheritance is practiced in both economies, although seemingly not to the same extent in the village where the problem is presently put off with the giving of shares in fields rather than the actual property itself. However, the results of inheritance are quite different in the two societies. Among the nomads a small number of animals is commensurate with the status of a new household and can be the means for its full economic autonomy.

In the latter part of Chapter VI it was demonstrated that nomadic pastoralist families of all wealth categories, including the lowest, are able to adjust not only total production in response to population, but, more importantly, can increase the productivity of individual workers within the tent. No attempt was made here to repeat these statistical tests with the Nogaylar Yörük population as not only are acceptable measures of output hard to come by and dubious at best, but even a cursory look at the distribution of wealth by household size and type was sufficient to show that such applications would be meaningless (see Fig. 19 for distribution of land among households).

Among the village population, inheritance rarely establishes a viable domestic unit that can avoid laboring on someone else's fields to provision itself. The large landowners, including two or three Yörük in the village, seem to be able to expand their field holdings through purchase or lease to keep pace with anticipated division. While the large herd owner faces many, if not all, of the risks of herd depletion that his poorer neighbors do, the large landowner does not. To the contrary, he is able to mortgage his fields

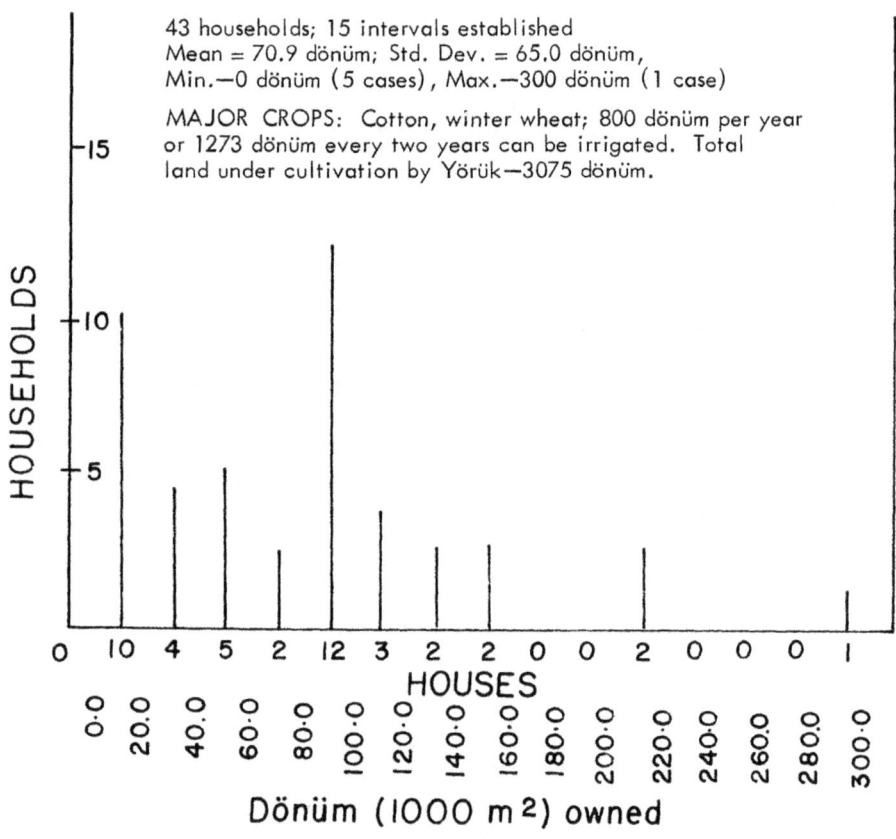

Fig. 19. Land use by family in Nogaylar Köyü (Yörük).

NOMADIC SETTLEMENT AND SOCIAL LIFE 213

to buy more land, secure in the fact that his holdings are sufficient to carry him through a series of poor harvests. He is able to purchase tractors (all six are owned by members of the dominant lineage, five of whom are of one sublineage) which can be hired out profitably when not used on his own fields. Thus he can maximize more fully the labor that his co-resident sons can provide and which is not otherwise productive in a highly mechanized agricultural system. Although the initial distribution of land by the state provided each Yörük household with over 80 dönüm of arable land, the land held by the eight households not of the dominant lineage averages only 12.8 dönüm. Furthermore, no member of these lineages has been able to purchase land since settling, although members of the dominant lineage (three households) have bought considerable land to supplement the amount originally given by the state. Table 48 shows the concentration of animal production in the hands of the lineage which is both longest settled and which has the largest landowners. Although not described here, variation within the lineage by wealth in land correlates highly with wealth in sheep. Table 48 further illustrates an apparent anomaly in that families of the lineages longest settled and which hold the most land also were among those which continued to migrate to summer pastures after settlement. This, of course, is understandable in light of what has been said already about the nature of village Yörük animal production.

The fact that inheritance cannot be sufficient in most cases to support a newly separated household unit is recognized by the youth of the village. This realization has led to a certain amount of muted inter-generational conflict which seemingly cuts across both genealogical and factional lines, although it is not publicly admitted. The landless youth and married sons of moderately wealthy families are pushing for rights of cultivation in the village mer'a (commons) much of which is arable. The present leading family of the Yörük, which is also the politically dominant one, is strongly opposed to this idea, as the mer'a serves established interests as an important source of animal income. Perhaps just as importantly, it serves established political interest in that some Yörük of the İzmirli lineage, while not resident in the village proper, make use of the commons at no cost and vote in the highly partisan village elections. Elimination of the mer'a, or substantial reduction of it, would mean its division among both Yörük and non-Yörük poor, as well as the diminishing of livestock production. Quite apart from this, it is obvious that even should it be divided, relief of pressure on the land would be shortlived.

TABLE 48

NOGAYLAR YÖRÜK HOUSEHOLDS BY LINEAGE
(45 houses: data collected November 1969)

Name of Patrilineage (Kabile)	K	H	I	T	A	Total
Number of Households	4	1	35	1	2	43
Mean Number of Sheep per Household	9.5	0.0	72.9	12	10.0	60.2
Standard Deviation	14.0	0.0	84.0*	0.0	4.1	79.7
Mean Age of Head of Household	46.5	51.0	43.4	50.0	37.5	43.7
Standard Deviation	11.9	0.0	12.0	0.0	10.6	11.6
Mean Number of Years Settled	10.8	20.0	17.8	20.0	12.0	16.9
Standard Deviation	1.5	0.0	4.5	0.0	11.3*	5.1
Mean Number of Sheep Owned when Family Settled	10.0	60.0	278.7	150.0	50.0	200.6
Standard Deviation	20.0	0.0	333.7*	0.0	7.1	307.8
Mean Number of Years Family Continued to Yayla after Settlement	0.0	14.0	8.9	0.0	0.0	7.5
Standard Deviation	0.0	0.0	8.6*	0.0	0.0	8.4
Mean Amount of Land Owned per Family (in dönüm)	4.75	60.0	81.9	40.0	37.5	70.9
Standard Deviation	7.1	0.0	66.4*	0.0	33.0*	65.0

*Note extreme variation within the lineage.

Political Economy: An Overview

If we take a view of political behavior which includes such actions as the mutual support of kinsmen in confrontations with non-kin or more distantly related families, the favored treatment a person might expect from close kin, or the preferential extension of credit within lineages, we have considerably expanded the scope of the discussion. This is necessary in order to understand many post-settlement developments in Nogaylar with respect to both formal office and the daily relations of households. Much of this has emerged in the course of the analysis, but might be restated here.

Although in Nogaylar Köyü there are the political offices and mahalle (ward) divisions common to most of Anatolia, these are phrased in terms of a genealogical referent. The Yörük half of the village can accurately be described as a tribal system whereby internal groupings or factions use a rationale of common descent. In reality, as we have noted, not all members are of the same descent group and the daily actions of some households' members are best understood in terms of economic clientship to their richer neighbors, not as the mutual support seen of kinsmen. The factions here are the two sub-lineages and are not simply the expression of clusters of people whose economic strategies differ. While genealogically defined kabile or lineages are fundamental to nomadic Yörük society, it is only in sedentary Yörük communities that the system of multi-lineage factions has developed.

The picture presented of nomadic Yörük political organization is of a segmentary society with no hereditary positions of leadership at any of the levels of possible grouping beyond the co-residing family. Although there are divisions of wealth which are important in determining who will fill certain achieved statuses within the tribe, these are not replicated from one generation to another. Most families undergo significant variations in wealth as they start with a small patrimony, build up their herd, and then see the flocks decimated by disease, forced sales, and high bride price payments to secure wives for their sons. In the same way, a family's wealth in animals varies even during the annual cycle, increasing every spring from the winter low point, declining again in the fall as older animals and male yearlings (*kısır* and *toklu*) are sold off. Labor is critical to the proper maintenance of the family herds, and sons can be incorporated usefully as income producers through the tending of correspondingly larger herds. Inheritance, then, does not involve the splitting up of a fixed number of animals among the sons, but the sharing of approximately the same number among fewer and fewer persons as each son leaves the household in succession and as the herd is replenished following each division. This fact, dependent on the high rate of sheep reproduction, is important in understanding the loose, virtually non-hierarchical political organization of the nomadic Yörük.

Lineage leaders (ağa) frequently profit from the cash credit needs of their kinsmen and can use this favored economic position to gain cheaper effective access to grazing. Nevertheless, there is no way for them either to perpetuate themselves as a stable class or to acquire formal office. The high degree of economic mobility and the inability of any person to restrict the access of others to resources enables nearly every family to achieve a position of relative economic independence. Even where a man must borrow heavily to replenish his herds at a high rate of interest, he does so without the overt symbols of clientship that are associated with many Mediterranean peasant systems. The physical mobility of the debtor, together with the inability of the creditor to make use of his services, precludes harsh treatment of a man at the hands of those to whom he owes money or animals. When there is a foreclosure the creditor most likely will receive fewer animals than were sold. Although traditional economic mobility is being eroded by increasing pasture fees and pressure on grazing land, it is still relatively high compared to that of most sedentary populations in the region. Nogaylar is a case in point.

In Nogaylar we have considered the Yörük portion of that village. Since this segment of the village commands the majority of votes, it has controlled all elected offices since the first election after the arrival of the nomads. The man who has held the elected office of muhtar (headman) since this time is the man who, when the Yörük were still nomadic, was thought of as lineage leader, or ağa. In both cases leadership had much to do with wealth, as this person was the largest herd owner of his lineage. However, as the lineage leader he exercised no stipulated duties and had no legal standing under Turkish law.

The establishment of formal office and the ağa's election to it is a departure from the nomadic lineage system. Also it appears to be the basis for the emergence of factions which, although expressed in terms of kinship and descent, are in practice becoming client-supported hierarchical structures, particularly within the most powerful section (see Barth, 1953:132 ff. and Aswad, 1968:95 ff.). Certainly the leader of the dominant lineage or faction is aware of his position in the patron-client dyad. For example, the unrelated shepherd of the ağa in nomadic days has, since settlement, become "the ağa's man." He and his family reside in a well well-constructed two-story house given to him by the ağa, and, being a living testimonial to the ağa's wealth and generosity, they are also staunch supporters. Another family, similarly unrelated and one of the latecomers to the village, is employed by the muhtar as village watchman (*bekçi*), but is also a general handyman for the ağa. It was observed in the study that the ağa could openly be critical of the actions and behavior or adult members of his own faction in a manner that would scarcely be tolerated among the nomads. There is little question that a substantial gap separates the standard of living and ability to manipulate public affairs of the wealthier families from the landless and the poor Yörük.

Although we have given weight in the discussion to the development of client-like ties, it should not be assumed that these negate or preclude the use of tribal affiliation as a means of political organization. Kinship and descent have functions other than simply serving as the ideological rationale for factions. Ties of kinship and descent, particularly the latter, continue to bear their previous burden in the areas of self-defense and in meeting opposition from outside the group. In one sense we might say that the tribe or "tribalism" has taken on increased political significance as a vehicle for political organization since settlement. This perhaps unexpected development is clearly a result of the continual confrontation of Yörük with members of the Çerkes mahalle at close quarters in Nogaylar.

We have noted that relations between Yörük and non-Yörük have been poor since the onset of settlement. Attempts on several occasions, particularly by the leader of the Yörük, to normalize the situation through social exchange, intermarriage, and even by alternating the office of muhtar between the two mahalle have all failed, largely due to internal dissent on both sides. No brides have been given or taken between the two populations, and little social intercourse or economic exchange has occurred apart from the cash sale of land to wealthy Yörük, which also has ended in disagreement over water rights. Even though the new mosque represents a communal effort, it seems more an outcome of competition than cooperation, and no imam or *hoca* until now has been able to survive for long the rivalry between the two groups. At the time of the study there was no such officeholder, nor had the people of Nogaylar been able to agree on a hoca for the *Kuran Kursu* whose new cement building stands vacant near the village school.

An Overview of Sedentarization and Social Change

The analysis has described the structural framework of settlement in the İslahiye region, discussed why some pastoral nomads leave tent life while others do not, and has approached the problem of social change subsequent to sedentarization. This latter was attempted with special reference to how structured interpersonal relations have been altered in response to fixed residence and to land as a resource in the village economy. Changes both in the domestic cycle and in formal political organization were seen in this light.

The discussion, however, has not dealt extensively with what might be called the immediate cause of settlement. Foremost among these is the increasing shortage of grazing land as population pressures reduce the amount of vacant or marginal land (*kĭrac*) available to livestock. Paralleling this is the drastic rise in grazing (*otlak*) fees in the last two decades. One reason for this is with modern agricultural technology less land is left fallow or empty during the months of winter grazing in the plains and foothills around İslahiye, thus reducing the absolute amount of land open to the Yörük. Secondly, the income that large land owners derive from nomad grazing fees is insignificant when compared with that provided by crop production, which, through modern technology, need leave little land fallow or unplanted. Furthermore, the risk of animal damage to the crops mounts as the fields left fallow diminish in size. The value of animal manure declines as commercial fertilizers become readily available to farmers. Thus some owners either charge an otlak price on a take-it-or-leave-it basis or do not bother to rent tracts of fallow land at all. It is the shortage of winter, not summer, grazing that limits nomadic pastoralism and increases the cash overhead of those who herd. Alongside of this is the newly begun speculation in winter pasture rights by sedentary and nomadic wealthy Yörük whereby winter pastures are leased early in the season (mid-summer) and later subleased at higher prices to nomads who have difficulty in finding suitable grazing.

Another problem facing nomadic pastoralists is that of moving the herds up to summer pastures along the Pĭnarbaşĭ-Maraş road.

Although the road is now open to migration, it has been closed during certain years in the past and is always strictly controlled by forestry officials. This is the reason that comparatively few herds of goats are found, even among Sarīkeçili who traditionally specialized in them. While forestry officials have little fault to find with the sheep herders, whose animals do not cause much damage to trees, villagers along the route frequently suffer crop damage. Often this damage is minor, but is used as an excuse to exact high cash payments from the passing nomads. Villages have also started to impose an illegal road tax (*yol* or *bekçi parasi*) of five to 10 T.L. on each herd that passes. Since a flock may traverse several village territories in an evening of movement, it amounts to a sizeable penalty, and one that is not visibly proportionate to the damage caused. The problem of theft has already been described.

All this works to limit the absolute number of sheep that can be carried throughout the year by the pastoralists. This also raises the mean number of animals needed to support a family near self-sufficiency. Where formerly, it is said, 50 sheep were adequate for economic independence, and this contention is indirectly confirmed by the rise in the mean number of animals inherited over the past 25 years (see Chapter IV), now 100 animals are a bare minimum for a mature family. The overall mean is 268 sheep owned per family among the present-day nomads. This is a response to the increased expenses associated with nomadic pastoralism and the high risks of theft, disease, and inclement weather. These are the pressures most acutely felt by the nomadic Saçīkara Yörük and underlie any individual family's decision to settle.

These pressures are common to the entire nomadic society, but not every household settles or wishes to do so. Some families have returned to nomadic pastoralism after settling, and in Sayburun Köyü two married youths who feel that farming is impossible with the land they have access to are working to build up herds adequate to support themselves without recourse to agriculture. These are, however, isolated cases and the trend is toward increasing settlement, while the average herd size per nomadic family continues to rise.

Most nomadic settlement in Turkey, however, has been in the form of related families settling as a group in a pre-existing community, not as isolated households entering a village or town where there were no other tribe or lineage members. There are several reasons for this, some of which were only tangentially dealt with in the analysis.

The Yörük tribal structure, with its marked preference for marriage with near kin, especially patrikin, encourages a family considering settlement to do so near other related Yörük. Also, reliance on the network of kinship for certain types of defense and support figures in deciding where to settle and gives preference to settlement near other Yörük. But the overriding reason for group settlement in the area of study, and in many parts of the Near East, arises from the interplay of ethnic boundaries. These define populations by numerous excluding criteria and result in the well documented heterogeneity of rural Turkish society.

Nomads in any part of Turkey rarely are able to settle in areas completely devoid of other ethnically distinct populations. In some areas they themselves constitute a majority, perhaps best illustrated by a number of stretches along the Mediterranean coast between Mersin and Fethiye. In regions where they are a minority, ethnicity strongly channels would-be settlers to communities where, if not close kin, at least other Yörük are established in sizeable numbers. It appears that many villages in Turkey, settled on government granted land, are populated by closely related families, often by sections of a single tribe, and that the close kin ties uniting families in these communities are not simply the result of subsequent intermarriage, but date from the time of settlement.[6]

Land is in great demand everywhere and many lack this vital commodity. Even when title to land is held by offices of the Turkish State, rarely are the fields themselves not under cultivation by people who, although having no legal right, do exercise an effective claim through custom or force. In some cases the government itself, through the Land Commission or the Ministry of Settlement, initiates settlement of landless families on such fields. In the cases studied here involving Yörük, the rich men of the Yörük initiated the government grant by locating hazine (treasury) land, determining that there existed no legal title for the land and then pressuring government officials to open it for settlement. This was the pattern followed not only in the İslahiye district, but also in Konya Province in the villages settled by Yörük of the Saçıkara tribe. In each instance the land, prior to settlement, was being farmed by non-Yörük who held no valid title, but who had effective control of the land, preventing other local residents

---

[6] See Hütteroth (1968:passim), Tanyol (1961:17 ff.), and Wenzel (1937:passim) for descriptions of such settlements.

from use of it. These non-Yörük were invariably large land owners.

In settling, the Yörük not only had to convince the government to make the distribution, but they had to face up to strenuous opposition from the non-Yörük villagers, led by the ağas, where the land was located. In three villages the Yörük, in settling, also made possible the acquisition of free land by local non-Yörük poor. These were in no position to start proceedings against their own ağa, but could take advantage of the situation once the Yörük had legally disputed their claims to village lands. In Nogaylar and a village in Konya, the non-Yörük landowning ağa was utilizing not only quantities of government land (hazine) but also the village commons, or mer'a, for his benefit. The coming of the Yörük with government support resulted in the distribution of formerly privately used but publicly owned land to Yörük and non-Yörük alike. However, the hostility generated in this process strengthened ethnic boundaries to the extent that significant intergroup social ties did not emerge. On the contrary, in Nogaylar Köy, once land was distributed to non-Yörük, pre-existing client-patron ties to the village ağa were re-established by the recipients despite the fact that they gained their fields essentially because of Yörük interference. Settlement in any of the villages visited would have been extremely difficult if it had not been done in numbers of cooperating families. The several examples known in the İslahiye region where Yörük attempted to take up farming as isolated households in non-Yörük communities have all ended in failure, even though land was purchased and not granted by the government.

Following settlement, the continual competition with non-Yörük in Nogaylar has in many ways strengthened the descent group or tribal structure. This competition, together with the nature of land as a restricted resource, has given a new territorial bias to the formerly strictly descent defined kabile. Also, this has its expression in political factions which are new to the Yörük of the twentieth century (although perhaps they were evident in earlier periods where political office among the nomads carried its own financial rewards for the winners).[7] These factions, even though

---

[7] Factions of large coalitions were, by Yörük accounts, common in earlier periods when political office recognized by the Ottoman State carried its own rewards. See also İnalcık (1951), Orhonlu (1969), and Sümer (1967 a, b), historians who have analyzed the political structure of Ottoman and pre-Ottoman Turkish tribes in Anatolia.

they are phrased as genealogically-based groupings, encompass non-descent members in stable coalitions and tend to be internally hierarchic. This is a departure from Yörük nomadic practices in two ways. First, among the nomadic Yörük, although lineages frequently attract members not related by descent, it is rare that this is done on a stable basis from one season to the next and, if so, leads to the complete genealogic merging of the smaller with the larger and the loss of the smaller lineage's name as a descent unit. Among Yörük villages visited, even after several generations (especially in Antalya), descent group identities are often preserved after members are encompassed in larger factions. Secondly, the nomadic pastoral economy precludes, for the most part, the formation of fixed categories of wealth. Following sedentarization and reflecting the new agricultural economy, the households within the Yörük sections of the villages studied have become fixed in terms of wealth and economic mobility. Patron-client ties between the wealthiest Yörük of Nogaylar and non-descent group families, as well as with members of his own lineage, become important.

It is apparent that what is at issue in Yörük adaptation to new resources and sedentary community life is not massive change in formal institutions or social rules. What emerges as important in the analysis is, rather, how economic processes, and concomitant individual strategies, transform a society evidencing great economic mobility and non-hierarchical political relations into one in which upward economic mobility is limited, and where social lines can be expected to reflect those of economic differences.

VIII
CONCLUSION

THE fundamental premise of the preceding analysis is that major aspects of the Yörük nomadic pastoral adaptation are closely determined by the nature of Yörük relations with other populations pursuing sedentary modes of production. It is possible to describe the regional system of joint land use in which the Yörük participate as a highly mutualistic one. That is, the nomads are using land which other specialized modes of production do not directly exploit, or which they use in a seasonal schedule that permits the maintenance of Yörük flocks on fallow land during certain times of the year. Because the Yörük are able to exploit a continuous series of such grazing sites as they move between the extremes of their migratory cycle, each associated with variations in floral conditions, they contribute to overall regional production. The number of animals any village can support is limited by conditions during the time of the year when grazing is the poorest or by the amount of forage that can be stored. The nomads visit each pasture when it is close to its peak carrying capacity.

The regional system of joint land use is mutualistic in another way. All exchange, in the broadest sense, is value equivalent: the nomads pay for pasture and for damage caused by their animals to the fields of the agricultural populations from whom they obtain grazing.

The area included in and lying between the winter and summer pastures of the Saçıkara Yörük, and related tribes, represents a succession of ecological zones, each related to altitude as one proceeds upward from the inland Amik Plains. This zonal diversity is expressed in a series of village types: they range, roughly, from highly mechanized commercial wheat, cotton and rice growing villages in the lowlands, which singularly or in aggregate are commonly dominated by large landlords; through foothill and middle slope communities which practice run-off irrigation and dry field grain agriculture and horticulture. At the highest altitudes, both in Maraş and in Kayseri provinces, villages at the upper limits of agriculture exploit a grain and mixed crop subsistence economy with limited irrigation, strongly supplemented by sedentary cattle and small animal pastoralism. Ethnic diversity is notable, but except when taken in the broadest sense does not correspond to differences in the local ecology. No ethnically defined population other than the Yörük has a monopoly of any mode of production. That the Yörük are the only pastoral nomadic population is not due to any characteristic of their adaptation, but arises from the fact that other nomadic populations were forcibly settled.

Virtually all access to grazing is negotiated with non-Yörük, as there are only two Yörük villages, both of which are in the area of winter pasture and are open to grazing by members of the local lineages only. One of these villages, Nogaylar, is described in considerable detail in Chapter VII. There is a certain amount of direct peasant-nomad exchange of foodstuffs, and nomads often purchase inexpensive manufactured products from village peddlers while in the higher summer pastures. More commonly, Yörük economic transactions take place in the market places along their migratory route, often with settled Yörük shopkeepers who extend credit.

The nomadic Yörük have a migratory schedule that takes the herds through villages at times complementary to the agricultural cycle. Land for winter pasture is rented for cash payment from village landlords in the lowland plain, and the animals are put on fallow grain, cotton, or rice fields following harvest in September and October.

Prior to 1949 grazing was, by all accounts, free in most areas, with payment, if any, consisting of inconsequential gifts of cheese and butter. Now grazing fees exacted with government assistance are a major form of capital outlay for the nomads, and the cash requirements of grazing payments have led to elaborate on-going credit transactions within the tribes. It has also raised the herd size needed to support a family unit from about 50 in the previous generation to over 100 animals at the present time (average herd size is 268 sheep). This pressure has caused many families to settle. It is also likely that inflation of pasture fees will continue, and that total nomadic herd production might well be impaired, and that fewer animals will be maintained than can be supported by the resources available.

Yörük animals would often be better served by staying longer in the lowlands than is presently possible due to the danger of crop damage. Grazing along the route to summer pastures is often poor, although it would not be if village agriculture were not so extensive. If government control were not as firm as it is now, it would be safe to say that much marginal agricultural land would revert to grazing as the risk of animal damage would make it unprofitable. Furthermore, pastures now rented would almost certainly be claimed by force.

Formerly, Yörük tribes, if they were not clearly dominant, were strong enough and mobile enough to avoid paying grazing fees and fines for crop damage. At that time the amount of land under cultivation in the area of both summer and winter pastures was less, by local accounts, and that land which was cultivated was restricted to land of the best quality. Part of the increase in agriculture is due to technological advances and the reclaiming of swamp lands throughout the area. Another reason for pressure on grazing in the winter quarters is the increase in village population concomitant to the clearing of the land, and a rising birth rate due to the eradication of malaria within the last 20 years. But it is nevertheless true that if government control were not effective, the Yörük migratory schedule would be different in an attempt to make optimum use of grazing in each of the altitudinal zones through which they pass. Optimal grazing times do not always coincide with harvest and fallow field cycles.

The high degree of mutuality is not the consequence of strictly economic forces at work. The Yörük entered the area at the turn of the century and migration into the region continued through World War II. This was a result of pressure on traditional Yörük grazing lands along the southern Anatolian coast. Prior to the arrival of the Yörük, the forced sedentarization of Kurdish and Türkmen tribes tribes starting in 1865, had been largely accomplished, a project which arose from the government's desire to bring politically threatening tribes under control. As in Iraq and elsewhere, the leaders of these tribes were given title to large tracts of formerly tribal land, and many of their descendants are found among the largest landlords of the region today. The Yörük, when they came into the region, filled an economic niche of pastoral nomadism which had been vacated for strictly political reasons. The grazing land still remained, as did open routes of access between summer and winter pasture.

The present pattern of interaction and exchange is largely a matter of relative power. The Yörük were permitted to enter the region and to remain nomadic as they were never a threat to the state as the more powerful Türkmen and Kurdish tribes had been. The Yörük are in many ways representative of the adaptation of a politically weaker entity to the demands of a stronger one.

The Yörük migratory schedule is adapted to the agricultural cycles of the various villages, not because it is the optimum for grazing, or because it coincides with other productive requirements of the Yörük. It is a political adjustment.

Similarly, the pasture fee represents the strength of local law enforcement agencies, together with village interest in making maximum use of lands to which they hold title. No household or group of tents can acquire access to grazing by force even though they might well be able to overpower an individual village should violence occur.

This is by way of saying that nomadic pastoral patterns of land use are often best intelligible as adaptive responses to other communities and the state. The migratory cycle, residential pattern, and many aspects of internal organization of the Yörük often become clearer when approached from this perspective.

BIBLIOGRAPHY

Alkim, Bahardir U.
    1969   The Amanus Region of Turkey. Archaeology, Vol. 22: 280-89.

Aswad, Barbara Carlene Black.
    1968   Land, Marriage and Lineage Organization among Sedentarized Pastoralists in the Hatay, Southern Turkey: A Diachronic Analysis. Unpublished doctoral dissertation, University of Michigan.

    1971   Property Control and Social Strategies: Settlers on a Middle Eastern Plain. Anthropological Paper No. 44, The University of Michigan Museum of Anthropology. Ann Arbor.

Ayoub, Millicent K.
    1959   Parallel Cousin Marriage and Endogamy: A Study in Sociometry. Southwest Journal of Anthropology, Vol. 15: 266-75.

Bacon, Elizabeth E.
    1958   Obok; A Study of Social Structure in Eurasia. Viking Fund Publications in Anthropology, No. 25. Wenner-Gren Foundation for Anthropological Research. New York.

Barth, Fredrik
    1953   Principles of Social Organization in Southern Kurdistan. Universitets Ethnografiske, Museum Bulletin No. 7. Brødrene Jørgensen A/S. Oslo.

    1954   Father's Brother's Daughter Marriage in Kurdistan. Southwestern Journal of Anthropology, Vol. 10: 1964-71.

    Ecological Relationships of Ethnic Groups in Swat, North Pakistan. American Anthropologist, Vol. LVIII: 1079-89.

    1959-60   The Land Use Pattern of Migratory Tribes of South Persia. Norsk Geografisk Tidsskrift, Vol. XVII: 1-11.

    1961   Nomads of South Persia: The Basseri Tribe of the Khamseh Confederacy. Humanities Press. New York.

    1962   Nomadism in the Mountain and Plateau Areas of South West Asia. In: The Problems of the Arid Zone: 341-55. Proceedings of the Paris Symposium, Arid Zone Research No. 18. UNESCO. Paris.

1964 Capital, Investment and the Social Structure of a Pastoral Nomad Group in South Persia. *In*: Capital, Saving and Credit in Peasant Societies. Raymond Firth and B. S. Yamey, Eds. Aldine Publishing Company. Chicago.

Barth, Fredrik, ed.
1969 Ethnic Groups and Boundaries. Little, Brown and Company. Boston.

Bartsche, Gerhart
1934-34 Das Gebiet des Erciyes Dağı und die Stadt Kayseri in Mittel-Anatolien. Jahrbuch der Geographischen Gesellschaft zu Hannover: 87-202. Hanover.

Bates, Daniel G.
1971a The Role of the State in Peasant-Nomad Mutualism. Anthropological Quarterly, Vol. 44: 109-31.

1971b The Yörük of Southeastern Turkey: A Study of Land Use and Social Organization. University Microfilms. Ann Arbor Michigan.

1971c Güney-Doğu Anadolu'da Göçebe Yörük Yerleşmeleri Üzerine Bir Çalısma. *In*: Türkiye: Coğrafi ve Sosyal Arastirmalar. Tümertekin, Mansur, Benedict, eds. Istanbul Üniversitesi Edebiyat Fakültesi: 245-92. Istanbul.

1972 Differential Access to Pasture in a Nomadic Society: The Yörük of Southeastern Turkey. Journal of Asian and African Studies, Vol. VII: 48-59.

Batu, Selahattin.
1962 Koyunculuğun Esaslari. Ankara Üniversitesi Veteriner Fakültesi Yayınları: 136. Rüzgardi Matbaa. Ankara.

Beşikçi, İsmail.
Doğuda Değişm ve Yapısal Sorunlar. Doğan Yayınlari: 4. Bilimsel Araştirmalar Dergisi: 4. Ankara.

Bohannan, Paul.
1957 An Alternate Residence Classification. American Anthropologist, Vol. 59: 126-31.

Çagatay, Saadet S.
1950 Türk Lehçeleri Örnekleri. Ankara Üniversitesi Dil ve Tarih-Coğrafya Fakültesi Yayınları: 26. Türk Tarih Kurumu Basimevi. Ankara.

Chayanov. A. B.
n.d. The Theory of Peasant Economy. R. D. Irwin for the American Economic Association. Homewood, Illinois.

Coon, Carleton S.
1958 Caravan: The Story of the Middle East. Rev. ed. Holt, Rinehart and Winston. New York.

BIBLIOGRAPHY

Cunnison, Ian.
    1966   Baggara Arabs: Power and the Lineage in a Sudanese Nomad Tribe. Clarendon Press. Oxford.

Dönmez, Yusuf
    1963-64   A Yörük (Nomadic) Settlement West of Karasu. Review of the Geographical Institute of the University of Istanbul, Nos. 9, 10: 161-79.

Dorian, Nancy C.
    1970   A Substitute Name System in the Scottish Highlands. American Anthropologist, Vol. 72: 303-19.

Downie, H. M. and R. W. Heath
    1970   Basic Statistical Methods, 3rd ed. Harper and Row. New York.

Dyson-Hudson, Neville
    1972   The Study of Nomads. *In*: Perspectives on Nomadism. William Irons and Neville Dyson-Hudson, eds, Brill. Leiden.

Eberhard, Wolfram.
    1953*a*   Nomads and Farmers in Southeastern Turkey: Problems of Settlement. Oriens, Vol. 6: 32-49.

    1953*b*   Types of Settlement in South-East Turkey. Sociologus, N.F. 1: 49-64.

    1954   Change in Leading Families in Southern Turkey. Anthropos, Vol. 49: 992-1003.

Evans-Pritchard, E. E.
    1940   The Nuer: A Description of the Modes of Livelihood and Political Institutions of a Nilotic People. Clarendon Press. Oxford.

    1963   The Sanusi of Cyrenaica. Clarendon Press. Oxford.

Fortes, Meyer
    1953   The Structure of Unilineal Descent Groups. American Anthropologist, Vol. 55: 17-41.

Fox, Robin
    1967   Kinship and Marriage: An Anthropological Perspective. Penguin Books. Baltimore.

Fried, Morton H.
    1957   The Classification of Corporate Unilineal Descent Groups. Journal of the Royal Anthropological Institute, Vol. 87, Part 1: 1-29.

Frödin, John
    1943-44   Les Formes de la Vie Pastorale en Turquie. Geografiska Annaler, Vols. XXV, XXVI: 219-272

Geertz, H. and C. Geertz
1964 Teknonymy in Bali: Parenthood, Age-Grading and Genealogical Amnesia. Journal of the Royal Anthropological Institute, Vol. 94: 94-108.

Gökbilgin, M. Tayyib
1957 Rumeli'de Yürükler, Tatarlar ve Evlad-i Fathihan. Istanbul Üniversitesi Edebiyat Fakültesi Yayınlarından, No. 748. Osman Yalçın Matbaası. Istanbul.

Gökçen, İbrahim
1946 Saruhan'da Yörük ve Türkmenler. Marifet Başımevi. Istanbul.

Goodenough, Ward H.
1955 Residence Rules. Southwestern Journal of Anthropology, Vol. 12: 23-37.

Goody, Jack, ed.
1962 The Developmental Cycle in Domestic Groups. Cambridge Papers in Social Anthropology, No. 1. Cambridge University Press. Cambridge.

Gould, Andrew
"Brigands and Pasas". A paper read at the Middle Eastern Studies Association meetings, Denver, November 1971.

Gulliver, P. H.
1966 The Family Herds: A Study of Two Pastoral Tribes in East Africa, The Jie and Turkana. Routledge & Kegan Paul. London.

Haaland, Gunnar
1969 Economic Determinants in Ethnic Processes. In: Ethnic Groups and Boundaries. Fredrik Barth, ed. Little Brown and Company. Boston.

Herzog, Rolf
1963 Seschaftwerden von Nomaden: Geschichte, Gegenwärtiger Stand Eines Wirtschaftlichen Wie Sozialen Prozesses und Möglichkeiten der Sinnvollen Technischen Unterstützung. Westdeutscher Verlag. Köln und Opladen.

Hütteroth, Wolf-Dieter
1959 Bergnomaden und Yaylabauren im Mittleren Kurdischen Taurus. Marburger Geographische Schriften, Heft 11. Marberg.

1961 Beobachtungen zur Sozialstruktur Kurdischer Stämme im Östlischen Taurus. Zeitschrift für Ethnologie, Band 86: 23-42.

1968 Landliche Siedlungen im Südlichen Inneranatolien in der Letzten Vierhundert Jahren. Göttinger Geographische Abhandlungen, Heft 46. Göttingen.

Inalcik, Halil
  1951   Osmalı̆ Imparatorluğunun Kuruluş ve Inkişaf Devrinde
          Türkiye'nin Iktisadi Vazıyeti. Belleten 60: 629-84. Ankara.

Irons, William G.
  1965   Livestock Raiding among Pastoralists: An Adaptive Interpretation Papers of the Michigan Academy of Science, Arts and Letters, Vol. 50: 393-414. Ann Arbor.

  1969a   The Turkmen of Iran: A Brief Research Report. Iranian Studies, Vol. 2: 27-38.

  1969b   The Yomut Turkmen: A Study of Kinship in a Pastoral Society. University Microfilms, Ann Arbor.

Istatistik Umum Mürdürlüğü/Central Statistical Office.
  1957   Başvekalet: 1955 Genel Nüfüs Sayı̆mı̆. %10 Örnekleme Usulü Ile Elde Edilen Türkiye Neticeleri. Yayı̆n No. 327. Ankara.

Jarring, Gunnar
  1939   On the Distribution of Turkic Tribes in Afghanistan. An Attempt At Preliminary Classification. Lunds Universitets Arsskritt. N.F. Avd. 1, Bd. 35, No. 4. Lund Universitet. Lund.

Johansen, U.
  1959   Die Alpfrau: Eine Damonengestalt der Türkischen Völker. Zeitschrift der Deutschen Morganlandischen Gesellschaft, 109: 303-16.

  1965   Die Nomadenzelte Sudostanatoliens. Bustan: Zeitschrift für Kultur, Politik und Wirtschaft der Islamischen Ländern, No. 7: 33-37.

Johnson, Douglas L.
  1969   The Nature of Nomadism. Department of Geography Research Paper No. 18. University of Chicago. Chicago.

Khadduri, Majid and Herbert Liebesney
  1955   Law in the Middle East, Vol. 1. The Middle East Institute. Washington, D.C.

Kolars, John F.
  1962   Community Studies in Rural Turkey. Annals of the Association of American Geographers, Vol. 52: 476-89.

  1963   Tradition, Season, and Change in a Turkish Village. Department of Geography Research Paper No. 82. University of Chicago. Chicago.

  1966   Locational Aspects of Cultural Ecology: The Case of the Goat in Non-Western Agriculture. Geographical Review, Vol. LVI: 577-84.

König, Wolfgang
    1962   Die Achal-Teke; Zur Wirtschaft und Geselleshaft einer Turkmenen-Gruppe im XIX Jahrhundert. Akademic-Verlag. Berlin.

Köprülü-Zade, Mehmed Fuad
    1935   Türk Halk Edebīyatī Ansiklopedisi. Istanbul.

Krader, L.
    1963   Social Organization of the Mongol-Turkic Pastoral Nomads. Indiana University Publications. Uralic and Altaic Series, Vol. 20. Mouton. The Hague.

Lambton, Ann K. S.
    1953   Landlord and Peasant in Persia; A Study of Land Tenure and Land Revenue Administration. Oxford University Press. London.

Lattimore, Owen
    1962   Inner Asian Frontiers of China. Beacon Press. Boston.

Levy, Reuben
    1965   The Social Structure of Islam. The University Press. Cambridge.

Lewis, G. L.
    1950-55   The Secret Language of the Geygelli Yürüks. Zeki Velidi Togan'a Armăgan: 214-26.

    1967   Turkish Grammar. Clarendon Press. Oxford.

Lewis, I. M.
    1961   A Pastoral Democracy: A Study of Pastoralism and Politics Among the Northern Somali of the Horn of Africa. Oxford University Press. London.

Moroney, M. J.
    1965   Facts from Figures. Pelican Books. Baltimore.

Mueller, John H. and Karl P. Schuessler
    1961   Statistical Reasoning in Sociology. Houghton Mifflin Company. Boston.

Murdock, George P.
    1948   Social Structure. MacMillan. New York.

Murphy, Robert F. and Leonard Kasdan
    1959   The Structure of Parallel Cousin Marriage. American Anthropologist, Vol. 61: 17-29.

    1967   Agnation and Endogamy: Some Further Considerations. Southwestern Journal of Anthropology, Vol. 23: 1-14.

Nicholas, Ralph W.
    1965   Factions: A Comparative Analysis. In: Political Systems and the Distribution of Power, M. Banton, Ed. American Sociological-Association Monographs, 2. London.

Orhonlu, Cengiz
    1969   Osmanlï Imparatorluğunda Aşiretleri İskan Teşebbüsü, 1691-1696. Istanbul Üniversitesi Edebiyat Fakültesi Yayinlarï, No. 998. Istanbul.

Patai, Raphael
    1955   Cousin-Right in Middle Eastern Marriage. Southwestern Journal of Anthropology, Vol. 11: 371-90.

    1965   The Structure of Endogamous Unilineal Descent Groups. Southwestern Journal of Anthropology, Vol. 21: 325-50.

Pehrson, Robert N.
    1966   The Social Organization of the Marri Baluch, compiled and analyzed from Pehrson's notes by Fredrik Barth. Viking Fund Publications in Anthropology, No. 43. Wenner-Gren Foundation for Anthrpological Research. New York.

Percy, Earl
    1901   Highlands of Asiatic Turkey. Edward Arnold. London.

Peters, E. L.
    1960   The Proliferation of Segments among the Bedouin of Cyrenaica. Journal of the Royal Anthropological Institute, Vol. 90: 29-53.

Planhol, Xavier de
    1950*a*   Estivage et Exploitation des montagnes en pisidie. Bulletin de l'Association de Geógraphes Francais, Nos. 208, 209: 81-88.

    1950*b*   La Garde du Bétail dans la Plaine Pamphylienne. Bulletin de l'Association de Geógraphes Français, Nos. 212, 213: 129-137.

    1954   La Vie de Montagne dans le Sandras Dağ (Carie Meridionale-Turquie). Revue de Geógraphie Alpine, Vol. XLII: 665-673.

    1958   De la Plaine Pamphylienne aux Lacs Pisidiens: Nomadisme et Vie Paysanne. Bibliothèque Archéologique et Historique de l'Institute Français d'Archéologie d'Istanbul, Tome III. Paris.

    1959   Geography, Politics and Nomadism in Anatolia. International Social Science Journal, Vol. IX: 525-31.

    1963   A Travers les Chaines Pontiques: Plantations Côtières et Vie Montagnarde. Bulletin de l'Association de Géographes Français, Nos. 311, 312; 2-12.

    1965   Les Nomades, la Steppe et la Foret en Anatolie. Geographische Zeitschrift, Vol. LIII: 101-16.

    1966   Aspects of Mountain Life in Anatolia and Iran. *In*: Geo- as Human Ecology: Methodology by Example. S. R. Eyre and G. R. J. Jones, eds. Edward Arnold. London.

Planhol, Xavier de and Inandik, Hamit
    1959   Etudes sur la Vie de Montagne dans le Sud-Ouest de l'Anatolie: Le Vesil Göl Dağ et le Boz Dağ. Revue de Geographie Alpine, Vol. XLVII: 375-89.

Randolph, R. and A. Coult
    1968   A Computer Analysis of Bedouin Marriage. Southwestern Journal of Anthropology, Vol. 24: 83-99.

Refik, Ahmet
    1930   Anadolu'da Türk Aşiretleri, 166-1200. Istanbul.

Sahlins, Marshall D.
    1968   Tribesmen. Foundations of Modern Anthropology series. Prentice-Hall. Englewood Cliffs.

    1972   Stone Age Economics. Aldine-Atherton. Chicago.

    n.d.   The Domestic Mode of Production in Primitive Societies: Social Inflections of the Chayanov Slope. Unpublished manuscript.

Salzman, Philip C.
    1971   Movement and Resource Extraction Among Pastoral Nomads: The Case of the Shah Nawazi Baluch. Anthropological Quarterly, Vol. 44: 185-97.

Schorger, William D.
    1969   The Evolution of Political Forms in a North Moroccan Village. Anthropological Quarterly, Vol. 42: 263-86.

Service, Elman R.
    1964   Primitive Social Organization. Random House. New York.

Smith, M. G.
    1956   Segmentary Lineage Systems. Journal of the Royal Anthropological Institute, Vol. 86: 39-80. London.

Stirling, Paul
    1963   The Domestic Cycle and the Distribution of Power in a Turkish Village. In: Mediterranean Countrymen. J. Pitt-Rivers, ed. Mouton. Paris.

    1965   Turkish Village. Weidenfeld and Nicolson. London.

Sümer, Faruk
    1967a   Kara Koyunlular, Cilt 1. Türk Tarih Durumu Basĭmevĭ. Ankara.

    1967b   Oğuzlar (Türkmenler), Tarihleri-Boy Teşkilatĭ-Destanlar. Üniversitesi Dil ve Tarih-Coğrafya Fakültesi Yayĭnlarĭ 170. Ankara.

Sweet, Louise E.
    1960   Tell Toqaan: A Syrian Village. University of Michigan Anthropological Paper No. 14. Ann Arbor.

Camel Pastoralism in North Arabia and the Minimal Camping Unit. *In*: Man, Culture and Animals: Animals in Human Ecological Adjustments. Anthony Leeds and Andrew P. Vayda, eds. American Association for the Advancement of Science. Washington, D.C.

Swidler, W. W.
    1972   Some Demographic Factors Regulating the Formation of Flocks and Camps Among the Brahui of Baluchistan. *In*: Perspectives on Nomadism. William Irons and Neville Dyson-Hudson, eds. Brill. Leiden.

Tanoğlu, Ali
    1954   The Geography of Settlement. Review of the Geographical Institute of the University of Istanbul, No. 1: 1-17.

Tanoğlu, Ali, Sırrı Erinç and Erol Tümertekin
    1961   Türkiye Atlası (Atlas of Turkey; 1:800,000; Konya and Musul Sheets). Istanbul Üniversitesi Edebiyat Fakültesi Yayınları No. 903. Milli Eğitim Basımevi; Istanbul.

Tanyol, Cahit
    1952   Baraklarda Örf ve Adet Araştırmaları. Sosyoloji Dergisi, No. 7: 71-108. Istanbul.

    1961   Peşke Binamlısı Köyü. Sosyoloji Dergisi, Sayı 16: 17-52. Istanbul.

Tumertekin, Erol
    1959   The Structure of Agriculture in Turkey. Review of the Geographical Institute of Istanbul, No. 5: 77-93.

Tunçdilek, Necdet
    1962   Observation on Rural Settlement in Two Different Regions of Turkey. Review of the Geographical Institute of the University of Istanbul, No. 8: 47-56.

    1963-64   Yayla Settlements and Related Activities in Turkey. Review of the Geographical Institute of Istanbul, Nos. 9, 10: 58-71.

Wenzel, Hermann
    1932   Sultan-Dagh und Akschehir-Ova: Eine Landeskundliche Untersuchung in Inneranatolien. Schriften des Geographischen Instituts der Universität Kiel, Band 1. Kiel.

    1935   Forschungen in Inneranatolien, I: Aufbau und Formen der Lykaonischen Steppe. Schriften des Geographischen Instituts der Universität Kiel, Band 5, Heft 1. Kiel.

    1937   Forschungen in Inneranatolien, II: Die Steppe als Lebensraum. Schriften des Geographischen Instituts der Universität Kiel, Band 7, Heft 3. Kiel.

Wolf, Eric R.
> 1956 Aspects of Group Relations in a Complex Society: Mexico. American Anthropologist, Vol. 58: 1065-78.
>
> 1966 Peasants. Prentice-Hall. Englewood Cliffs.

Yalgĭn, Ali Riza
> 1950 Toroslar'da Karatepeli Bölgesi: Yurt ve Etnografya. Ulus Basĭmevi. Ankara.

Yasa, İbrahim
> 1969 Yirmibeş Yil Sonra Hasanoğlan Köyü. Ankara Üniversitesi Siyasal Bilgiler Fakültesi Yayĭnlarĭ, No. 270. Ankara.

Yengoyan, Aram A.
> 1964 Environment, Shifting Cultivation and Social Organization Among the Mandaya of Eastern Mindanao, Philippines. Unpublished Ph.D. dissertation. University of Chicago.

Vinogradov, Amal R.
> 1970 The Beni Mtir of the Middle Atlas: A Study in Moroccan Tribalism. University Microfilms. Ann Arbor.

2. Girl Leading Her Family's Camels

Plate 3. First Day of Spring Migration

Plate 4. Packing the Caldron

Plate 5. Hasan Baba, Prominent Member of the Satılar Lineage

Plate 6. Three Brides

Plate 7. Bride Making the Bread

Plate 8. Woman Washing Clothes

Plate. 9. Camp Group in Migration

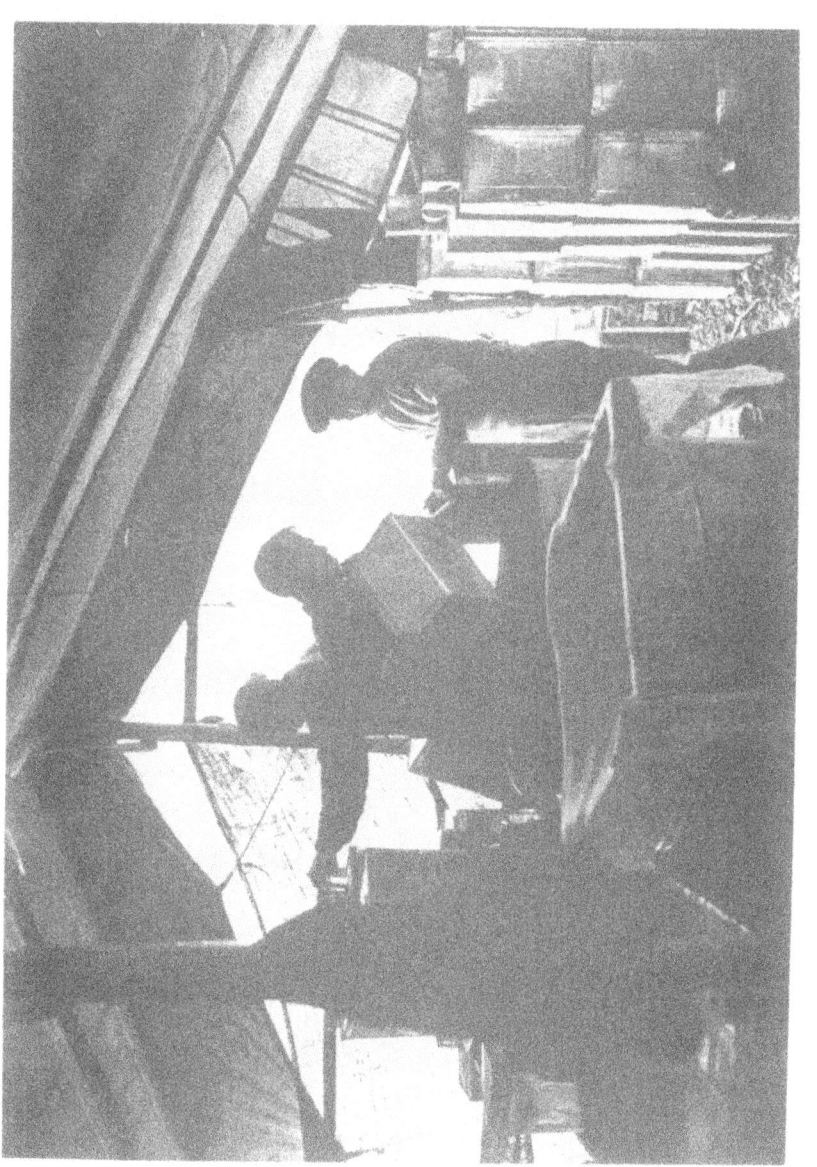

Plate 10. Cheese Makers in the Ağa's Dairy Tent

Plate 11. Preparing Wool for Felt Rug

Plate 12. Weaving a Rug for the Tent

Plate 13. Admiring Neighbor's Newly Born Camel

www.ingramcontent.com/pod-product-compliance
Lightning Source LLC
Jackson TN
JSHW070313120426
100741JS00007B/38